THE SOCIAL RESPONSE TO ENVIRONMENTAL RISK

Policy Formulation in an Age of Uncertainty

Recent Economic Thought Series

Editor:
Warren G. Samuels
Michigan State University
East Lansing, Michigan, U.S.A.

Others books in the series:

Feiwel, G.: Samuelson and Neoclassical
  Economics
Wade, L.: Political Economy: Modern Views
Zimbalist, A.: Comparative Economic Systems:
  Recent Views
Darity, W.: Labor Economics: Modern Views
Jarsulic, M.: Money and Macro Policy
Samuelson, L.: Microeconomic Theory
Bromley, D.: Natural Resource Economics:
  Policy Problems and Contemporary Analysis
Mirowski, P.: The Reconstruction of Economic
  Theory
Field, A.: The Future of Economic History
Lowry, S.: Pre-Classical Economic Thought
Officer, L.: International Economics
Asimakopulos, A.: Theories of Income
  Distribution
Earl, P.: Psychological Economics;
  Development, Tensions, Prospects
Thweatt, W.: Classical Political Economy
Peterson, W.: Market Power and The Economy
DeGregori, T.: Development Economics
Nowotny, K.: Public Utility Regulation
Horowitz, I.: Decision Theory
Mercuro, N.: Law and Economics
Hennings, K. and Samuels, W.: Neoclassical
  Economic Theory, 1870 to 1930
Samuels, W.: Economics as Discourse
Lutz, M.: Social Economics
Weimer, D.: Policy Analysis and Economics

The Social Response to Environmental Risk

Policy Formulation in an Age of Uncertainty

Edited by
Daniel W. Bromley

Kathleen Segerson

Kluwer Academic Publishers
Boston/Dordrecht/London

Distributors for North America:
Kluwer Academic Publishers
101 Philip Drive
Assinippi Park
Norwell, Massachusetts 02061 USA

Distributors for all other countries:
Kluwer Academic Publishers Group
Distribution Centre
Post Office Box 322
3300 AH Dordrecht, THE NETHERLANDS

Library of Congress Cataloging-in-Publication Data
The Social response to environmental risk: policy formulation in an
  age of uncertainty/edited by Daniel W. Bromley, Kathleen Segerson.
      p.   cm. — (Recent economic thought series)
    Includes bibliographical references and index.
    ISBN 0-7923-9208-6
    1. Environmental policy. 2. Risk assessment. I. Bromley, Daniel
W., 1940–   . II. Segerson, Kathleen, 1955–   . III. Series.
  HC79.E5S57 1992
  363.7′056—dc20   91-25119
                                                     CIP

Contents

Contributors

Professor Daniel W. Bromley
Department of Agricultural Economics
University of Wisconsin-Madison
Madison, WI 53706

Professor Sharon Dunwoody
School of Journalism and Mass Communication
University of Wisconsin-Madison
Madison, WI 53706

Douglas Easterling
Risk and Decision Processes Center
Wharton School
University of Pennsylvania
Philadelphia, PA 19104

Patrick W. Hamlett
Division of Multidisciplinary Studies
North Carolina State University
Raleigh, NC 27695

Professor Howard Kunreuther
Risk and Decision Processes Center
Wharton School
University of Pennsylvania
Philadelphia, PA 19104

Professor Lola Lopes
Department of Management and Organizations
University of Iowa
Iowa City, IA 52242

Professor Kathleen Segerson
Department of Economics
University of Connecticut
Storrs, CT 06268

Professor V. Kerry Smith
Department of Economics
North Carolina State University
Raleigh, NC 27695−8109

Professor W. Kip Viscusi
Department of Economics
Duke University
Durham, NC 27706

Professor Edward Woodhouse
Department of Science and Technology Studies
Rensselear Polytechnic Institute
Troy, NY 12181

Preface

We have undertaken this volume in the belief that there is now sufficient research completed on environmental risk to justify a retrospective assessment of what is known. Our authors and our intended audience are eclectic indeed. Environmental risk assessment receives increasing attention in the media today. The populace is practically assaulted with stories, with anecdotes, and with conflicting evidence.

It is our hope that these chapters will provide the reader with a comprehensive glimpse of a fast-growing field in public policy. No complete survey of the literature would be possible or meaningful. We offer here instead the integrative thoughts of some of the most respected analysts in the field. We believe that the coverage is coherent, the perspectives are illuminating, and the individual treatments deserving of careful study.

We are grateful to Warren Samuels of Michigan State University who is editor of the Kluwer series on recent economic thought. We are also grateful to our Kluwer editor, Zach Rolnik. Both have been gracious in their toleration of unconscionable delays.

The Social Response to Environmental Risk

Policy Formulation in an Age of Uncertainty

1 ENTITLEMENTS AND PUBLIC POLICY IN ENVIRONMENTAL RISKS

Daniel W. Bromley*

[all rights] are conditional and derivative ... they are derived from the end or purpose of the society in which they exist. They are conditional on being used to the attainment of that end.

— R. H. Tawney, *The Acquisitive Society*

The Problem

In this volume we address a wide range of issues pertaining to risk in environmental policy. The chapters to follow are concerned with individual perceptions of risk, the valuation of environmental risks, the ways in which risks are reported and discussed in the media, the alternative governmental roles in addressing environmental risks, and public policy issues involving risks—biotechnology hazards, hazardous waste facilities, and occupational hazards. Underlying all of these issues are important questions concerning individual and group exposures to environmental risks.

This first chapter is concerned, therefore, with alternative entitlement structures—property rights—in environmental policy. We start with this subject because the status quo structure of entitlements determines which parties to environmental disputes bear unwanted costs, which parties bear the transaction costs of institutional change through new environmental policy, and which parties are able to call upon the power of the state to protect their interests. To have a "right" is to have the capacity to call

---

* Daniel W. Bromley is Anderson-Bascom Professor of Applied Economics and Acting Director of the Institute for Environmental Studies, University of Wisconsin, Madison.

1

upon the state to protect one's current or future interests in particular areas. Because many environmental disputes are recent or because new knowledge has only recently demonstrated the real cause of observed environmental problems,[1] much environmental policy operates in an un-regulated domain where the legal rights of the contending parties is unclear. Environmental policy is, at bottom, about determining which party shall receive protection from the state. When protection is forth-coming, that party acquires a *right*.

I will be concerned with several topics in this chapter. First, I will offer a stylized environmental conflict to illustrate how the status quo — yet presumptive — entitlement structure defines the way in which the problem is perceived and addressed by the conflicting interests. Second, I will develop the concept of entitlements, and in doing so will explain both their static as well as dynamic characteristics. Finally, I will turn to a discussion of the perceptions of entitlements in environmental situ-ations involving risks. Here, I suggest that perceptions of risk will interact with perceptions of entitlements — real or imagined — to produce unique behaviors on the part of public decision makers in matters of environ-mental policy.

The Issues Before Us

To illustrate the role of entitlements in the assessment of environmental risk, consider as an example the chemical contamination of a river im-portant for commercial fishing. Assume an industrial chemical manufac-turer is currently discarding waste residues into the river without regard for the interests of the fishing industry. Under this status quo setting the entire public discussion of risks will focus on the concentration of chemical residues in fish. Various experts will comment on the significance of the levels of certain chemicals in the fish. Others will advise on the number of servings per month of fish that can reasonably be considered safe. Experts will disagree, of course, and so the argument will persist. During this time the chemical factory will be able to continue its practice of discharging its manufacturing residues into the river.

In the interest of resolving this policy problem, the chemical plant — or the chemical industry — may support research into the tolerance levels of laboratory animals to these chemicals. The debate will rage, and scientific experts will participate in discussions to disseminate information to citizens. In the meantime, there will be economic loss to the local fishing industry as the safety of eating the fish is questioned. The media may report the hard luck of families dependent the fishing industry. There will also, most assuredly, be reports about the families dependent upon employment in the chemical plant. The problem will be redefined — reframed in the words of Sharon Dunwoody (chapter 4) — as one of jobs versus a pure environment. Alternatively, the problem will be defined as jobs for fishing families versus jobs for chemical workers. Some will even seek to cast the issue as a choice between letting the market work or bowing to government intervention. That is, the status quo — in which chemical residues are dumped into the river — will be regarded by some as letting the market work. Government *interference in the market* will, in all probability, be the term used to refer to a proposed change in the current situation to protect the interest of the fishing families and those who consume fish.

The strange convolution of facts and concepts that emerges from this stylized environmental conflict will tend to dominate public policy discussions and hence the ultimate resolution of the problem. The owners of the chemical factory will no doubt claim that they have a right to dispose of manufacturing residues as they have been doing since the plant was built. Those who fish in the river will claim that they have a right to be free from chemical contamination of fish; after all, their grandfathers started fishing long before the chemical factory was built. While these conflicting claims of a right are incoherent, as will be seen later there is a more fundamental problem. Specifically, while such rights claims tend to dominate discussions of environmental policy, little attention is paid to entitlements. There are two related aspects of this problem.

First, the status quo entitlement structure is taken as the legitimate starting point for legal — as well as political — deliberations. Second, each party — each interest — to any dispute will enlist specific language that will bolster its claim. In the United States few words pack as much emotional appeal as *rights*. This should not surprise us. Our political history is cluttered with rights claims — a "right to keep and bear arms," a "right to the pursuit of happiness," a "right to property," a "right against unreasonable searches," a "right to due process," a "right to free speech," and more. Indeed, even the recent debates over smoking in public is dominated by those claiming that they have a right to smoke, while others claim that they have a right to breathe clean air. These self-serving appeals are not at all helpful, primarily because they betray a fundamental confusion over what constitutes a right. I will be concerned here with clarifying the concept of a right. Of equal importance, I will illustrate how the status quo rights structure dominates the nature of the debate over environmental risks.

To provide glimpse of this, consider once again the previous example.

Suppose we imagine a different status quo entitlement structure — one in which the chemical factory is prohibited from discharging any of its residues into the river. Under this entitlement structure it follows that a very different technical process would be followed by the plant — one in which discharging residues into the river is not part of the manufacturing process. This new legal regime — an entitlement structure — would certainly be an effective incentive for technical innovation in the chemical industry so that residues are processed within the plant rather than being discharged into the nearest river. Of equal importance, it would mean that any discussions to alter the status quo legal regime would put the burden of proof on the chemical industry rather than on consumers of fish (and the fishing industry).

While the debate would still rage over the safety of fish exposed to chemical residues, notice that the consumers of fish would not be exposed to a health risk during that debate. It is also worth noting that the interests of the chemical factory in discharging its wastes would become very much like the debates over the siting of hazardous waste facilities (see chapter 7). In these latter debates, it is the producer of such wastes who must search for disposal sites for the unwanted materials. The transaction costs fall on the producer, and the major desire of such producers is to induce reluctant communities to accept the wastes. While the search goes on, those opposed to such dumping are protected from unwanted disposal of hazardous wastes. These individuals stand protected by the presumptive rights in the status quo.

A more fundamental difference must also be noted. We saw, previously, that if the chemical factory were suddenly to be prevented from dumping toxic residues into the river, the situation would most likely be characterized as one of government interference with the factory. Those who accepted this description might also be tempted to suggest that the chemical factory had a right to dump wastes into the river and that the new policy represented an interference with that right. As noted, such assertions represent a fundamental confusion over what a right is. Until such confusions are addressed, it will be impossible to develop a coherent approach to the problem of entitlements and environmental risks.

Before turning to that, we must address the so-called Coase Theorem. Specifically, some will argue that it does not matter which party — the chemical factory or the fishing industry — is protected by entitlements in the status quo. Those who believe this will claim that as long as there is a market the ultimate outcomes will be identical. This position, fueled by a possible desire to defend market solutions to externality problems, has been amply exposed as incorrect. Coase postulated, as a heuristic, a world of zero transaction costs, and a world without income (or wealth) effects from the transfer of property rights. Under these circumstances he recognized that there could be no externalities.[2] That is, when transaction costs are zero, there can be no externalities for the simple reason that all possible gains from trade, perfectly calibrated because of zero transaction costs, will have been exploited. Hence under the strict Coasean assumptions, it is logically necessary to recognize that we have, in fact, the Coase Tautology.[3]

Surprisingly, there are individuals who still believe that the initial assignment of property rights makes no difference. A major part of the confusion over the Coase Theorem arises, I believe, because of unclear language. Some will claim that eventual *resource allocation* is unaffected by the status quo legal setup. Others will claim that *efficiency* will result regardless of the initial assignment of property rights. If by "resource allocation" one means the input mix that will bring forth a particular total production of fish and chemicals in the previous example, then this is clearly untenable, as all those cited in footnote 2 have illustrated. If by "efficiency" one means something less sweeping than identical output mix in the economy, then the adherents to the Coase Theorem appear to be on firmer ground. Unfortunately, appearances can be deceiving.

Specifically, of what value is it to claim that both contaminated fish and uncontaminated fish (or chemicals dumped in rivers as opposed to being processed elsewhere) are instances of "efficiency"? While efficiency is certainly nice, two efficient outcomes — one that renders fish unsafe for human consumption, the other that keeps toxins out of fish — provide scant ground for coherent policy. As Randall [1974] notes, the hyper-Coaseans were (and are) keen to show that externality policy is not about the ethical dimension of one outcome versus the other, but is, rather, a matter of pure efficiency analysis. However, the assertion that efficiency will be unaffected by the status quo entitlement structure — when coupled with the ineluctable fact that resource allocation will most certainly differ — means there is no efficiency basis for deciding which entitlement structure is best. Inevitably, therefore, externality policy reduces to an issue of whose interests the state will protect — the chemical company or consumers (and harvesters) of fish.[4]

There will be more discussion along these lines later. For now, our interest is in the way that entitlements affect the subsequent discussions about environmental risks, and the policy implications that flow from such considerations. For that, we must turn attention to entitlements.

Entitlements

An entitlement is the constellation of rights and duties that defines the legal position of parties to any particular conflict. Earlier, I noted that the term *right* is venerable in the English language, a term that is wheeled in whenever an individual seeks to buttress a specific environmental dispute. While the term *right* is used without hesitation to cover all manner of situations, the legal meaning of *right* is very clear and carries with it quite unambiguous political entailments. Specifically, *a right is the capacity to call upon the state to protect one's interests in a particular outcome or situation*. Rights only have meaning when there is some authority that agrees to defend the holder of a right in a particular situation. If I have a right in some situation, it means I can turn to the state to see that my claim is protected. It should be clear that the claim of a factory that it has a right to dump its chemical residues by virtue of a long history of that behavior is simply unfounded. Likewise, the claims of the fishing industry that its members have a right to catch uncontaminated fish since they were there first is equally ludicrous. Neither party has a right to either action until some authority within the state — either the legislature or the courts — says that it does. Indeed, disputants go to the legislature or the courts precisely for this reason.

This concept is, for some reason, difficult for many to comprehend. I can only speculate that the word *right* is so much a part of our everyday language that it has become trivialized and less meaningful. Perhaps the prominent place of "natural rights" doctrine in American political and economic thought has something to do with this. Those who believe the natural rights doctrine will be inclined to accept the idea that rights exist prior to the state. If the chemical factory has been dumping its poisonous residues for, say, 63 years, and if the extent of that poison is only now comprehended, then collective action by the government to prohibit continued dumping seems to suggest an interference with some putative right of the chemical factory.

Such logic, while helpful to those seeking to defend the status quo — or those hoping to be bought out (compensated) if asked to change their existing behavior — does not really illuminate the choices we face in environmental policy. If one accepts that particular logic, then the perpetrator of any action, no matter how undesirable, stands to gain financially if suddenly required to stop. This view obviously flies in the face of the constitutional distinction between actions that constitute a taking of property and the exercise of the police power. More will be said on this later. For now, it is enough to recognize that rights can only exist when there is a system to insure that the right holder is protected from the claims of another. If the right holder does not have recourse to some authority, then adverse claims can only be deflected by the threat of force or appeal to conscience. A system that depends upon force or moral persuasion is not a civil society, it is brutish anarchy.[5]

A right is a triadic relationship that encompasses the object of my interest (whether a physical object or a stream of benefits arising from fortuitous circumstances), plus all others in the polity who have a duty to respect my right. Rights are *not* relationships between me and an object, but they are rather relationships between me and others *with respect to that object*. Rights can only exist when there is a social mechanism that gives duties and then binds individuals to those duties. The effective protection I gain from this authority is nothing other than a correlated duty for all others interested in my claim.

Where does that duty originate? Kant would argue that it is in the mind of all others with an interest in my situation (or the object under my control). This is what Kant meant by intelligible possession. By way of contrast, Locke argued that prior collective consent is not required for individual expropriation of valuable resources. He maintained that the absolute right to appropriation derives from the need for all people to secure their sustenance, and from the right of all people to the fruits of their own labor. These two conditions justify the private appropriation of the earth's bounty, quite prior to any social contract. Using this view one might speculate that the fishing community in our example — by dint of being there first — had a more robust claim than did the chemical plant.

Within economics there is an obvious affinity for the Lockean view since the private appropriation of natural resources is thought necessary and sufficient for a market to emerge among resource owners. However, the claim of the fishing community is undermined by the need for an efficient solution to the dispute. That is, it may be more efficient to permit the chemical factory to continue to discharge its toxic wastes, thereby causing the demise of the fishing industry. We should not be surprised if many individuals — and not a few policymakers — are unimpressed with this particular notion of the efficient solution.

Some individuals will be inclined to notice that the production — oriented actions of the fishing industry are not being called into question here; the members of the industry are simply doing what they have always done. In fact, members of both industries are doing what they have always done, but now new knowledge reveals that the traditional behavior of dumping chemical wastes harms another party. The Lockean view would favor the fishing industry, but economics now abandons its Lockean position by suggesting that we should balance the benefits and costs of two situations: (1) allowing the continued dumping of chemicals, or (2) prohibiting that dumping.

There is, in this economic assessment, a sense of Kantian logic. Kant's position on property rights is that Locke confused empirical possession with *de jure* or intelligible possession (Williams, 1977).[6] That is, while physical appropriation is necessary for something to become mine—for me to be able to control its benefit stream—physical appropriation is not sufficient. Possession cannot establish ownership. Kant argued that this confusion in Locke means that Locke failed to see that a social convention— a social contract—is logically prior to real ownership. That is, only intelligible possession constitutes a right to property. If the necessity of a social convention is understood to be the core of intelligible possession— a property right—then two conclusions follow from this fact. The first concerns the relations between rights and the state, while the second concerns the instrumental nature of rights.

Rights and the State

It is essential to recognize that all rights flow from the state; it is the collective will that bestows rights and duties. Natural rights, so fundamental to Locke, form no logical foundation for rights in general, and property rights in particular. By definition, when one has a right in something it means that the benefit stream arising from that situation is consciously protected by the state. The state gives and takes away rights by its willingness—or unwillingness—to agree to protect one's claims in something. A *property right* is the socially sanctioned control of a benefit stream. When I purchase a piece of land, its price is a reflection of the present discounted value of all of its future benefit streams. By purchasing the land I am really purchasing the benefit stream—that is, my property, the thing I actually own. Land is called 'property' in everyday usage, but the essence of property is the benefit stream that I now own, and that the state agrees to protect by defending my claim in that stream.

When one has property it means that the state recognizes your rights in something, and it acts on that right by giving all others a duty to regard your right. Returning to the example, the ability of the chemical plant to discharge its wastes as opposed to spending money to purge its effluent of such compounds means that a benefit stream exists (in the form of cost savings), which the chemical factory now controls. This benefit stream is manifest in the lower operating costs of discharging untreated chemicals into the river. In the status quo ante, the present value of these savings may or may not be protected by a right. It is the essence of such environmental disputes to determine whether the interests of the chemical industry or the interests of the fishing industry will receive the official protection of the state in the form of a right. If the chemical industry gains protection, then it remains free to discharge its residues into the river. If the fishing industry gains protection, then it acquires the right to force the chemical industry to dispose of its residues without harming the fishing industry.

Rights as Social Instruments

Second, property rights are instrumental variables and, of necessity, are subject to change when new conditions warrant. This instrumentality must be understood to include not only those rights clearly established by the courts or the legislatures, but also those presumed rights that individuals claim are theirs (Sax, 1983). To return to the example, recall that both parties claim to have a right to continue their traditional practices. If made to stop discharging chemical wastes, the factory owner will most assuredly insist that some right has been infringed upon. Compensation will no doubt be demanded. If the chemical factory manages to prevail, then it is the fishing industry that will claim its rights have been violated. Compensation will be demanded in this case as well.

The important point here is that collective action is concerned precisely with defining the domain of individual choice. That domain, seen as both liberation and constraint of individual action, reflects the outcome of collective perceptions regarding what sort of world the citizens wish to inhabit. If the interests of the chemical industry weigh more heavily than the interests of the fishing industry—and of those who eat fish—then one choice domain will result. On the other hand, if the interests of the fishing industry and consumers of fish are thought more important than those of the chemical industry, a different choice domain will result. The economist can find each choice domain to be consistent with efficiency. Which choice domain and its associated outcome is consistent with social optimality, however, requires knowledge of the relevant social welfare function (Bromley 1989b; Lang 1980; Mishan 1980). The Kantian element here is the realization that rights—or property rights—are the product of civil society making conscious choices.

Rights as Legal Correlates

The recognition of rights as social instruments derived from collective determinations of the state, suggests that we now turn to the content of rights as a structure of correlated obligations or duties. The seminal work on rights and duties is that of Hohfeld [1917]. In the Hohfeld scheme a right means that one party—call it Alpha—has an assurance that another party—Beta—will behave in a certain way toward Alpha. The assurance comes from the willingness of the state to compel Beta to behave in a certain way toward Alpha. In the chemical discharges example, a right for the fishing industry would mean that the chemical industry had a *duty* not to discharge pollutants into the river. Notice that a component of Alpha's standing is Beta's standing; Alpha has the right, Beta has the duty.

The second legal correlate is that of *privilege* and *no right*. When a party, say Alpha, has privilege, we mean that it is free to act without regard for the interests of Beta. Should Beta seek relief from the courts for this unwanted imposition, Beta would be told that it had no right to ask the court to cause a change in Alpha's behavior. Alpha's protection through Beta's no right means that Alpha's behavior is protected by the unwillingness of the collective power to interfere. Imagine that the fishing community sought an injunction against the chemical discharges of the chemical factory. The fishing industry would be told, under the status quo legal regime, that it had no right to expect the court to enjoin the chemical discharges.

This description is a static picture at a moment when the environmental problem first appears. When scientific evidence begins to suggest a possible problem with chemicals accumulating in fish, the contending parties will stand defined by a structure of legal correlates. In the example, we would say the fishing community has no right to prevent chemical discharges, and therefore the chemical industry is free to continue its dumping without regard for the harm visited on the fishing community and the consumers of fish. In the Hohfeld terminology, the chemical industry has privilege.

With the appearance of new evidence detrimental to the putative safety of fish, this status quo legal setting comes under challenge from those engaged in fishing and from those who seek chemical-free fish. Those economists inclined to laissez faire will suggest that the two groups should be allowed to bargain out their differences without interference from the state.[7] For reasons spelled out elsewhere in this volume, such bargaining is most unlikely. Rather, public policy will focus on either (1) altering the status quo legal regime or (2) sustaining the status quo legal regime. Indeed, the intense scrutiny and discussion to attend just such environmental disputes is precisely concerned with changes in, or defense of, the status quo legal relations between the contending parties. Let us turn briefly to that consideration.

Public Policy, Institutional Change, and New Legal Correlates

Environmental policy must be understood to represent a challenge to the prevailing institutional structure in an economy. Such structure provides the legitimate domains of choice for actions with environmental import. Recall that the economy is a set of ordered relations which indicate (1) what individuals must or must not do — Hohfeldian duty, (2) what individuals may do without the interference from others — Hohfeldian privilege, (3) what individuals can do with the aid of the collective power of the state — Hohfeldian right, and (4) what individuals cannot expect the collective power of the state to do in their behalf — Hohfeldian no right.[8]

Because public policy is about institutional change, we must address the dynamic aspect of this problem. If the fishing community is able to marshal sufficient support for its challenge to the chemical industry, and thereby force termination of chemical discharges, then we would say that the fishing community had power in the Hohfeld sense. That is, the fishing community had the capacity to force the chemical industry into a new legal situation that is disadvantageous to the latter. Costs of disposal that had heretofore been avoided by the chemical industry must now be borne by that industry as it searches for alternatives to the traditional practice of merely discharging its residues into the river. The chemical industry, because it was forced against its will to alter its waste-handling practices, is said to have liability at the hands of the fishing community.[9]

On the other hand, if the chemical industry is successful in preventing a change in the legal relations vis-a-vis the fishing community, then Hohfeld would regard this as a situation of immunity. The correlate of immunity, no power, means that the fishing community was unable to create a new legal relation affecting the chemical industry. The four legal relations from Hohfeld are shown in table 1.1.

These four legal relations are reducible into two further categories, which are either active (positive) or passive (negative). The right/duty and the power/liability relations are active in that they represent imperative relations subject to the authority of the state. On the other hand, the privilege/no right and immunity/no power relations are passive in that they are not themselves subject to direct legal enforcement. Instead, they set the limit of the state's activities in that they define the types of

Table 1.1.   The Four Fundamental Legal Relations

	ALPHA		BETA
Static Correlates	right		duty
	privilege		no right
	* * * * * * * * *		
Dynamic Correlates	power		liability
	immunity		no power

(After Hohfeld 1917).

behavior that are beyond the interest of the state. As seen in the case of privilege and no right, the state declares that it is none of its direct concern if Alpha imposes costs on Beta. In a sense, we have here legal relations that are statements of no law. Note that every right Alpha has upon Beta is reinforced by accompanying pressure on the courts to compel Beta to perform his/her duty with respect to Alpha.

Policy prescriptions suggesting we should leave it to the market imply that bargaining over environmental matters should occur within the prevailing institutional arrangements. Because there is no implied threat to the prevailing structure of entitlements, such prescriptions seem Pareto safe.[10] On the other hand, policy prescriptions that imply a change in the status quo entitlement structure appear quite extraordinary and are thought to entail government intervention. It is no surprise that policy change is controversial.

Externalities, Private Costs, and Social Costs

Environmental policy is often confounded by the particular language that characterizes many such disputes. One sees repeated reference to private benefits and costs in conflict with social benefits and costs. That is, the individual takes actions whose private benefits are said to exceed the social benefits, or whose private costs are said to be less than the social costs. To label these effects private and social, however, is to cloud the essential feature of environmental problems and may cause us to err in the search for coherent solutions. At issue in environmental disputes is the private interest of one party (Alpha) against the private interest of another (Beta). Environmental policy is concerned with the problems of determining whether the interests of Alpha will prevail or whether the interests of Beta will prevail. Alpha could be all of the chemical factories along a river, while Beta could be the fishing industry as well as those concerned about the safety of fish. Both parties will make a claim that they hope to have protection as an entitlement by the state. That is, each party will hope to secure protection over a benefit stream that we call property. That protection constitutes a *right*. Recall that entitlements are structures of rights and correlated duties, and that power is the ability to impose a new entitlement structure on others. Also note that the standard formulation of private versus public (or social) gives the impression that environmental matters are characterized by the wishes of the individual against the wishes of the collective — and that government then steps in to represent this collective interest. Using this view, it is easy to see how some believe that government is somehow interfering with the wishes of the individual in the name of some nebulous concern for the public interest.

A more careful consideration would reveal, however, that environmental problems — because they are usually a matter of the private interest of Alpha versus the private interest of Beta — are more properly regarded as triadic matters; Alpha, Beta, and the state. To protect the interest of Alpha is to interfere with Beta, while to protect the interests of Beta is to interfere with Alpha. The state must do something, for to do nothing is to side with the party protected by the presumptive rights of the status quo property arrangement (Samuels, 1971, 1972).

In our example, to counsel bargaining between the chemical industry and the fishing industry is to give a priori sanctity to the prevailing institutional setup. Recall that the status quo is one in which the fishing industry claims it is harmed by the actions of the chemical industry, while the chemical industry pleads innocent of any wrongdoing. In the absence of a legal finding favorable to the fishing industry, this situation would require the fishing industry to offer economic inducements to the chemical industry to change its waste-disposal practices. Yet such payments cannot be justified except under a presumptive entitlement structure in which the chemical industry is free to continue to discharge its residues until the real risks of chemical-laden fish are understood. Even then, we certainly expect the chemical industry to wage a spirited and perhaps costly campaign against any change in the prevailing setup.

The problem here is that the existing institutional setup was never ratified as legitimate in the presence of the potentially damaging chemical wastes. Rather, the institutional setup simply existed because — until the presence of the chemicals was determined to be potentially dangerous —

there was no reason for an alternative structure. The institutional structure did not account for the physical interdependence between chemicals and fish because, until recently, there had been no interdependence. Now, for the state to avoid interfering with the chemical industry, it must interfere with the long-run viability of the fishing industry. This is not a matter of the private interests of the chemical industry versus the public interests of clean water; it is a matter of the economic interests of two private parties — and the consumers of their respective products.

I now turn to the relationship between different entitlements and the perception of environmental risk.

Entitlements, Obligations, and Choices Regarding Environmental Risks

The literature on environmental policy sees two stylized choices before us. Either we rely on atomistic bargaining of the affected parties or we turn to collective action to set rules of behavior and performance. Those favoring atomism are able to invoke arguments showing that efficiency will be secured, bungling bureaucrats will be absent, and the citizenry will be well served. Those favoring collective action are able to invoke arguments showing that third-party interests will be better protected, that transaction costs will not stand in the way of clear social improvements, and that public decisions can overcome the myopia of market solutions. The student of environmental policy must then choose sides depending upon which attributes of the two poles hold the most appeal.

When uncertainty enters, as it surely must, the postulated symmetry of expected value theory of the von Neumann-Morgenstern variety becomes a contested auxiliary assumption in the construction of a coherent empirical model. The presence of uncertainty forces us to ask whether atomistic agents will regard the value of gains and losses the same as how gains and losses will be seen by public decision makers. By definition, atomistic agents make decisions in light of their own interests. Under the assumption that those independent decisions carry no external benefits or costs for others, then the aggregate of all such decisions will produce outcomes that constitute Pareto optimality.

However, atomistic actions can only occur within an institutional structure that is collectively determined. That is, the fishing industry and the chemical industry can bargain under the status quo institutional setup in which chemical residues are being discharged, or else they can bargain under the alternative institutional setup in which discharges are not allowed without the permission of the fishing industry. Uncertainty is of interest here because we now have reason to believe that the preferred institutional setup is very much influenced by the perceptions of individuals respecting probabilistic gains as opposed to probabilistic losses. To anticipate things somewhat, the theoretical symmetry of expected utility theory is not borne out by empirical work.

The issue of alternative entitlement structures and the appropriate policy response can be illustrated by constructing a payoff matrix of four possible policy outcomes predicated upon two states of nature and upon two possible decisions about the continued discharge of chemicals into the river. Specifically, there are two states of nature to consider: (1) chemical accumulation in fish is clearly dangerous to human health — call this S1, and (2) chemical accumulation in fish is completely harmless — call this S2. I pose this stark dichotomy to simplify the discussion, while recognizing that such absolute polarity is rare in environmental policy.

The policy problem is equally simplified by considering only two possible collective actions: (1) ban chemical discharges or (2) do nothing. The choice process is confounded by our incomplete knowledge of whether S1 or S2 represents the actual state of nature that will prevail. The expected-utility decision maker would seek estimates of benefits and costs for the four possible outcomes, she would proceed to assign weights based on their probability of occurrence, and the appropriate choice would be derived accordingly. Our task here is to consider whether this well-accepted practice accords with how the choice would be seen by those responsible for public policy. Consider table 1.2.

We have two classes of outcomes in table 1.2 — two 'correct' decisions, and two 'incorrect' decisions. The correct decisions are I and IV; picking the policy that produced either would be a considerable relief for those charged with doing the right thing. Unfortunately, it is difficult to know whether S1 or S2 will be the true state. In much environmental policy, the decision maker is, I suggest, more concerned with the two 'wrong' decisions: (1) doing nothing when in fact there is a real threat — case II, or (2) banning the chemical discharges when in fact there is no threat — case III.

I have suggested elsewhere that indeed policy makers would be inclined to attach quite different values to the four possible outcomes (Bromley, 1989a). This conclusion is supported by the imaginative work in prospect theory pioneered by Daniel Kahneman and Amos Tversky.[11] In that work we find important insights concerning perceptions of risk and public policy.

One implication of this work is that public decision makers may not regard losses and gains symmetrically. If that is the case, the existing

Table 1.2. The Choice Environment

	BAN CHEMICAL DISCHARGES	DO NOTHING
REAL THREAT	I	II
S1		
NO THREAT	III	IV
S2		

entitlement structure takes on added importance. That is, the expected value decision maker will choose the action that produces the greatest expected payoff, while the decision maker concerned to minimize maximum regret will choose the action that promises the smallest expected opportunity loss. Under conventional treatments of risk analysis, the expected payoff is simply the obverse of the expected opportunity loss. However, this symmetry seems to contradict empirical reality.

Specifically, recent developments in the theory of risk analysis provide an opportunity to illustrate the importance of status quo institutional arrangements in problems in which uncertainty is present. In prospect theory, one partitions the decision problem into two parts: (1) framing the actions, outcomes, and contingencies; and (2) evaluating the choices to be made. When this is done, the experimental evidence indicates that people do not behave as expected utility theory predicts. In an illustration of the certainty effect, Kahneman and Tversky found that 80 percent of their respondents preferred a sure gain of 3,000 units to the following choice: a 4,000-unit gain with probability of 0.8 or a zero gain with probability of 0.2. The expected value of the sure thing is 3,000 while the expected value of the gamble is 3,200. Yet the sure thing was the dominant choice. When concerned with losses as opposed to gains they found the opposite effect. That is, a sure loss of 3,000 units was preferred by only 8 percent of the respondents, while a 4,000-unit loss with probability 0.8 or a zero loss with probability of 0.2 was preferred by 92 percent. In the positive domain the certainty effect contributes to risk aversion so that a sure gain is taken rather than a larger, but probable, gain. In the negative domain the certainty effect leads to risk-seeking preferences for a probable loss over a smaller — but certain — loss.

This distinction between the positive and negative domains is relevant because, unlike conventional investment analysis, many instances of collective action in environmental policy require that expenditures be undertaken now to protect against probable losses in the future. It is important to understand that expected payoffs from productive investments differ from expected losses from failure to make defensive investments.

Risk aversion and risk seeking have different dimensions when choices involving gains are compared with choices involving losses. Tversky and Kahneman refer to loss aversion as the situation in which there is a discrepancy "between the amount of money people are willing to pay for a good and the compensation they demand to give it up (Kahneman and Tversky, 1979, p. 74)."[12] While loss aversion may capture what is at work here, these differences reflect underlying perceptions regarding entitlements and the presumed rights of the status quo. That is, if one is already in possession of something there is a presumption that the item is the property of the individual faced with its loss. Put somewhat differently, one is thought to have a right to that particular situation or outcome.

Public decision makers will often seem to be taking actions that will minimize losses as opposed to actions that will maximize gains; for this they are often thought to be irrational. Yet it may well be that those in a position to make collective decisions are willing to gamble to avoid certain losses, but are risk averse in the domain of gains, preferring a certain small gain to a chance at a much larger one. The Minimax Regret Decision Criterion from expected utility theory addresses the difference between the payoff from the correct decision and the payoff from the actual decision. Because of the presence of irreversibilities in many choices and the social stigma of being thought to make wrong choices, it is reasonable to suppose that many policy makers—just as with most participants in the Kahneman and Tversky experiments—reject the formal equality of the expected value of gains and losses.

This would make them more amenable to a strategy that seems to minimize their maximum regret. If choice II in table 1.2 is the one promising the greatest regret—that is, doing nothing when in fact there are important implications from chemical discharges—then that choice is the least desirable option. In fact one can postulate a ranking among the four choices in table 1.2 as follows: IV p> I p> III p> II (where p> reads "is preferred to"). Unlike the arena within which atomistic decision makers operate, public decision makers are under some obligation to take decisions that will avoid probabilistic losses. They are, as Kahneman and Tversky found, likely willing to engage in probabilistic choice to avoid large losses, but most unlikely to engage in gambles to attain large gains.

Perhaps risk-averse choices in the face of certain gains reflects a particular attitude of rights toward the expected gains. If that is so, then decision makers may see no reason to engage in probabilistic undertakings that may enhance those gains but which may also reduce the gains to zero. On the other hand, when decision makers are faced with certain losses unless something is done, they may be quite unwilling to sit idly by without undertaking actions to attempt to reduce those certain losses — even with the remote prospect of even greater losses.

The different perceptions of gains and losses, and the fact that much environmental policy is concerned with defensive actions, seem important for how we analyze collective choice situations. The essential issue here is quite simple. The entitlement structure that is presumed to prevail will influence the framing of the choice problem and also the evaluation of the putative efficiency of alternative policy options. An entitlement structure that seems to permit individuals to engage in certain polluting behaviors will clearly color the way in which the decision problem is cast and evaluated. Similarly, if politicians perceive an implicit entitlement structure in which individuals are thought to have a right to something, we should not be surprised to observe actions that display scant interest in taking chances with that perceived right. This difference is reflected in the economics literature in which the willingness to pay for items has been found to be quite different from the willingness to accept compensation for the pending loss of something (Knetsch and Sinden, 1984). If one is thought to have a right, then it implies that the willingness to accept compensation for the loss of that right is germane. On the other hand, if someone else holds that right, then we must ascertain one's willingness to pay to acquire the object in question.

Conclusions

The defining characteristic of public decision making is, I suggest, that the citizenry expects to be informed about some risks, protected from others, and compensated for yet others. In essence, most individuals accept the idea that it is better to be safe than sorry. This means that collective action is unlikely to regard alternative entitlement structures — one permissive of possibly harmful chemical discharges, the other restrictive of such discharges — as equally attractive. Public policy remains concerned with the welfare of the collective. Individual members of society do not take this matter lightly, and public decision makers seem to be inclined to act accordingly. In the context of our discussion here about alternative entitlement structures, one can expect to see institutional setups that err on the side of caution when ecological and health effects are probabilistic.[13]

Notes

1. One may recall the recent ability to demonstrate causality linking the use of chlorofluorocarbons to holes in the earth's ozone layer.

2. Many of those who were attracted to the laissez-faire policy implications of the Coase Theorem — the so-called hyper-Coaseans — have been less circumspect.

3. For a sample of the literature exposing the fallacy in the alleged neutrality of the Coase Theorem, see Bromley [1978, 1989b, 1991], Dahlman [1979], Dick [1976], Marchand and Russell [1973], Mishan [1969, 1974, 1975], Randall [1972, 1974], and Schap [1986].

4. There is, of course, a difference in the value of output from the two different entitlement structures. But the value of output does not translate, automatically, into some clear measure of efficiency. See Bromley [1989b, 1990].

5. There is a literature within economics that regards possession as evidence of property rights. See Demsetz [1967] and Sugden [1986] for arguments along such lines. This confusion of physical possession with Kantian intelligible possession is rejected here.

6. By intelligible possession Kant meant the social recognition of the property claim of the owner. In my terms this is the triadic aspect of rights that recognizes the owner and the claim against all others.

7. See Buchanan [1972] for arguments along such lines in relation to the famous Virginia cedar-rust disputes reported in Samuels [1971, 1972].

8. These elaborations are from Commons [1968, 1990].

9. Note that liability is used here in a different sense from that often seen in the environmental economics literature.

10. It is instructive to contemplate the normative content of the conclusion that environmental disputes should be resolved through bargaining within the existing entitlement structure. Most economics, loath to appear normative, will insist that this recommendation is not a personal value judgment but follows from the compelling efficiency gains to be had from volitional bargains. This is certainly Buchanan's point [1972]. But such efficiency gains must be seen as embedded within a value system that places zero weights on all considerations other than the maximization of net economic value as measured by willingness to pay and willingness to accept compensation. Efficiency is not value free, it is simply consistent with value judgments widely held among economists. Because of this apparent consensus, it appears to entail objective science rather than a value judgment (Bromley, 1990). To quote one writer: "Pareto optimality is optimal with reference to those value judgments that are consistent with the Pareto principle (Ng, 1983, p. 30).

11. See Kahneman and Tversky [1979], and Tversky and Kahneman [1981, 1987].

12. Also see the work by Knetsch and Sinden [1984].

13. I have elsewhere elaborated on the idea that the nature of the perceived damage arising from externalities is the fundamental issue in assessing the appropriate entitlement structure (Bromley, 1991).

References

Bromley, Daniel W. 1991. *Environment and Economy: Property Rights and Public Policy*. Oxford: Basil Blackwell.

Bromley, Daniel W. 1990. "The Ideology of Efficiency: Searching for a Theory of

Policy Analysis," *Journal of Environmental Economics and Management* 19, 86–107.

Bromley, Daniel W. 1989a. "Entitlements, Missing Markets and Environmental Uncertainty," *Journal of Environmental Economics and Management* 17 (September), 181–94.

Bromley, Daniel W. 1989b. *Economic Interests and Institutions: The Conceptual Foundations of Public Policy.* Oxford: Basil Blackwell.

Bromley, Daniel W. 1978. "Property Rules, Liability Rules, and Environmental Economics, *Journal of Economic Issues* 12 (March), 43–60.

Bromley, Daniel W., and Ian Hodge. 1990. "Private Property Rights and Presumptive Policy Entitlements: Reconsidering the Premises of Rural Policy," *European Review of Agricultural Economics.* 17 (Spring), 197–214.

Buchanan, James N. 1972. "Politics, Property and the Law: An Alternative Interpretation of Miller et al. v. Schoene," *Journal of Law and Economics* 15 (October), 439–452.

Coase, Ronald. 1960. "The Problem of Social Cost," *Journal of Law and Economics* 3 (October), 1–44.

Commons, John R. 1990. *Institutional Economics.* New Brunswick, NJ: Transaction Publishers.

Commons, John R. 1968. *Legal Foundations of Capitalism.* Madison: University of Wisconsin Press.

Dahlman, Carl J. 1979. "The Problem of Externality," *Journal of Law and Economics* 22 (April), 141–162.

Demsetz, Harold. 1967. "Toward a Theory of Property Rights," *American Economics Review* 57 (May), 347–59.

Dick, Daniel T. 1976. "The Voluntary Approach to Externality Problems: A Survey of the Critics," *Journal of Environmental Economics and Management* 2 (February), 185–195.

Hohfeld, W. N. 1917. "Fundamental Legal Conceptions as Applied in Judicial Reasoning," *Yale Law Journal* 26, 710–770.

Kahneman, Daniel, and Amos Tversky. 1979. "Prospect Theory: An Analysis of Decision Under Risk," *Econometrica* 47, 263–291.

Knetsch, Jack, and J. A. Sinden. 1984. "Willingness to Pay and Compensation Demanded: Experimental Evidence of an Unexpected Disparity in Measures of Value," *Quarterly Journal of Economics* 99, 507–521.

Lang, Mahlon. 1980. "Economic Efficiency and Policy Comparisons," *American Journal of Agricultural Economics* 62 (November), 772–77.

Marchand, James R., and Keith P. Russell. 1973. "Externalities, Liability, Separability, and Resource Allocation," *American Economic Review* 63 (September), 611–20.

Mishan, E. J. 1980. "How Valid Are Economic Evaluations of Allocative Changes?" *Journal of Economic Issues* 14 (March), 143–161.

Mishan, E. J. 1975. "The Folklore of the Market," *Journal of Economic Issues* 9 (December), 681–752.

Mishan, E. J. 1974. "The Economics of Disamenity," *Natural Resources Journal* 14 (January), 55–86.

Mishan, E. J. 1969. "Welfare Economics: An Assessment," *Humanities Press*, Atlantic Highlands, N.J.

Munzer, Stephen. 1990. *A Theory of Property*. Cambridge: Cambridge University Press.

Ng, Y-K. 1983. *Welfare Economics*. London: Macmillan.

Randall, Alan. 1974. "Coasian Externality Theory in a Policy Context," *Natural Resources Journal* 14 (January), 35–54.

Randall, Alan. 1972. "Market Solutions to Externality Problems: Theory and Practice," *American Journal of Agricultural Economics* 54 (May), 175–183.

Samuels, Warren. 1972. "In Defense of Government as an Economic Variable," *Journal of Law and Economics* 15 (October), 453–459.

Samuels, Warren. 1971. "The Interrelations Between Legal and Economic Processes," *Journal of Law and Economics* 14 (October), 435–450.

Schap, David. 1986. "The Nonequivalence of Property Rules and Liability Rules," *International Review of Law and Economics* 6, 125–132.

Sugden, Robert. 1986. *The Economics of Rights, Co-operation and Welfare*. Oxford: Basil Blackwell.

Tawney, R. H. 1948. *The Acquisitive Society*. New York: Harcourt Brace.

Tversky, Amos, and Daniel Kahneman. 1987. "Rational Choice and the Framing of Decisions," In Robin Hogarth and Melvin Reder (eds.), *Rational Choice*. Chicago: University of Chicago Press.

Tversky, Amos, and Daniel Kahneman. 1981. "The Framing of Decisions and the Psychology of Choice," *Science* 211 (January), 453–58.

Waldron, Jeremy. (ed.) 1984. *Theories of Rights*. Oxford: Oxford University Press.

Williams, Howard. 1977. "Kant's Concept of Property," *Philosophical Quarterly* 27, 32–40.

2 ENVIRONMENTAL RISK PERCEPTION AND VALUATION: CONVENTIONAL VERSUS PROSPECTIVE REFERENCE THEORY

V. Kerry Smith*

The definition of the commodity is a central issue in modeling people's choices in the presence of uncertainty. To appreciate why, we need to consider the modeling strategy inherent in virtually all microeconomic descriptions of people's values for commodities. Using tradeoffs to infer values is usually the first idea introduced in describing individual behavior with microeconomics. A commodity's value is measured by how much of some other good a person will give up to get more of the defined commodity. This concept is, of course, the essence of a marginal rate of substitution.[1]

The conventional economic model for individual behavior in the presence of risk assumes that people choose lotteries, and the rule for selecting them involves optimizing a von Neumann-Morgenstern (VNM)

* V. Kerry Smith is University Distinguished Professor, Department of Economics, North Carolina State University.

23

utility function. While this function has specific properties that influence its predictive power, the model is basically the same as that for behavior under conditions of certainty. VNM restructured their description of preferences to allow a lottery to play the same role as a commodity. The value the model implies for a lottery is described in terms of other goods people would trade for an increment to the lottery.

Two aspects of this approach to describing people's behavior cause problems in applying it to situations involving environmental risks. First, there is no natural way to define and measure increments to a lottery. As a result, the economic models used to value changes in lotteries focus on changes in either the probabilities or the outcomes that define each lottery. Much of the literature on private decisions involving lotteries concerns choices about insurance or financial assets. With the exception of life insurance choices, the outcomes at risk are usually well-defined monetary values. Often people have the opportunity to gain experience through repeated transactions, and markets provide incentives that discipline incorrect perceptions of the probabilities inherent in such lotteries.

Such mechanisms are not available for environmental lotteries. Both the probabilities and the outcomes are different. Environmental lotteries are usually described in terms of exposures to substances that involve serious, often life-threatening, health effects. A partial list includes hazardous and nuclear waste, air pollutants, and pesticide residues on food. There are many others. Both the exposure probabilities and the conditional probability of a health outcome given exposure are not widely understood by people.[2] Because the outcomes often involve death, no opportunities exist to gain experience. And, in many of these examples, a different type of "time" compounds the problems in conceptualizing environmental lotteries as commodities. *They never seem to end.* Once hazardous substances are released into the environment, or a person is exposed to a potentially harmful pollutant, the outcome is not resolved until the individuals dies.[3]

The second problem with treating environmental lotteries as commodities arises from the ex ante nature of the tradeoff inherent in determining values for them. Exchanges are between some numeraire and attributes of a process that is not resolved when the tradeoff is defined. The lottery can involve risk of a chronic health impairment that has never been experienced, yet by specifying a conventional ex ante marginal rate of substitution, we assume people can consider incremental tradeoffs between the odds of the disease and dollar expenditures to avoid such impacts. Of course, assuming these tradeoffs are possible is less important if individuals have prior experience with the outcomes at risk. However, as noted earlier, this is unlikely for many types of environmental risks.

Therefore, it should not be surprising that economic analyses of efficient policies for dealing with environmental risks seem to be at odds with what people want. The Environmental Protection Agency (EPA) recently sought to rate environmental risks and found wide discrepancies between the public's identification of important environmental risks and those selected by the EPA's technical experts [U.S. Environmental Protection Agency, 1987]. Motivated by concerns about using economics to evaluate policies involving environmental risk, Machina [1990] recently recommended that we treat departures from the "strictures of probability theory" arising from the formation of risk perceptions differently than systematic departures from the predictions of expected utility theory. In his view, the former should be corrected and the latter should not be corrected. This paper is about some of the issues that underlie Machina's conclusion — the connections between risk perceptions and valuation.

Environmental risks require that people acquire information and learn about the events at risk, including the processes underlying them. However, we know very little about how people perform these tasks. In the next section, I summarize some findings from the available research. Overall, these results suggest that the framing of information about the process causing the risk can influence both perceptions and behavior. Moreover, people's preferences influence how they acquire this information, form risk perceptions, and value actions intended to reduce the perceived risk.[4] Unfortunately, attempts to replace the conventional expected utility framework have not been successful in describing this multifaceted process as a complete unit. Nonetheless, it is possible to illustrate how risk perceptions and values are connected.

I develop this connection later by comparing how the value of a change in risk can be described using a conventional expected utility model versus Viscusi's [1989, 1990] recently proposed prospective reference theory (PRT). PRT recognizes that individuals' risk perceptions are distinct from the experts' technical estimates. They reflect each individual's prior beliefs, the information they receive about the process, and the relative degree of confidence they assign to each. To demonstrate the links between perceptions and values, I use the PRT model to define a locus that describes how the values of a policy change would vary with the weights involved in defining subjective risk perceptions.

Drawing implications for environmental risk policy is certainly dangerous, especially after arguing that the conventional theory used to evaluate policy is incompatible with what people do, and noting that the empirical evidence is incomplete. Nonetheless, the last section describes how coordinating the available instruments might improve the efficacy of environmental risk policies.

Economic Research on the Risk Perception Process

Despite the wide acceptance of the expected utility model for describing individual behavior under uncertainty, and the general recognition that experience must condition each person's beliefs about uncertain events, remarkably little economic research has been undertaken to describe how people form risk perceptions. Viscusi and O'Connor's [1984] evaluation of how chemical workers updated their risk perceptions and wage requirements in response to hypothetical product labels appears to be the first such study. Psychologists have expressed long-standing interest in these problems and have often criticized the expected utility (EU) framework.[5] Nonetheless, the recent research on risk perception is different from their experiments, which have been designed to explore the limits of people's ability to process information.

Two types of studies characterize the recent work. The first type involves hypothetical behavior and follows the general format of contingent valuation (CV) studies. (See Mitchell and Carson [1989] for a general overview of the CV method.) These surveys seek to elicit how risk perceptions or contingent behavior or both respond to different hypothetical information treatments. The second type of research involves actual risks and the effects of different information programs. Because the risks are real, these studies have usually been conducted as part of evaluating the effectiveness of risk communication programs.

Both types of research suggest that people's risk perceptions systematically respond to information. The content and framing of the information can influence respondents' risk perceptions, stated behavior, and actual behavior.

Studies Using Contingent Behavior

Most current research that uses hypothetical situations to study how people's risk perceptions respond to information is associated with experiments by Viscusi and his collaborators. As noted earlier, the first of these (Viscusi and O'Connor [1984]) considered chemical workers and their perceptions of job risks from handling chemicals in the workplace. To evaluate how workers' risk perceptions responded to information, the study elicited each respondent's perception of job risk using a simple scale with the average risk to manufacturing workers identified as an anchor on the scale. Each respondent was interviewed before and after they read hypothetical labels describing new products. Respondents were asked their wage requirements and whether they would remain at their jobs if the hypothetical product they read about replaced the chemicals currently involved in their workplace. Viscusi and O'Connor's analysis of the risk updating process, as well as of the other behavioral responses asked of these respondents, strongly supports a rational response (and therefore conventional EU theory where learning and perception are treated as exogenous). These results are reported in more detail in chapter 8.

Viscusi's continuing research in this area reveals a subtle but systematic change in this conclusion. With each progressive reduction in the way the information presented to respondents connected risks to precautionary behavior, as well as with changes in the structure of the behavioral questions asked of them, support for the conventional framework's separation of risk perception and behavior lessened.

Viscusi, Magat, and Huber's [1986] study reinforced Viscusi and O'Connor's analysis. However, it was a highly structured evaluation of responses to a single source of risk. These authors interviewed respondents about their precautionary behavior in using two hypothetical household products. Labels for each product varied in the amount of risk information and its prominence on the label. Each respondent in a shopping mall intercept survey was shown one product label and asked about product use patterns to avoid prompting them to focus on the risk-related questions. While specific risk perceptions were not elicited, questions about general risk attitudes and precautionary behavior were asked. Both sets of responses supported the conclusions drawn in Viscusi and O'Connor's earlier study of chemical workers' risk perceptions. However, when the experimental situations introduced multiple-risk sources (see Viscusi, Magat, and Huber [1987]) or used questions relying on open-ended memory tasks related to the information from hypothetical product labels (see Magat, Viscusi, and Huber [1988]), the cognitive factors frequently identified by psychologists as important to how people process risk information were found to influence both experiments' findings. With multiple risks, departures from a rational model's predicted behavior seemed to be related to cognitive factors in a respondent's understanding of risk information. This was reinforced in the last study. Magat, Viscusi, and Huber [1988] concluded that the experiments indicate "an upper bound on individuals' ability to process risk information" that may well interfere with their overall ability to use that information.

The most recent study investigating the influence of information on risk perceptions and behavioral intentions, that of Weinstein, Sandman, and Roberts [1989], follows the overall design of the Smith, et al. [1990]

New York radon study (discussed later) but asks people about their risk perceptions and behavioral intentions in response to hypothetical radon and asbestos readings, different types of information about the risks they produce, and mitigation responses. The sample consisted of New Jersey homeowners with telephone listings who agreed to receive one of fifty-six different information treatments designed for the study along with a questionnaire. Thirty-four percent of the 8,500 households contacted agreed to participate. About two-thirds of those agreeing (1,948) returned questionnaires.

Table 2.1 describes the differences in the seven information treatments used in the study. Each treatment involved a four-page brochure — one for radon and one for asbestos. The last page in each brochure was altered to incorporate information identified as the design feature. Each respondent was asked to evaluate their circumstances using one of four hypothetical exposure levels for the substance serving as the source of

Table 2.1. Weinstein Sandman, Roberts Evaluation of Risk Communication Materials

Treatment Number	Key Issue	Description
1	Risk Probabilities	Information about expected lifetime mortality expressed as deaths per thousand people at various levels of exposure.
2	Risk Probabilities and Comparisons	Same information as Treatment 1 with comparative information describing risks from cigarette smoking.
3	Probabilities in Graphic Format	Treatment 1 displayed using a histogram.
4	Standard	Information about the recommended action level for the source of risk.
4	Standard, Risk Probability and Comparisons	Combines Treatment 4 with Treatment 2.
6	Standard and Advice	Treatment 4 with detailed action advice and verbal levels for the four range of exposure levels.
7	Standard, Advice, Risk Probabilities and Comparisons	Combines Treatment 2 with Treatment 6.

risk for their treatment. Thus, fifty-six different possibilities rise from the source of risk (2) x level of exposure (4) x information attributes (7).

Respondents were asked to evaluate the brochures, including their perceptions of risk seriousness, the likelihood of illness, and their intentions to take action if they were to receive the hypothetical radon or asbestos readings described in the questionnaire as imaginary. The authors draw rather strong conclusions from their analysis of the responses to these information treatments. Those most relevant follow:

1. People respond differently when a level specified as requiring some action is presented based on variables likely to be related both to risk perception and remediation plans.
2. People receiving probability information did 'a better job of estimating illness probabilities.' However, comparisons of the risks assigned by respondents to radon versus asbestos were not correctly scaled in terms of their absolute levels by either group.
3. Respondents receiving comparative risk information reduced their risk averse reactions to the materials.

While these conclusions support the argument that preferences, information, and perception are linked, they should not be taken as the result of conventional statistical tests with the survey data collected. The most appropriate conclusion to be drawn from the analysis is that the findings are the researchers' qualitative judgments based on simple statistical summaries of the response distributions. The findings may not be as conclusive as the authors imply. Nonetheless, when their findings are combined with the work of Viscusi and his co-authors, which was based on fewer information alternatives but more rigorous testing, the record from contingent behavior studies clearly supports a link between risk perceptions and behavior. This may be the result of predetermined risk perceptions influencing behavior, or in some situations perceptions and behavior may be jointly determined.

Studies Using Risk Communication Programs

Research findings that rely on responses to hypothetical situations inevitably face the criticism that reports based on people's interpretations of hypothetical situations — and their contingent responses — may not be reliable guides to their actual responses to risk information.[6] Policy interest in using information programs has encouraged new opportunities to provide further insight into how people form risk perceptions as part of evaluating the effectiveness of risk information programs.. These studies can be distinguished by two design features: (1) the ability to observe a sample of people update their risk perceptions and undertake activities in response to information about specific types of risks, and (2) the experimental control over the information provided to the sample. In what follows, I will summarize the results of four studies — all associated with radon risk — that investigated the influence of information on risk perceptions.[7]

Reed Johnson and I (see Smith and Johnson [1988]) conducted one of the first efforts to evaluate how people respond to information about a real risk. Staff at the Maine Medical Center designed an epidemiological study relating lung cancer to radon exposure. They interviewed a sample of individuals who participated in the study, as well as a control sample of households who requested tests of air or water as part of the Radiological Health Program offered by the Maine Department of Human Services.[8] Both indoor air and water were monitored for radon for all of the 230 households agreeing to telephone interviews about their risk perceptions, mitigating activities, and socioeconomic activities. Interviews were conducted after each household received its radon readings along with the same eleven-page information booklet describing the sources of radon, its health risks, and possible mitigation strategies. Respondents were asked their perceptions of radon's risks at the time of the interview and what their perceptions of radon's risk were prior to receiving the monitoring results and pamphlet.

The results supported Viscusi and O'Connor's updating model. These households' risk perceptions were influenced by their radon readings and by whether they had undertaken some form of mitigation before they were asked about their risk. Experience with a cancer patient in the household also increased the weight respondents assigned to their prior perceptions (i.e., before receiving the monitoring results and pamphlet). Unfortunately, the retrospective nature of the risk perception question and the inability to observe how different types of information affected these respondents, limit this study's usefulness as support for my overall argument that risk perception must be treated as an important determinant of behavior.

The last three studies do allow this issue to be investigated more directly. Two of them involve my joint research with Bill Desvousges initiated in 1985 to investigate the performance of different types of risk communication programs in New York and Maryland. Because the New York study is still underway (the surveying of participating households is finished but empirical analysis of the panel data describing their responses continues), I will review those findings last.

The Maryland risk communication program was initiated after some preliminary results were available from the New York study (see Smith et al. [1987]). The Maryland program sought to develop and evaluate practical information programs that could eventually be distributed to individual states in an effort to promote radon testing (see Desvousges, Smith, and Rink [1989]). Three Maryland towns were selected for analysis—Hagerstown, Frederick, and Randallstown. The first two communities received different public information programs developed jointly by the EPA's Program Evaluation Division and the Research Triangle Institute. The third community served as a control. Table 2.2 describes the two programs. For program evaluation, three sets of telephone interviews were conducted in each community. These included baseline surveys of random samples of approximately 500 individuals in each community in December 1987 (before the program). Then two follow-up surveys were conducted concurrently in April 1988 (after the program). These follow-up interviews involved repeat contacts with those originally interviewed, along with independent samples of another 500 individuals in each town.

The analysis I will summarize here focuses on two aspects of the panel sample's responses that provide one way of gauging the effectiveness of an information program: (1) evaluating how well they learned the key elements of the program's intended messages and (2) examining the factors that explain respondents' radon testing decisions. Three features of these findings relate to my overall argument about the connections between preferences, risk perception, and behavior regarding environmental risks. First, the most extensive information program (in Frederick) had a consistently significant, positive effect (at least at the 10% level) on learning for both of the targeted questions. Information questions were asked during a baseline survey and then again after the program to promote testing. Moreover, this effect can be distinguished from any prior knowledge. Hagerstown's smaller-scale program apparently did not transfer sufficient information to improve respondents' knowledge on these issues.

Second, our study examined whether an independent radon information program had a separate effect on learning. A week-long public service television special on radon was initiated by WJLA, a Washington, D.C., television network. Two of our sample towns were in this station's viewing area. To attempt to account for this influence, we asked respondents during the second interview if—and how—they had heard about radon. If they identified the WJLA program or simply stated "from television," both answers could be considered as reflecting WJLA's program.

Third, table 2.3 reports our findings on whether the information programs affected behavior. This response measured whether respondents

Table 2.2. Design Features of Maryland Public Information Program

| Community | Role in EPA Test | Elements of Treatment[a] | | | | Impact of Independent WJLA Program[b] |
		Media	Mailings	Outreach		
Randallstown	Control	None[c]	None[c]	None[c]		10 kits
Hagerstown	Treatment #1	PSA to three radio stations every two weeks; project-designed posters ran in newspaper one week in February; four additional articles in paper	Pamphlet inserted in utility bills during February/March billing cycle	None		93 kits
Frederick	Treatment #2	PSA to two radio stations every two weeks; five of eight articles in local newspaper project-related	Pamphlet inserted in utility bills during February/March billing cycle	Posters (4) in locations around town; nine presentations to community groups between January and March 1988; organized Radon Awareness Week; arranged for Mayor and Aldermen to visit their homes		669 kits

[a] The primary messages emphasized in the public service announcements (PSA), posters, public meetings, etc. were

- Randon is a serious health risk. *You* may be at risk. The only way to find out is to test.
- Testing is easy and inexpensive.
- Radon problems can be fixed.

[b] Independent of the EPA project, a Washington, D.C., television station, WJLA, conducted a month-long campaign to encourage people to test their homes for radon during January/February of our study period. The campaign had multiple components, with coordination by television and newspapers, and availability of radon test kits at a reduced price at Safeway Supermarkets. The campaign began on January 12, included a three-part news series during the week of January 18, and ended with another three-part series during the week of February 15–19. Advertisements for the effort appeared in the *Washington Post* and on television. 100,000 radon test kits were purchased, with 70,000 returned for analysis. Television ratings indicated an audience of 76,000 viewers. The television programs targeted the Washington, D.C., viewing area. Residents of Frederick were most likely to watch the station arising the programs. Hagerstown residents could view WJLA, but reception is poor without cable. Randallstown is outside the viewing area, but reception is good. Numbers refer to the radon test kits returned from each community.

[c] None refers to the fact that there were no project-initiated information materials presented in public media mailings or meetings. Some independent newspaper articles did appear in a local paper.

Table 2.3.   Determinants of Radon Testing: Maryland Panel Sample[a]

Independent Variables	Before Information Programs	After Information Programs
Family Income (in Dollars)	$.26 \times 10^{-5}$	$.29 \times 10^{-5}$
	(0.648)	(0.661)
Years of Education	.052	−.062
	(1.668)	(−1.765)
Age	−.005	.002
	(−0.774)	(0.473)
Sex (1 = Male)	−.059	
	(−0.414)	
Health Attitude (Concerned about Health = 1)	.328	−.007
	(2.333)	(−0.042)
Number of Years at Address	$.36 \times 10^{-3}$	
	(0.052)	
Have Basement and Use It for Living Space	−1.59	.057
	(−1.075)	(0.366)
Total Correct Answers Baseline Radon Quiz	.202	
	(5.480)	
Hagerstown (= 1)		.078
		(0.368)
Frederick (= 1)		.437
		(2.243)
Talk about Radon Prior to Baseline (= 1)		.345
		(2.232)
Saw WJLA Program (= 1)		.091
		(0.427)
Inverse Mills for Baseline Testing		−2.168
		(−2.466)

[a] These models are probit estimates. The numbers in parentheses below the estimated coefficients are rations of the coefficient to the estimated asymptotic t-ratio.

[b] An inverse Mills ratio is included in the probit model for the new testing decisions to reflect the selection effects of losing those who tested at the baseline. Bivariate probit models for both testing decisions did not converge.

who had not previously monitored their homes for radon later decided to do so because of the public information program. Column 1 in the table reports a probit model describing the determinants of decisions to test for radon prior to the baseline survey. Column 2 reports a comparable analysis of the untested households at the time of the baseline interview who appeared to respond to the program by undertaking some type of monitoring for radon.

The positive and significant coefficient for the qualitative variable used to designate the Frederick program suggests a direct connection between the information program and new testing decisions. This implies an increase of nearly five percentage points in the probability of testing because of the program in Frederick (.03 to .076). Only a few other factors appear to influence these decisions, including (1) prior knowledge of radon (reflected by the qualitative variable for discussing radon) and (2) the inverse Mills ratio used to account for the selection effects associated with the untested households at the time of the baseline interview (see Heckman [1979]). The model in Column 1 was used to estimate this term. While these models are best interpreted as reduced form relationships, they do indicate a behavioral link between the decision to monitor a home for radon and the form of the information program used to describe radon's risk as part of an effort to encourage increased testing. Moreover, this impact could well be understated because the information programs do appear to raise a household's level of awareness of radon, and this appears to increase the likelihood of monitoring at a later time.[9]

Golding, Krimsky, and Plough [1990] adopted a similar design in their study of the effects of information programs in three towns in Massachusetts — Clinton, Fitchburg, and Worcester. Worcester served as the control community. The other two received two different information programs about radon through their local newspapers. Each town was assumed to be served exclusively by its local newspaper. In Clinton, four technical articles appeared in the local newspaper, each covering a different aspect of radon: its source and nature, monitoring, health effects from exposure, and finally, mitigation. In Fitchburg, four articles covered the same concepts but used a dramatized account of one person's attempt to understand and cope with these aspects of radon.

Baseline and follow-up telephone interviews were conducted before and after the newspaper articles appeared in the two towns receiving the information and in the control community. Both panel and independent samples were composed to evaluate the effects of the programs. Unfortunately, the sample sizes for the follow-up interviews (both the panel and the independent groups) were small.[10] The authors did not find differences in the effects of the two types of programs on respondents' decisions to test for radon. Indeed, the information programs did not appear to have a significant effect on testing decisions. As with the Weinstein et al. [1989] analysis, these conclusions are difficult to evaluate. The authors did not appear to consider multivariate analysis in evaluating the programs and relied instead on simple univariate tests and graphical descriptions of the data. With these small samples and rather small differences in the responses to questions about intentions to test or mitigate, their conclusions are probably correct. That is, statistical tests with such small samples are unlikely to reveal an effect that is not apparent from the summary data.

The converse is, of course, not necessarily true. Effects that seem to be present in simple descriptive summaries may not be associated with information treatments. Moreover, the criticism that relates to this study arises from the conclusion of no effect when the samples are too small to detect one. The differences between the information treatments may be small enough to require larger samples to be estimated accurately. This is especially true when individuals' demographic and economic characteristics influence how they respond to information programs. Thus, we cannot conclude that Golding et al.'s method for framing is not important. Instead, this variation in framing may have such small effects that it requires a more discriminating test.

The last study to be reviewed is the most extensive and, in some respects, nearly as specialized as the evaluation of the Maine sample described earlier.[11] The New York State Energy Research and Development Authority (NYSERDA)/EPA study of the influence of informational materials on perceptions of radon risks and associated mitigation decisions began before much of the risk communication research summarized above. Because aspects of this study's results have been summarized in several earlier papers (see Smith, et al. [1988, 1990] and Smith and Desvousges [1990]), I will focus this summary and overview on three aspects of the study: (1) a brief description of the design, (2) a summary of the influence of information on risk perceptions, including new evidence from the last interview after mitigation decisions, and (3) some highlights of the evidence on the influence of information on respondents' mitigation decisions.

In 1985, the New York State Energy Research and Development Authority initiated a monitoring project to measure indoor concentrations of radon in detached single-family homes in seven geologic zones in the state. The study design selected a random sample of 2,300 New York homeowners who had no plans to move in the next year and placed three radon monitors in each home—two in the living area and one in the basement. One of the living area monitors was removed after about two months, and the other monitors were removed after one year.

With EPA support and NYSERDA cooperation, this monitoring project was used as an opportunity to evaluate the effectiveness of risk communication materials.[12] The design was adjusted to conform to the NYSERDA protocol for providing the participating households information about their radon readings. To meet this objective, four information brochures were designed, each varying the mode of presentation of risk information. They can be distinguished by two design attributes: (1) the extent of quantitative information (i.e., quantitative versus qualitative) and (2) the degree of encouragement given to respondents to evaluate how their personal circumstances might affect the risks they experience from radon (i.e., command versus cajole). Four different variants were composed by pairing the design alternatives from each attribute. In addition, the EPA booklet *A Citizen's Guide to Radon* and a one-page fact sheet were also considered as alternative information treatments.

Each household received its radon readings in two steps—first the two-month readings from the living area monitor and then the annual readings for the remaining living area and basement monitors. In addition, they received one of the six information treatments. This treatment was randomly assigned with an important constraint—households with two-month radon readings higher than one picocurie per liter were not allowed to receive the one-page fact sheet and were randomly assigned one of the five remaining alternatives. Those with readings at or below one picocurie were randomly assigned to the six treatments, with about half given the fact sheet and the remainder divided randomly among the five other alternatives.[13]

The analysis of the effects of these informational materials is based on four interviews of the same adult decision maker. This member of the household was randomly selected during a baseline interview conducted six months before the results for the two-month readings were sent to each household. The schedule for the information distribution and interviews, along with percentages of households completing each survey, are given in table 2.4.

Table 2.5 summarizes the primary results applying the Viscusi-O'Connor updating model for risk perceptions to each of the three updates. Because of the experimental design, the panel nature of the sample, and the application to real risks, these findings provide the strongest support to date for a systematic risk updating process that is influenced both by information and by how it is conveyed to individuals. The radon readings were positive and significant determinants of risk perceptions when they were new information. The two-month reading was new for the first update and had a positive, significant influence on stated risk perceptions. Thereafter, we would expect this reading's effect to be incorporated in the prior risk perceptions term (i.e., those formed at the first update), and this is what the model implies. Because the annual living area reading confirms the two-month reading, it is not new information.

Table 2.4.   Description of Interviews for NYSERDA Radon Risk Study

Interview/Mailing	Format of Interview	Percent Completion	Date
Baseline	Telephone	97	May/June 1986
Distribute two-month readings and information treatment	–	–	December 1986 /January 1987
First Followup	Telephone	91	December 1986 /January 1987
Distribute annual readings and information treatment[a]	–	–	January 1988 /February 1988
Second Followup	Mail[b]	74	March 1988
Final Followup	Telephone	91[c]	February 1989

[a] Our analysis of the participating households' responses to the one-page fact sheet after the first follow-up interview indicated that they had become overly concerned about their radon readings and wanted additional information. Because their responses to learning and risk perception questions and questions intended to measure their demands for more information provided strong support for the need for intervention, we modified the design in subsequent contacts with this group. They were randomly assigned to one of the five remaining information treatments. All other households received the same information treatment that they were assigned prior to the first followup.

[b] In implementing the mailed survey we generally followed Dillman's [1978] suggestions. However, after two mailings and reminder postcards, we used a telephone contact (rather than a certified letter) to attempt to increase response rates.

[c] This estimate is calculated based on households with completed and correct radon readings—1825 of the originally 2300 recruited for the sample.

The annual basement reading was surprising for most households—over twice as high as the living area readings. The second risk update reflects this aspect of the basement reading as new information with a positive and significant coefficient.

The information treatments also affect risk perceptions in ways that are consistent with people systematically responding to information. Those households that received quantitative risk information—the command/quantitative and cajole/quantitative booklets, both containing risk charts linking radon readings to estimates of the lifetime risk of premature death from lung cancer—reduced their risk perceptions in comparison to households with comparable radon readings that received the one-page fact sheet.

The informational materials are generally not influential thereafter. Again their effects are captured in the prior risk perceptions term. However, the second update produced an interesting response that did reflect a new effect from the informational materials. Because of the surprising basement reading, households receiving the command/qualitative brochures updated their risk perceptions differently from those receiving other materials. This brochure emphasized the EPA Action Guideline for radon (at four picocuries per liter) and provided no specific risk information. As a result, it established the Action Guideline as a threshold. We (Smith et al. [1990]) conjectured that this treatment probably led respondents to treat the Action Guideline as a 'threshold for safety,' and therefore these households interpreted their basement readings differently. This hypothesis was informally confirmed (as noted earlier) by the Weinstein et al. [1990] independent results evaluating the effects of specific action guidelines for people's behavioral intentions and perceptions of both radon and asbestos risks.

The last two columns in the table report some preliminary results from the last interview. At this point, people had nearly a year to take action and revise their risk perceptions. Overall the average risk perception is lower and somewhat less influenced by the perceptions stated a year earlier. The first model considers only the prior risk perception and a qualitative variable for mitigation. This specification implicitly assumes that the effects of the information treatments and radon readings would already be incorporated in the prior risk perception measure because both were received before these were stated. These estimates treat the mitigation variable as endogenous and are counterintuitive. Those who reported undertaking some form of mitigating behavior report higher (on average) levels of risk perception after the mitigation was undertaken than before. Because this contradicts intuition, we investigated a variety of more detailed specifications. The last column reports one of these. After incorporating a proxy measure for years of exposure in additive and interactive form with mitigation, we find a *negative* and significant term for the interaction effect between mitigation and years of exposure, and a *positive* but insignificant effect for mitigation entered in linear form.

It is possible that people reacted to the lifetime nature of the risk and adjusted their response to mitigation based on the time they lived in their homes and were exposed to radon before receiving information about radon's risk. This type of response is consistent with Ippolito's [1981] explanation of the opposing effects of information about cancer-causing hazards on the aggregate patterns of consumption of hazardous goods that nonetheless contribute positively to utility. She argued on theoretical grounds for two opposing influences. Using her model for this case would suggest that people who are ignorant of radon's presence in their home and its risk should act to reduce the risk when informed of the hazard. If

Table 2.5.   Updating of Radon Risk Perceptions: NYSERDA Sample[a]

Selected Independent Variables	First Followup[b]	Second Followup[b]	Final Followup N2SLS[c]	Final Followup N2SLS[c]
Prior Risk Perception	.063 (3.228)	.458 (10.897)	.074 (4.427)	.076 (4.313)
Two-Month Radon Reading (living area)[d]	.024 (2.927)	−.031 (−0.760)		
Annual Radon Reading (living area)[d]		0.013 (1.004)		$.69 \times 10^{-2}$ (1.055)
Annual Radon Reading (basement)[d]		.006 (2.355)		$.59 \times 10^{-2}$ (2.134)
Command/Quantitative	−.084 (−2.048)	.021 (0.583)		−.025 (−0.820)
Command/Qualitative	−.030 (−0.721)	.088 (2.448)		−.022 (−0.710)
Cajole/Quantitative	−.122 (−2.974)	−.002 (−0.007)		$-.13 \times 10^{-2}$ (−0.043)
Cajole/Qualitative	−.059 (−1.486)	−.020 (−0.585)		$-.96 \times 10^{-2}$ (−0.295)
EPA Citizen's Guide	−.018 (−0.427)	−.001 (−0.671)		
Mitigation			.229 (2.691)	.097 (0.464)
Radon Basement and Use Basement				$.37 \times 10^{-2}$ (1.054)
Originally Received Fact Sheet				.019 (0.780)
Mitigation* Years at Address				−.017 (−2.384)
Years at Address				$-.22 \times 10^{-4}$ (−0.074)
Threshold				.063 (1.701)
Radon Is Not a Problem				$-.13 \times 10^{-2}$ (−0.062)
Need to Know More				.074 (1.435)
Sample Size	785	785	853	853

[a] These results are based on a model assuming currently stated risk perceptions (R_t) is a linear function of immediately prior statements of risk perceptions (R_{t-1}) plus variables describing information respondents received. The numbers in parentheses below the

Table 2.5. Contd

estimated parameters are ratios of the coefficients to their estimated asymptotic standard errors. The models reported are not the complete specifications.

[b] These estimates were derived using the two-limit Tobit framework of Rosett and Nelson [1975]. See Smith et al. [1990] for a complete description of the model and results.

[c] These estimates are derived using a nonlinear 2SLS estimator proposed by Barrow, Cain and Goldberger [1981] to allow for the potential for simultaneity of the dummy variable for reported mitigation and the final risk perception.

In this model, the information brochure qualitative variables refer to the "final" brochure received. In the case of households receiving the fact sheet, this changed after our analysis of the results from the first follow-up survey. For all others it did not change. The variables are measured relative to the EPA *Citizen's Guide*. In the earlier models, and omitted category was the fact sheet.

The variable "Originally Received Fact Sheet" is a dummy variable to evaluate whether initial receipt of the fact sheet influenced households' updating even though they received new information prior to this interview. Our investigation of this issue with the annual updating indicated the treatment of this effect did not alter our conclusions from the annual updating model (see Smith et al. [1990]).

"Mitigation" is a qualitative variable for people reporting they had undertaken some form of mitigation *since* the annual readings were sent and that follow-up survey was conducted to reduce radon levels.

"Radon Basement and Use Basement" refers to an interaction variable between the annual radon reading for the basement and a variable initially collected asking households if they used their basements for daily activities (=1) or not (=0).

"Years at Address" is as implied the number of years the household has lived at the address.

"Threshold" is a qualitative variable that takes the value of unity when the individual initially received a radon reading (three-month for the living area) less than four picocuries and then received an annual basement reading exceeding four.

"Radon Is Not a Problem" is a qualitative variable that is unity for individuals responding that this attitude is one they strongly agree or agree with and zero otherwise.

"Need to Know More" is a qualitative variable for strongly agreeing or agreeing with the statement expressing connection between knowledge of radon and ability to control it (zero otherwise).

These results are based on joint research currently in process with Bill Desvousges and John Payne.

[d] These statistics correspond to the average and range of readings for households in our sample based on each monitor.

the initiation of some health effect is delayed after exposure, these individuals also could perceive that their risks of cancer had already increased and choose — because of shortened life expectancy — to postpone action in favor of other consumption activities. The net effect in Ippolito's life-cycle description of rational behavior with these types of risk could be in either direction. While these estimates are broadly consistent with her arguments, it is important to acknowledge that they are quite sensitive to the specification of the model used to describe the role of mitigation as a determinant of risk perceptions.

The last aspect of the NYSERDA experiment concerns the influence of information on risk mitigation. As with the case of risk perceptions, the empirical evidence indicates a clear link between the information respondents received and their mitigation responses. Because most of the sample had low radon readings, we did not expect a large fraction to undertake any form of mitigation. Equally important, the expenditures for mitigation do not seem to imply a smooth continuous relationship. Consequently, mitigation was defined in categorical terms as (1) taking no action, (2) acquiring information, or (3) modifying the house to reduce radon concentrations. Using a multinomial logit model, both the radon levels and the type of information affected the likelihood of either acquiring more information, or of taking some action to reduce radon concentrations.

Information that identifies clear thresholds for action increases a person's inclination to undertake some form of mitigation. This was especially true for respondents who perceived that they crossed the threshold implied by the EPA's action guidelines. That is, when we considered the responses of households with two-month readings below four picocuries and annual basement readings above the Action Guideline, they had increased likelihood of mitigating in addition to the effect contributed separately by the level of the basement reading. When informational materials served to reduce the emphasis placed on the EPA's action guidelines without specific quantitative risk estimates (as in the case of the cajole/qualitative booklet), the likelihood of mitigation was also reduced.

Implications

Empirical analyses of the risk perception process for real sources of risk are inherently limited. Controlling the level of serious risk experienced by people and manipulating the information they have to understand the risk, is ethically unacceptable in most situations. Only where the risk arises from natural sources, and the information alternatives are considered equally effective, can we investigate how differences in real risks and the information provided about them might affect people's risk perceptions. As the earlier summary indicates, these requirements limit the issues that can be considered. This is one reason why research on risk perception has posed hypothetical situations.[14] Overall, the findings of both strategies support an economic model of risk perception and behavior that links the two processes.

The Treatment of Risk Perceptions and Ex Ante Valuation

Once we acknowledge that risk perceptions reflect objective information about the events at risk, *and* each individual's beliefs about the process, then the task of defining ex ante values identifies a fundamental conflict. Are the departures of each person's risk perceptions from the objective probabilities a matter properly regarded as inherent in preferences? Answering in the affirmative would imply that we should accept them as we accept consumer sovereignty in defining ex post, measures of people's values. Or do these risk perceptions reflect mistakes? This is the issue addressed by Machina [1990]. His argument is best captured in the following:

> reporting a length, width, and area of a room that are not commensurate implies an internally inconsistent description of the room and is simply wrong; preferring purple polka-dot carpeting, however, is a matter of clients' tastes, to which they have every right if it is their living room. In the case of health or environmental risks, this would correspond to the distinction between measuring the detrimental effects of a drug or a pollutant versus determining the individual patient's or society's attitudes toward bearing these consequences (p. 174).

The issues are not as clear-cut as this interpretation of his argument would imply. One could give several different interpretations to his reasoning. I believe he is arguing for checks to be imposed on subjective risk perceptions so that they satisfy fairly weak conditions for consistency. Correcting "mistakes" in this context seems more acceptable than treating perceptions that differ from those of experts' assessments as mistakes. Indeed, Machina's justification would support a continued reliance on consumer sovereignty. He explains his position noting:

> Why do I feel that departures from the structures of probability theory should be corrected but that (systematic) departures from the strictures of expected utility theory should not? Because the former involve the determination of the risks involved in an option, which is a matter of accurate representation, whereas the latter involve the client's willingness to bear these risks, which is a matter of preference (p. 174).

Nonetheless, others could interpret his position as calling for corrections to the risk perceptions. I believe this approach would be inconsistent with preferences because people's perceptions depend in part on their preferences.

As Fischhoff [1989] observes, while there are "actual risks" (i.e., probabilities of undesirable outcomes), we will never know what they are.

> All that anyone does know about risks can be classified as perceptions. Those assertions that are typically called actual risks (or facts or objective information) inevitably contain some element of judgment on the part of the scientists who produce them. *In this light, what is commonly called the conflict between actual and perceived risk is better thought of as the conflict between two sets of risk perceptions. Those of ranking scientists performing within their field of expertise and those of anybody else* (p. 270, emphasis added).

In the absence of a comprehensive description of individual behavior that explains the connections between preferences, perceptions, and behavior, ex ante benefit measurement has largely been forced to adopt one of two strategies: (1) ignore the difference between experts' estimates of risk and peoples' perceptions and use expected utility theory to define ex ante values or (2) postulate an alternative structure to describe preferences that allows experts' estimates of risk to enter preferences in a nonlinear form and derive values from these functions.

For the most part, these approaches have been treated as mutually exclusive alternatives. However, this is not necessary. Indeed, it is possible to extend Viscusi's [1989] recent proposal—integrating a risk updating model with ex ante consumer choice—to provide the basis for comparisons that illustrate how using either strategy will affect the value assigned to policies, whether they are intended to influence the outcomes at risk or the size of the risks.

Prospective Reference Theory Versus the Conventional Approach

A simple two-state characterization of individual decision making illustrates how Viscusi's PRT framework can be used to compare the implications of treating risk perception in different ways. Two types of valuation tasks will be considered—valuing changes in some outcome and valuing changes in risk. Following the conventions of most of the literature on ex ante valuation, I assume preferences are state dependent.[15] To avoid another set of issues that is not central to the reasons for comparing Viscusi's framework with the conventional approach, I will focus on the option price measure for valuing each type of change.[16]

Individual utility is represented by $U_i(Y_i)$ ($i = A, B$ where the interpretation of the different states will depend on the particular application of interest), and Y_i represents income in state i. What is important about the assumption of state dependency is that the marginal utility of income varies with state. As a rule, the U_i are interpreted as indirect utility functions, and the focus is on a change in outcome that is assumed to be outside each person's control but valued. This is represented by adding an argument, Q, to U_i as $U_i(Y_i, Q)$. The model considers a change in Q from some reference level. Here I will denote the original level Q_0 and the new level $\overline{Q}$. The value of this change is defined in ex ante terms because the model assumes a person does not know which state will govern his (or her) preferences.[17] The realized state is determined by random process with P designating the probability for state A and $(1 - P)$ the probability for B. The distinction between the conventional and Viscusi models rests with the representation of the probabilities.

For a conventional expected utility model, the probabilities are treated as objective information and therefore are exogenous parameters in defining ex ante monetary values for the change in Q. When each individual is assumed to maximize expected utility, the maximum amount that would be paid (as an option price, OP) for a change from Q_0 to $\overline{Q}$ is defined by equation 1. It represents the reduction in income (Y) that would be agreed to, regardless of state, to realize the change from Q_0 to $\overline{Q}$. With such a payment, the expected utility is the same as it would have been if Q remained at Q_0 and no payment were made.

$$PU_A(Y - OP, \overline{Q}) + (1 - P)U_B(Y - OP, \overline{Q})$$
$$= PU_A(Y, Q_0) + (1 - P)U_B(Y_i, Q_0) \qquad [1]$$

The definition in (1) assumes that the change in Q is assured if the payment is made. In some cases the change from Q_0 to $\overline{Q}$ may not be assured. It might take place only in one state, say A. Equation 2 defines the option price, $\widetilde{OP}$, for this situation.

$$PU_A(Y - \widetilde{OP}, \overline{Q}) + (1 - P)U_B(Y - \widetilde{OP}, Q_0)$$
$$= PU_A(Y, Q_0) + (1 - P)U_B(Y, Q_0) \qquad [2]$$

There is still a change in outcome, but it is not assured. Both possibilities have been discussed in the option price literature (see Bishop [1982], Smith [1983], and Freeman [1985, 1989]).

A third possibility considers the ex ante value of a probability change. Continuing to assume the change to $\overline{Q}$ is desirable, increasing its probability would have a positive value. Here the usual case presented in the literature modifies the reference case, so it is not assured Q_0, but instead $\overline{Q}$ and Q_0 with a different set of probabilities than the new situation. The corresponding option price OP^* is given by (3), where θ is the change in the probability being valued.

$$(P + \theta)U_A(Y - OP^*, \overline{Q}) + (1 - P - \theta)U_B(Y - OP^*, Q_0)$$
$$= PU_A(Y, \overline{Q}) + (1 - P)U_B(Y, Q_0) \qquad [3]$$

Of course, simultaneous changes in both P and Q could also be envisioned. Such cases would involve modifying both aspects of the lotteries. Thus, these alternative specifications illustrate the problems in defining an increment to the commodity that is valued — the lottery. The marginal effect on the option price of a change in the probability component of the lottery (holding expected utility constant) can be defined from (3) as $\dfrac{dOP^*}{dP}$ (when θ is allowed to approach zero).

$$\frac{dOP^*}{dP} = \frac{U_A(Y, \overline{Q}) - U_B(Y, Q_0)}{PU_{AY} + (1 - P)\,U_{BY}} \qquad [4]$$

$$\text{where } U_{iY} = \frac{\partial U_i}{\partial Y}$$

The effects of marginal changes in Q would also be defined in a similar fashion and compared with ex post values (see Freeman [1989]).

This is the conventional treatment. The difficulties arise in implementing any of these three definitions when people do not accept the objective probabilities provided to them by the experts. That is, a policy change involves either a change in Q or in P, and consumers believe the probabilities are different from the experts' evaluations. This situation is most pronounced when the policy involves a change in probability. Increasing P would correspond (because state A has been described as favorable) to policies that reduce risks of exposure to hazardous wastes through drinking water, pesticides on food, or even the likelihood of poor visibility conditions at a national park when the scenic vista is important to the enjoyment of a visit.

Two problems result from these discrepancies. First, to the extent indirect methods can be used to measure $\widetilde{OP}$ or OP^*, they will be based on what people perceive the probabilities to be, *not* the experts' estimates (see Freeman [1991]). Second, and equally important, even if we could recover enough information to measure the elements in equations 2, 3, and 4, whose probabilities do we use to measure $\widetilde{OP}$, OP^*, or $\dfrac{dOP^*}{dP}$? If we interpret Machina as calling for alignment of people's subjective perceptions with the experts' estimates, then we should use the experts' estimates.[18]

With regard to the second question, Viscusi's prospective reference theory (PRT) offers an alternative approach. While it may seem simply to restate the weighting function used in prospect theory (Kahneman and Tversky [1979]), PRT does more in its description of subjective probabilities and does not restrict value functions. It replaces P in each of the preceding expressions by a function of P, say $\Pi(P)$, as prospect theory would. However, the distinction arises in how that perceived probability function is interpreted. It is treated as a linear function of a reference risk level, say P_0, and the P which can be interpreted as the experts' assessment of the risk. Equation 5 provides an example:

$$\Pi(P) = \frac{\gamma P + \alpha P_0}{\gamma + \alpha} \qquad [5]$$

Where γ and α represent weights describing the informational content associated with experts' risk assessments versus each person's reference risk level or prior beliefs. While the model does not explain the source of these weights or how they change in response to different events at risk, it does provide a basis for describing how the ex ante values analysts use are affected by how we resolve problems with the formation of subjective risk perceptions.

PRT and the Ex Ante Valuation of Outcomes

PRT treats each individual's objective function as if it were a weighted average of two expected utility functions, and this is why it provides a direct way to illustrate the effects of perceptions on ex ante values. The PRT description of the reference ex ante level of well being, k, for the initial definition of option price (i.e., r.h.s. equation 1) would be given by equation 6.

$$k = P\left(\frac{\gamma}{\gamma + \alpha}\right) U_A(Y, Q_0) + (1 - P)\left(\frac{\gamma}{\gamma + \alpha}\right) U_B(Y, Q_0)$$

$$+ P_0\left(\frac{\alpha}{\gamma + \alpha}\right) U_A(Y, Q_0) + (1 - P_0)\left(\frac{\alpha}{\gamma + \alpha}\right) U_B(Y, Q_0) \quad [6]$$

This is derived by substituting $\Pi(P)$ for P on the right side of equation 1 and regrouping terms so k can be reexpressed as a weighted sum of two expected value (EU) functions — one using P and the other (P_0 as in (7).

$$k = \left(\frac{\gamma}{\gamma + \alpha}\right) EU(Y, Q_0, P) + \left(\frac{\gamma}{\gamma + \alpha}\right) EU(Y, Q_0, P_0) \quad [7]$$

The counterpart to the first valuation definition for OP defined for PRT would be

$$\left(\frac{\gamma}{\gamma + \alpha}\right) EU(Y - OP^V, \overline{Q}, P) + \left(\frac{\alpha}{\gamma + \alpha}\right) EU(Y - OP^V, \overline{Q}, P_0) = k$$

$$[8]$$

where OP^V corresponds to the PRT definition of OP.

The reason for adopting this reformatting is that it illustrates how assumptions about the role of perceptions define a locus of valuation concepts. That is, by recognizing that each component of the pair of terms in (6) describes an expected utility function with different assumptions about probabilities, each could be used to define an option price for some improvement (i.e., Q_0 to $\overline{Q}$) to hold expected utility at k. Because the weights sum to unity, the locus will follow the concave shape displayed in Figure 2-1 and the OP for (P_0 and the OP for P will define one point on the locus. Changing the EU associated with P_0 or P and defining new OP's (for given P_0 and P) can also be considered as ways to define points on the locus, provided the weighted values of the EU's for each case sum to k. Alternatively, the points could be described as representing the effects of alternative weighting schemes. Figure 2.1 illustrates the idea.

Because the utility functions are well-behaved, this locus looks like a Graham [1981] willingness-to-pay locus. However, it is not the same concept. Intersections with a 45° line correspond to using Viscusi's PRT to describe people's behavior *and* assuming that ex ante values for policy changes should correspond to how they would value those policies even if their values are based on incorrect perceptions.

The schedule's slope reflects the fundamental issue — any intervention in how each person evaluates risk involves separating the components of a lottery in order to define an increment for use in defining an ex ante value, and that separation will be arbitrary because both perceptions and the valuation of outcomes are reflected in changes in $OP(P)$ and $OP(P_0)$. This can be illustrated by substituting in equation 8 the definitions for $OP(P)$ and $OP(P_0)$, each holding expected utility constant at k and taking the total derivative.

$$\frac{dOP\ (P)}{dOP(P_0)} = \frac{\alpha EMUY(P_0)}{\gamma EMUY(P)} \quad [9]$$

where $EMUY(P)$ and $EMUY(P_0)$ are the expected marginal utilities of income when P and P_0 are taken as the description of risk respectively.

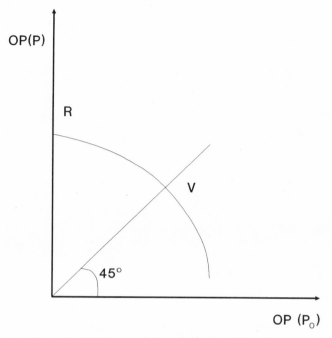

Figure 2–1.   Viscusi's PRT locus of the valuation-risk perception trade-off.

PRT and Ex Ante Valuation of Risk

Equation 8 also allows a description of how the probability describing people's risk perceptions influences the valuation of a risk change. The *PRT* counterpart to the relationship in (4) can be used to describe how the valuation of risk would differ from the conventional model. Equation 10 provides that description.

$$\frac{dOP^V}{dP} = \frac{\dfrac{dOP^*}{dP}}{\left[1 + \dfrac{\alpha EMUY(P_0)}{\gamma EMUY(P)}\right]} \qquad [10]$$

Thus, the size of the discrepancy between a perception-based measure of the value of a risk change in comparison to one that assumes people use experts' probability assessments depends on two factors: (1) the differential

weight given to experts' versus prior information and (2) the relative size
of the expected marginal utilities of income under the individual's prior
perceptions versus the experts' assessments of the risk. Because it is
difficult to conceptualize how large these differences are likely to be, I
calculated some examples using a variation on one of the specifications
proposed by Freeman [1989] in his comparison of ex ante and ex post
values. Table 2.6 summarizes the results for state dependent utility functions defined by equation 11. Here the event corresponds to some undesirable outcome that would yield a loss of Z in state A but no loss in
state B.

$$U_A = (Y - Z)^a$$
$$U_B = Y^{a + b}$$

[11]

Z corresponds to the ex post consumer surplus of having state A over
state B. In table 2.6 we describe it as a percent of income using 10 and
80 percent.

The most important determinant of the relative size of the value of a
risk change (i.e., comparing OP^V to OP^*) is the weight a person assigns
to experts' versus personal risk assessments. Only one set of parameters
for a and b were selected because the magnitude of the differences are
insensitive to the specification. While the same general pattern characterizes
all the cases when comparing the disparities between prior and experts'
assessments of risk, both the level and the size of the disparity do matter

Table 2.6.   Relative Size of Incremental Option Price Under PRT versus the
Conventional Framework

$\dfrac{\gamma}{\gamma + \alpha}$	(P, P^0)					
	(.1, .5)	(.1, .7)	(.3, .5)	(.3, .7)	(.5, .7)	(.5, .9)
Z/Y = 10% a = .5 b = .2						
.05	.010	.008	.031	.025	.034	.025
.25	.063	.051	.167	.138	.183	.211
.50	.167	.138	.375	.325	.401	.445
.90	.643	.590	.844	.813	.858	.878
Z/Y = 80% a = .5 b = .2						
.05	.010	.008	.031	.023	.038	.031
.25	.063	.048	.167	.132	.202	.169
.50	.167	.132	.375	.312	.431	.379
.90	.643	.577	.844	.804	.872	.846

in determining the relative size of the values assigned to risk changes. As with Freeman's [1989] comparison of ex ante and ex post values, different specifications for the utility function will influence the factors judged to be important in determining values in a PRT framework. My point is simply that depending on how we choose to interpret the risk perception process, the size of the differences can be substantial.

Policy Implications

By selecting a position on how to deal with divergences between experts' risk assessments and everyone else's risk perceptions, we also choose a valuation measure. This applies even when we adopt a model like Viscusi's *PRT* that treats risk perception and valuation as being separately determined. All that needs to be added is recognition that people have their own perceptions and they weigh experts' assessments along with their initial risk perceptions.

I have used Viscusi's PRT framework to derive a new locus of possible ex ante values for changes in outcomes. While the shape of the locus will depend on the assumed features of each person's preferences and his (or her) relative weighting of information, clearly the treatment of perceptions can make the difference between positive and negative net values for actions under uncertainty. Moreover, if we accept the fact that the presentation (or framing) of information can influence its interpretation and use — as suggested in chapter 4 — then we acknowledge policy's ability to influence the relative weights assigned to experts' assessments and people's prior perceptions. This influence is certainly not complete. There are limits to how much public information programs can influence the confidence people will place in experts' judgments, and this seems to vary with the type of environmental risk.

This may seem to make the task of developing economic information on the ex ante value people place on policy so complex as to preclude its use in any practical applications. This is not my intent. Rather, I am suggesting that policy design under conditions of uncertainty must be reconsidered to include more than simply estimating values for policies that are defined independently from uncertainties in the processes to be affected by policy initiatives. Instead, the design should redefine the meaning of a policy to include three activities that are provided jointly to people. They would include (1) offering information about the sources of risk and the influence of policy actions on either the risk or the outcomes at risk, (2) designing actions to change the outcomes or risks in ways that recognize how people perceive the potential gain, and (3) providing opportunities for individuals to adjust in ex ante terms (through insurance mechanisms) to the level of protection or size of uncertain outcomes provided by the policy process.

The exact mix of these three activities would vary with what is at risk, as well as with the nature of the process giving rise to the risk. This three-fold strategy acknowledges that people's risk perceptions are not formed completely in isolation of the policy process, but information alone is limited in its effect. This strategy accepts consumer sovereignty, including the role of risk perceptions, even if it contradicts experts' perceptions. But it also recognizes that people's perceptions will be heterogenous and that providing safety for those who are most 'worried' may be inefficient. Nonetheless, it does not imply that offering those concerned opportunities to reduce risk (or its implications) at increased private cost would be incompatible with an efficiency objective.

Notes

1. Visualizing it is easy with nondurable goods. When we move to durables or services, explaining the implicit exchange becomes more difficult. "Time" usually becomes the quantitative metric that allows us to conceptualize tradeoffs. Such a modeling strategy treats the amount of time the durable is used or the service takes as the good exchanged for some other commodity.

2. This conclusion is consistent with evidence from laboratory experiments and contingent valuation experiments. Early work by Grether [1980] involving experiments with and without monetary incentives found behavioral departures from Bayesian learning. Experience and the financial incentives improved the adherence to a Bayesian framework. Camerer [1987] also found that experience with compound lotteries improves the performance of a Bayesian learning model. By contrast, McClelland, Schulze, and Coursey [1986] report substantial departures from a systematic learning process, especially with low-probability events. A substantial fraction of participants do not appear to learn, even with financial incentives and repeated trials.

3. Erikson [1990] highlights two features of what he describes as "toxic emergencies" that apply equally well to most environmental risks. First, they are unbounded in the sense of having no timeframe or ending. He describes this as using an analogy to rules of drama, characterizing them as a different sort of tragedy. Second, people cannot apprehend them through the unaided senses. Because of this feature, they are more frightening.

4. Risk will be used here to be synonomous with the probability of specific undesirable events.

5. See Slovic, Fischhoff, and Lichtenstein [1985], and Slovic [1987] for good overviews of this literature.

6. These critics generally overlook the ethical constraints that must be imposed on any 'experiments' in which people face real risks at varying levels with the analyst observing their response to these risks and controlling the information they receive.

7. These cases may not be completely hypothetical. For example, contingent behavior studies have asked respondents their perceptions of risk from specific sources and then presented hypothetical policies to address the source of risk. The perception relates to an actual risk, and the behavior is contingent on the situation described in the questions. This approach contrasts with Weinstein et al.'s study [1989] that used hypothetical information about the levels of radon or asbestos and asked responses. In this case, all answers relate to hypothetical situations.

8. Radon is a colorless, odorless gas that occurs naturally and is considered to be the second leading cause (after smoking) of lung cancer in the United States. See National Research Council [1988] for an evaluation of the EPA risk assessment model for radon.

9. We defined a variable indicating whether a respondent talked to a friend, neighbor, or co-worker about radon after the program and found that both the Hagerstown and Frederick programs raised awareness, as measured in these terms. To the extent this increased awareness independently contributes to the likelihood of monitoring, as the results in table 2.3 would imply, the programs may have further impact on monitoring decisions. See Appendix A, Desvousges, Smith, and Rink [1989].

10. The authors note that they set targets of fifty respondents as a threshold, after which the sampling would stop. To the extent the analysis envisions modeling categorical response variables and multivariate models that acknowledge a role for demographic and economic variables in addition to those describing the information programs, this plan is inadequate. The specific samples recruited by town are shown in table 2.7.

11. One reason I feel the sample is specialized follows from the NYSERDA criteria for entry to the sample: people who would place the monitors in their homes and had no plans to move for at least one year. The analysis did consider whether this criteria significantly affected risk perceptions using a variation on a Heckman [1979] selection model, and the results indicated it did not appear to influence any of the conclusions. See Smith et al. [1990] for the details.

12. The research design and planning for the project was jointly undertaken with Ann Fisher of the U.S. Environmental Protection Agency and F. Reed Johnson of the U.S. Naval Academy.

13. The level of one picocurie was selected because it is well below levels that remediation technologies at the time of the study could achieve and corresponds to the level experts estimated was the average level in the United States.

14. Studies involving laboratory experiments were not discussed because they must confront people with lotteries. As a result, they are not especially useful in any effort to evaluate how risk perceptions are formed when information about the process does not come to people in a form comparable to a lottery.

Table 2.7. SAMPLE

Town	Baseline	Dependent Followup	Independent Followup
Clinton	208	45	49
Fitchburg	202	38	55
Worcester (control)	81	51	—

15. Viscusi's original paper [1989] describing PRT assumed state independent preference. His discussion of applications to health risks (Viscusi [1990]) allows for state dependency. The central question in a state-dependent specification is the extent of differences in the marginal utility of income across states. See Arrow [1974] for the first identification and discussion of the significance of this assumption.

16. Option price measures use the expected value of the marginal utility of income in defining ex ante monetary measures of the value of some change. Other measures will depend more on the opportunities for ex ante adjustment in the form of insurance markets. See Graham [1981] and Smith [1990] for discussion of ex ante benefit measures.

17. Plummer and Hartman [1986] describe the way uncertain prices or income could be used to explain uncertain state dependent preferences. Of course, these are not the only possibilities, as the Cook-Graham [1977] discussion clearly suggests.

18. Machina [1990] would certainly accept other non-EU, objective functions, and these could incorporate probabilities in a nonlinear form, violating the independence axiom. What appears to be at issue in his recommendations is "correct" use of what he views as objective information about probabilities.

This may well be the best strategy for simple lotteries in which the process is known (e.g., rolling a die, drawing a colored ball from an urn, etc.), but it is not an appropriate characterization of the form of risk information in environmental lotteries.

References

Arrow, Kenneth J. 1974. "Optimal Insurance and Generalized Deductibles," *Scandinavian Actuarial Journal* 1, 1–42.

Barrow, B., G. Cain, and A.S. Goldberger. 1981. "Issues in the Analysis of Selectivity Bias." In E. Stromsdorfer and G. Parkas (eds.), *Evaluation Studies Review Annual*, Vol. 5. Beverly Hills, Ca.: Sage Publications.

Bishop, Richard C. 1982. "Option Value: An Exposition and Extension," *Land Economics* 58 (February): 1–15.

Camerer, Colin F., 1987. "Do Biases in Probability Judgment Matter in Markets? Experimental Evidence," *American Economic Review* 77 (December): 981–987.

Cook, Philip J., and Daniel A. Graham. 1977. "The Demand for Insurance and Protection: The Case of an Irreplaceable Commodity," *Quarterly Journal of Economics* 9 (February): 143–156.

Desvousges, William H., V. Kerry Smith, and Hillery Rink. 1989. *Communicating Radon Risk Effectively: Radon Testing in Maryland*. Final Report for EPA Cooperative Agreement No. CR-811075, Document No. EPA-230-03-89-048 Washington, D.C.: Office of Policy Planning and Evaluation, U.S. Environmental Protection Agency, March.

Dillman, Don A. 1978. *Mail and Telephone Surveys: The Total Design Method*. New York: John Wiley and Sons.

Erikson, Kai. 1990. "Toxic Reckoning: Business Faces a New Kind of Fear," *Harvard Business Review* (January/February): 118–126.

Fischhoff, Baruch. 1989. "Risk: A Guide to Controversy," Appendix C in

Improving Risk Communication. Report by Committee on Risk Perception and Communication. Washington, D.C.: National Academy Press.

Freeman, A. Myrick, III. 1985. "Supply Uncertainty, Option Price, and Option Value," *Land Economics* 61 (August): 176−181.

Freeman, A. Myrick, III. 1989. "*Ex Ante* and *Ex Post* Values for Changes in Risks," *Risk Analysis* 9(3): 309−317.

Freeman, A. Myrick, III. 1991. "Valuing Individuals' Changes in Risk: A General Treatment," *Journal of Risk and Uncertainty* 4 (April): 153−166.

Golding, Dominic, Sheldon Krimsky, and Alonzo Plough. 1990. *Radon Risk Communication in Context: An Experiment in Massachusetts*, Report to U.S. Environmental Protection Agency Center for Environmental Management. Boston: Tufts University, January 30.

Graham, Daniel A. 1981. "Cost Benefit, Analysis Under Uncertainty," *American Economic Review* 71 (December): 715−725.

Grether, David M. 1980. "Bayes Rules as a Descriptive Model: The Representativeness Heuristic," *Quarterly Journal of Economics* 95 (November): 537−558.

Heckman, James J. 1979. "Sample, Selection Bias as a Specification Error," *Econometrica* 47 (January): 153−161.

Ippolito, Pauline M. 1981. "Information and the Life Cycle Consumption of Hazardous Goods," *Economic Inquiry* 19 (October): 529−558.

Kahneman, Daniel, and Amos Tversky. 1979. "Prospect Theory: An Analysis of Decisions Under Risk," *Econometrica* 47(1): 263−291.

Machina, Mark J. 1990. "Choice Under Uncertainty: Problems Solved and Unsolved." In R. Brett Hammon and Rob Coppock (eds.), *Valuing Health Risks, Costs and Benefits for Environmental Decision Making.* Washington, D.C.: National Academy Press.

Magat, Wesley A., W. Kip Viscusi, and Joel Huber. 1988. "Consumer Processing of Hazard Warning Information," *Journal of Risk and Uncertainty* 1 (June): 201−223.

McClelland, Gary H., William D. Schulze, and Don L. Coursey. 1986. "Valuing Risk: A Comparison of Expected Utility with Models from Cognitive Psychology," University of Colorado, unpublished paper, September.

National Research Council. 1988. *Health Risks of Radon and Other Internally Deposited Alpha-Emitters.* Washington, D.C.: National Academy Press.

Plummer, Mark L., and Richard C. Hartman. 1986. "Option Value: A General Approach," *Economic Inquiry* 24 (July): 455−472.

Slovic, Paul. 1987. "Perception of Risk," *Science* 236 (April): 280−285.

Slovic, Paul, Baruch Fischhoff, and Sarah Lichtenstein. 1985. "Regulation of Risk: A Psychological Perspective." In R. Noll (ed.), *Regulatory Policy and the Social Sciences.* Berkeley: University of California Press.

Smith, V. Kerry. 1983. "Option Value: A Conceptual Overview," *Southern Economic Journal* 49 (January): 654−668.

Smith, V. Kerry. 1985. "Supply Uncertainty, Option Price and Indirect Benefit Estimation," *Land Economics* 61 (August): 303−307.

Smith, V. Kerry. 1990. "Valuing Amenity Resources Under Uncertainty: A Skeptical View of Recent Resolutions," *Journal of Environmental Economics and Management* 19 (September): 193–202.

Smith V. Kerry, and William H. Desvousges. 1990. "Risk Communication and the Value of Information: Radon as a Case Study," *Review of Economics and Statistics* 72 (February): 137–142.

Smith, V. Kerry, and F. Reed Johnson. 1988. "How Do Risk Perceptions Respond to Information? The Case of Radon," *Review of Economics and Statistics* 70 (May): 1–8.

Smith, V. Kerry, William H. Desvousges, John W. Payne. 1991. "Does Risk Information Influence Mitigation Behavior?" Working Paper, Resource and Environmental Economics Program, North Carolina State University.

Smith, V. Kerry, William H. Desvousges, Ann Fisher, and F. Reed Johnson. 1988. "Learning About Radon's Risk," *Journal of Risk and Uncertainty* 1 (June): 233–258.

Smith, V. Kerry, William H. Desvousges, Ann Fisher, and F. Reed Johnson. *Communicating Radon Risk Effectively: A Mid-Course Evaluation*. Report to the U.S. Environmental Protection Agency. Vanderbilt University. 1987.

Smith, V. Kerry, William H. Desvousges, F. Reed Johnson, and Ann Fisher. 1990. "Can Public Information Programs Affect Risk Perceptions?" *Journal of Policy Analysis and Management* 9 (Winter): 41–59.

Thaler, Richard, and Sherwin Rosen. 1976. "The Value of Saving a Life: Evidence from the Labor Market," In Nestor E. Terleckyi (ed.), *Household Production and Consumption*. New York: Columbia University Press.

U.S. Environmental Protection Agency. 1987. *Unfinished Business: A Comparative Assessment of Environmental Problems*, Vol. 1. Washington, D.C.: EPA.

Viscusi, W. Kip. 1989. "Prospective Reference Theory: Toward an Explanation of the Paradoxes," *Journal of Risk and Uncertainty* 2 (September): 235–264.

Viscusi, W. Kip. 1990. "Sources of Inconsistency in Societal Responses to Health Risks." *American Economic Review Papers and Proceedings* 80 (May): 257–261.

Viscusi, W. Kip, and Charles J. O'Connor. 1984. "Adaptive Responses to Chemical Labeling: Are Workers Bayesian Decision Makers? *American Economic Review* 74 (December): 942–956.

Viscusi, W. Kip, Wesley A. Magat, and Joel Huber. 1986. "Informational Regulation of Consumer Health Risks: An Empirical Evaluation of Hazard Warnings," *Rand Journal of Economics* 17 (Autumn): 351–365.

Viscusi, W. Kip, Wesley A. Magat, and Joel Huber, 1987. "An Investigation of the Rationality of Consumer Valuations of Multiple Health Risks," *Rand Journal of Economics* 18 (Winter): 465–479.

Weinstein, Neil D., Peter Sandman, and Nancy E. Roberts. 1989. *Communicating Effectively About Risk Magnitudes*. Final Report to the U.S. Environmental Protection Agency, EPA-230–08–89–064.

3 RISK PERCEPTION AND THE PERCEIVED PUBLIC

Lola L. Lopes*

The popular press has a fondness for stories about the risks of life. Death and destruction, pollution and pestilence, murder and mayhem: the more the merrier. So it has always been. Recently, however, reporters have uncovered a new kind of threat. According to numerous psychological experiments, it now seems likely that lay people do not understand statistics well enough to make intelligent use of all this information about death and destruction, pollution and pestilence, murder and mayhem. As a writer for the *Saturday Evening Post* recently summed matters up, "when it comes to risk, we are idiots" (Bryson, 1988, p. 31).

The *Post* article focused on mortality rates for a variety of activities, occupations, illnesses, and demographic variables. Mulling on the body counts, the author commented, "The remarkable thing is not that the world is full of hazards but that we are so bad at assessing them" (p. 31). As illustration, he offered the observation that although "one of the

* Lola L. Lopes is Pomerantz Professor of Business Administration and Professor of Psychology, University of Iowa. She acknowledges the helpful comments of Gary Gaeth, Don McCloskey, Gregg Oden, Jerry Rose, and Sara Rynes on an earlier version.

57

biggest fears for most people is of dying in an airplane crash .... statistically, [we] are more likely to be kicked to death by a donkey" (p. 31).

As the reporter no doubt intended, I was surprised by this claim, so surprised that I tried to check it out at the public library. I started with the airline data. The author put the chances of dying in an airplane crash at 1 in 100,000. Assuming that the statistic refers to the United States, this amounts to about 2,500 deaths per year (based on an estimated population of 250,000,000). The figure seemed high to me but it might have been correct if it included deaths in general aviation and (possibly) military aviation as well.[1] On the other hand, it could have been that the 1 in 100,000 figure was wrong and the correct value was actually closer to 1 in 1,000,000 or about 250 deaths per year. According to the almanac, this comes closer to the annual number of deaths on scheduled commercial flights in the United States, although it is still high.

Hoping to find some sort of converging evidence, I went to work on the other side of the equation. First, I wondered whether donkeys were more dangerous than I knew. This was possible, but not sufficiently so for the almanac to have data on the number of people killed by donkeys each year. In fact, it did not even have a category for people killed by animals each year. Having been sensitized by much research on what has been called "the base rate fallacy," I next considered that perhaps I was underestimating the number of donkeys in the United States. After all, if even a small percent were rogue donkeys, they could account for a considerable number of deaths. Unfortunately, the almanac had no listing at all for donkeys and the books on animal husbandry that I consulted (while filled with all sorts of useful information about donkeys) offered no insights on their numbers. Stymied, I finally gave up, frustrated that although years of statistical study had prepared me for working out Poisson probabilities involving comparable events (such as Prussian cavalry officers being killed by their horses), nothing had prepared me for finding out how likely I or anyone else was of being kicked to death by a donkey.

On the face of it, the *Saturday Evening Post* writer seems to suppose that the magnitudes of my fears and protective actions should be directly related to the magnitudes of *his* statistics. Given the likely inaccuracy of the latter,[2] I might reasonably disagree. Nevertheless, the general notion that some fairly simple relationship ought to exist between behavior and mortality rates is quite common among experts in psychological risk perception. As three of the indisputably dominant figures in the area (Paul Slovic, Sarah Lichtenstein, and Baruch Fischhoff) expressed matters in one of their first major articles on the topic, accurate intuitive knowledge concerning vital statistics that are "carefully tabulated and reported to the public" is of great importance to society since "citizens must assess risks accurately in order to mobilize society's resources effectively for reducing hazards and treating their victims" (Lichtenstein, Slovic, Fischhoff, Layman, and Combs, 1978, p. 551).

In what follows, I will describe some seminal research aimed at assessing the accuracy of lay people's knowledge about risks, and characterizing the ways in which their intuitive estimates differ from figures provided by experts. My intent is to illustrate some ways in which the research suggests a limited and unnecessarily pessimistic view of the lay person's understanding of risk.

1. How Much Do People Know about Hazards?

In the last decade, a variety of experimental approaches have been developed for determining how much people know about risks and how their knowledge differs from that of experts who deal with the same risks as professionals. The results of these experiments have been reported in psychological journals as well as in numerous chapters and articles in books and journals on public policy, technical risk assessment, medicine, computer science, law, and so forth, and in presentations made to various congressional and regulatory groups.

Very clearly, the assumption exists among academic researchers that the results bear profoundly and, in many cases, pessimistically on the degree to which ordinary citizens are capable of participating intelligently in societal decisions concerning the adoption and regulation of technologies, and the allocation of resources for maintaining and improving human lives. An alternative view is that the experiments tell us little about the layman either psychologically or politically, but tell us much about how certain professionals construe the world and their role in it.

1.1. Judged Frequency of Lethal Events

One of the earliest experiments on risk perception (as the topic has come to be known) asked people to make judgments about the lethality of 41 different causes of death. These included things like botulism, tuberculosis, collisions of motor vehicles and trains, suicide, heart disease, and so forth (Lichtenstein, Slovic, Fischhoff, Layman, and Combs, 1978).

The study was a thorough one involving multiple experiments and a variety of response measures, with both college students and members of the League of Women Voters as subjects. In all situations and with all subjects, comparison of intuitive responses with statistical data revealed that people have a great many misconceptions about the relative likelihood of some causes of death. Although most subjects were able to select the more likely cause of death when the true ratio was 2:1 or greater, they often misordered events with smaller true ratios, and their quantitative estimates were typically far off the mark. For example, students judged tornadoes to be more lethal than asthma even though the latter accounts for 20 times as many deaths, and deaths from accidents were judged to be about as likely as deaths from disease even though diseases claim about 15 times as many lives. Moreover, even when the direction of the judgment was correct, numerical estimates were likely to be way off, as for example, in estimating the likelihood of death by motor vehicle to be 356 times more likely than death by diabetes when the true ratio is only 1.4:1.

On the other hand, global evaluation of the data revealed that subjects' choices in paired comparisons were internally consistent (as judged by assessment of stochastic transitivity among triads of comparisons) and that direct ratings of event frequencies were generally related to actual frequencies with linear correlations of .89 or better. The main systematic discrepancy was a tendency to underestimate the likelihood of death due to high-frequency causes (such as heart disease and diabetes) and to overestimate the frequency of death due to low-frequency causes (such as tornado and botulism).

In discussing the results, the authors are sparing in compliments for the performances of their subjects. They acknowledge that "our subjects exhibited some competence in judging frequency" (p. 574) but suggest that "high correlations between direct estimates and true frequency across a million-to-one range of the latter variable are deceptive" (p. 574) and mask "large estimation errors" (p. 563). They go on to note that "unless the true frequencies of a pair of lethal events differed by more than a factor of two, there was no guarantee that subjects could correctly indicate which was the more frequent" (p. 574). Somewhat earlier they characterized ratios of estimates and true scores that were within a factor of 1.5 to be only "moderately good" (p. 572). In the end they concluded "people do not have accurate knowledge of the risks they face .... Improved public education is needed before we can expect the citizenry to make reasonable public-policy decisions about societal risks" (p. 577).

Is this performance good or bad? One possible evaluation offered by Fischhoff, Slovic, and Lichtenstein (1982) is that it is about as good as can be expected, given that the subjects were neither specialists in the hazards considered nor exposed to a representative sample of information. Although my inclination is to be more nearly awestruck by the accuracy of the subjects' performances, I cannot disagree with the assessment of the technical difficulties under which the lay person must operate in amassing data and generating responses to questions such as these.

One might ask, however, what the assumptions about people's statistical performances reveal about the researchers' attitudes toward the statistics. The most basic assumption concerns the meaningfulness and reality of the numbers themselves. By focusing on *accuracy* of *perception*, the researchers implicitly suggest that the statistics measure bona fide events that exist in a form that can be perceived much as we perceive other objects and events in the world. The analogy here (cf. Fischhoff, Slovic, and Lichtenstein, 1982, pp. 243—244) is to the topic of classical psychophysics in which measurable dimensions of physical stimulation (e.g., frequency, intensity, wavelength) are related to their psychological correlates (e.g., pitch, loudness, hue). Although it is clear that no physical receptor for risk is being proposed, the fact remains that categories such as botulism, tuberculosis, and collisions between motor vehicles and trains are assumed to exist sufficiently tangibly for their statistics to be apprehensible by means of unaided intuition.[3]

There are, however, at least two difficulties with the analogy. The first is that it assumes that people constitute a homogeneous reference group for which all statistics are equally interesting and applicable. In the case of physical stimulation, this is not a bad assumption. If we are concerned with basic responses in a controlled laboratory setting, Mr. Smith and Mr. Jones are likely to respond similarly to a 100-Hertz tone at 30 decibels (a soft, low tone) provided they have normal hearing. But Mrs. Smith and Mrs. Jones may respond differently to a question about the mortality rate for breast cancer if they differ in their vulnerability to the disease.

What should either woman know about breast cancer statistics? Should she be knowledgeable about the statistics for everyone or only for her own age group? Should her personal risk perceptions be different if her mother died of breast cancer? Should her concerns change if she decides to undergo hormone replacement therapy? Just as there is no simple answer to the question of what Mrs. Smith or Mrs. Jones should know about breast cancer, there is likewise no one category of breast cancer to be perceived, accurately or not.

The second assumption is that unbiased estimates of a risk's magnitude can be extracted from routine experience with the risk. This turns out not to be the case. One study (J. Christensen-Szalanski, Beck, C. Christensen-Szalanski, and Koepsell, 1983) compared the judgments of physicians and college students in estimating mortality rates for diseases. Although the physicians were more accurate overall than the college students, their responses were systematically biased in that they underestimated the mortality rates of the most common diseases and overestimated the mortality rates of the least common diseases. Moreover, analysis showed that the source of the bias was work-related exposure to the illnesses. Thus, physicians apparently based their mortality judgments partially on the frequency with which they encountered illnesses, particularly rare illnesses, even though such encounters did not often involve death.

In the end, it appears that the only people who can be said to be expert in their knowledge of mortality rates are the epidemiologists and statisticians who compile the rates for categories that they themselves define. And even here, it would be inappropriate to suggest that the statistical experts *perceive* the rates more accurately than lay persons or physicians since the soundness of their estimates reflects the soundness of the procedures they use to collect and analyze the data rather than the acuity of their statistical perceptions.

1.2.   What is Risky?

Modern political and economic institutions have been keeping statistics on deaths and injuries for many years. Yet it is only recently that there has been much interest in determining the degree to which lay people are intuitively attuned to the statistics. One critical reason for the increase in the apparent psychological relevance of vital statistics is that quantitative estimates are increasingly being promoted as appropriate and objective measures of the riskiness of various activities and technologies. Indeed, risk assessment is now a profession encompassing not only the actuarial sorts of mortality and morbidity counting that have long been the staple of insurance underwriting, but also highly speculative estimates of accident and fatality rates in complex systems involving new and still-evolving technologies.

Although risk experts seem comfortable with their own risk analyses, lay people often are not and increasingly voice their concerns in the public arena. Dismayed and annoyed, private industry and governmental bodies alike assume that the disagreements result from public misunderstanding of the relevant statistics.

A study by Slovic, Fischhoff, and Lichtenstein (1980a) reveals the inadequacy of this view. In the study, four different groups of subjects were asked to rate the risk of dying from various activities and technologies. Three of the groups were comprised of lay people (members of the

League of Women Voters, college students, members of a business and professional club) and the fourth was comprised of experts selected nationwide for their professional involvement in risk assessment. Because the results for the three lay groups were qualitatively similar, I will focus only on the data for the members of the League of Women Voters (League) and the professional risk assessors (Experts).

Overall, the final rankings of the League and the Experts were surprisingly similar for the 30 risks. Of the 30 pairs of ranks, 17 were within ±5 positions of one another. But there were some notable exceptions, most prominent of which was that League members ranked nuclear power as most risky while the Experts ranked it 20th. Indeed, the rankings of the Experts were close enough to available technical estimates of annualized fatalities that the authors deemed it reasonable to conclude that they "both knew what the technical estimates were and viewed the risk of an activity or technology as synonymous with them" (p. 192).

One possible interpretation of the large difference of opinion between the Experts and the League members on the issue of nuclear power is that League members think nuclear power is risky because they overestimate the frequency or likelihood of fatalities due to nuclear energy production. Slovic, Fischhoff, and Lichtenstein checked this possibility by asking additional groups of League members and students to estimate annual deaths in the United States due to each of the 30 activities. Their results clearly rejected the overestimation hypothesis. In fact, for League members, nuclear power actually had the lowest annual fatality estimate of all 30 activities and technologies.

If riskiness is something beyond annual fatality rates, what is it? Factor-analytic studies by Slovic (1987) and his colleagues have suggested that the subjective space in which risks lie is not the simple unidimensional continuum envisioned by risk assessors. Instead, risk appears to have at least two major, conceptually orthogonal factors: dread risk and unknown risk.

The high end of the dread risk factor is correlated with perceived lack of control, catastrophic potential, fatal consequences, and inequality of risks and benefits. Nuclear energy and nuclear weapons are the highest scoring technologies on dread. Comparable low-dread technologies are caffeine, aspirin, and power mowers.

The high end of the unknown risk factor is correlated with risks that are new, unobservable, and delayed in their manifestation of harm. Examples of high-unknown technologies are microwave ovens, electric fields, and nitrites. Low-unknown technologies are automobile accidents, fireworks, and bridges.

For the most part, technologies that are controversial tend to be in the high-dread, high-unknown quadrant. Examples include genetic engineering, pesticides, and anything to do with nuclear technology (including waste disposal, uranium mining, weapons fallout, and reactor accidents). The low-low quadrant includes activities such as smoking, drinking, and various forms of recreational activities (skiing, boating, snowmobiling, etc.).

It is along the high-high versus low-low diagonal that experts and lay people tend to have their most serious disagreements. For the most part, lay people resist the large scale and essentially involuntary risks in the high-high quadrant. Experts, however, believe that these risks are relatively minor and point to public acceptance of the individual and essentially voluntary risks in the low-low quadrant as evidence that either statistically comparable high-high risks ought to be acceptable (the revealed preference approach of Starr, 1969) or that lay people's preferences are too nonsensical to be heeded (see, e.g., Wildavsky, 1988).

Slovic's two-factor structure has been replicated in many studies spanning diverse samples of subjects and risks. There is no doubt that something like the dread risk and unknown risk factors do figure in people's perceptions of activities and technologies. The factors are real psychologically and must be dealt with as part of the political context in which societal decision making takes place.

But are the risk factors also real in the sense of being *objectively* real? For the most part, risk perception researchers think not and treat the factors as though they are purely *subjective*. For example, Fischhoff, Watson, and Hope (1984) present Slovic's risk dimensions by saying "[unknown risk] expresses aversion to uncertainty, and thus represents cognitive (or intellectual) aspects of concern, whereas [dread risk] captures a risk's ability to evoke a visceral response" (p. 129).

Lichtenstein, Gregory, Slovic, and Wagenaar (1990) also relegate public concerns to the subjective realm. Speaking of people's fear of technologies that can produce catastrophic outcomes (e.g., people's opposition to nuclear power plants), they advise societal decision makers to ignore public opinion if necessary and adopt policies that minimize the expected (or long-run average) number of deaths without regard to how deaths are distributed over incidents or over time. To behave otherwise, they claim, would be to allow a purely subjective preference to needlessly claim human lives. Likewise, they argue that "ambiguity and vagueness about probabilities ... are formally irrelevant in decision analysis" (p. 96) and should be ignored even though the public "might quite rightly trust probabilities based on abundant data more than probabilities assessed by experts lacking such evidence" (p. 97).

No one who has ever been seriously at risk can doubt the vividness and subjectivity of the experience. But it confuses effect with cause to suppose that the factors that trigger an emotional state are intrinsically subjective. Catastrophic potential, irreversible consequences, invisible and slow-acting effects, absence of verifiable operational data, lack of personal or political control, weak managerial accountability, untrustworthy public information: these are, indeed, the elements of an industrial thriller. But are they not also the quintessential elements of real (that is to say, objective) risk?

1.3. What is Risk?

Risk is a basic concept in many disciplines, but it is not always the same concept. Fischhoff, Watson, and Hope (1984) surveyed a set of measures that are used by risk assessors for quantifying objective risk. These include things like annual death toll, death per person exposed or per hour of exposure, loss of life expectancy, and lost working days. The authors note that seemingly objective measures such as these often mask political values. For example, the loss of life expectancy measure puts a premium on the lives of young people (who lose more life expectancy when they die) relative to measures such as annualized death toll that treat all deaths as equal.

The measures also mask theoretical assumptions that are embedded in the way some professionals think about risk and risk management. For all of these measures, risk is characterized as the mean (expected value) of a probability distribution in which the potential outcomes are numbers of deaths or numbers of days lost. This, in turn, implies that the negative social impact of deaths or losses of life expectancy increases linearly with the magnitude of the losses and independently of the manner in which deaths are distributed over time and place. This corresponds to "risk neutrality" in terms of a standard expected utility analysis and it conflicts with people's strongly felt desire to avoid situations (that is, probability distributions) in which catastrophic losses are possible.

The idea that distribution matters in defining riskiness has a long history in psychology, and there is much evidence that both variance and skewness affect perceived riskiness (Coombs and Huang, 1970b; Coombs and Lehner, 1981; Lopes, 1984; Luce, 1980; Pollatsek and Tversky, 1970). Distribution-based definitions are also common in both the theoretical and the practical assessment of financial risks. In portfolio theory, for example, risk amounts to variance, although skewness and skewed measures of variance (such as the semivariance) have also been advanced as appropriate measures of riskiness (Markowitz, 1959).

But aversion to high variance, negatively skewed risks (in which there is a small probability of a catastrophic outcome) is exactly what the dread risk dimension of Slovic's (1987) factor-analytic representation entails. Although Fischhoff et al. (1984) have glossed this dimension as involving a "feeling" of dread (p. 129) and a "visceral response" (p. 129), there is nothing in the data to argue against the interpretation that people's subjective notion of risk comes closer to that embodied in distributional theories than it does to distribution-free notions based solely on expected losses.

For authors such as Lichtenstein et al. (1990), catastrophe avoidance is an ethically troubling and socially expensive whim. Still, the desire to avoid catastrophes may reflect more than mere psychology. In animal populations, for example, single deaths spread over time and place can be accommodated easily by healthy species, but catastrophic losses may lead to extinction if the population falls below a critical level. Thus, for biological groups, the whole is truly more than the sum of its parts. If the same holds for social groups (and who could imagine that it does not), the dread that individuals have of catastrophes may signify the communal virtues of protecting valuable social entities (families, communities, indeed, whole peoples) from the threat of extinction.

The second assumption embedded in many technical risk assessments is the idea that uncertainty or ambiguity in probability measures is unimportant. Thus, risk indices computed on the basis of theoretical analyses are to be treated with the same respect as risk indices based on solid actuarial data. For example, a brand new technology for which experts estimate an average of one fatality per year is to be considered no more risky than an old technology in which years of accumulated experience have shown that there will be an average of one fatality per year.

Theoretical convenience notwithstanding, the problem of ambiguity in probability measures will not go away. Early objections to the dismissal of ambiguity in normative theory (Ellsberg, 1961) have slowly diffused into psychological theory (e.g., Curley, Yates, and Abrams, 1986; Einhorn and Hogarth, 1985). And there is also increased (if belated) recognition in the business literature that insurance firms (who make their profits by converting risks into certainties) act as though ambiguity matters and either charge a premium for risks in which probabilities are uncertain

(Kunreuther, 1989) or refuse outright to sell policies for risks involving highly speculative and potentially disastrous outcomes.

2. What Needs to be Known (and by Whom)

2.1. What People Should Know About Hazards

Taking these studies of risk perception as a set, it can be seen that behind them all is the implicit belief that quantitative data concerning hazards are meaningful, accessible, universal, and useful to citizens as absolute indicators of riskiness. There is no margin for disagreement or even for less than absolute accuracy: the only way the public can be seen as having adequate knowledge of risks is for the public to know the numbers. And although risk experts understand that they cannot impose their views on people in a democratic society, they do tend to define their problem as one of developing techniques for communicating correct assessments to an inexpert public.

An interesting contrast in the focus of expert risk communications can be found in the comparison between two booklets issued by the federal government in the mid-1980s. The first, "A Citizen's Guide to Radon: What It Is and What to Do About It" (1986), was issued jointly by the U.S. Environmental Protection Agency and the U.S. Centers for Disease Control. The authors of the booklet are unnamed and unmentioned except for the disclaimer that no one associated with the booklet "makes any warranty, guarantee, or representation . . . with respect to the usefulness or effectiveness of any information, method or process disclosed [in the booklet] or assumes any liability [for use of the provided information]."

The booklet spends some pages explaining what radon is and why it is dangerous, but it mostly discusses radon testing and the interpretation of test results. Two kinds of information are highlighted: numerical probabilities of lung cancer deaths attributable to radon exposure and risk-comparison figures that relate various radon exposure levels to other sources of lung cancer. For example, the fact that between 6 and 21 people out of 100 who are exposed to radon concentrations of 20 pCi/l for 75% of each day for 70 years eventually die of lung cancer is illustrated by presenting a panel of 100 little heads and replacing 13 of them with black squares. Additional panels of little heads are presented to portray 1–5 per 100, 14–42 per 100, and 44–77 per 100. Obviously, the authors suppose that simple numerical statements will not be understood.

On the other hand, a chart comparing the risks of radon with smoking and chest X rays is presented without comment or interpretation. Some of the items seem helpful (as, for example, the fact that the 20 pCi/l level of exposure is somewhere between smoking one and two packs of cigarettes per day). But other comparisons mystify, as for example, the fact that choosing to live indoors at average radon exposure levels (1 pCi/l) rather than outdoors (at 0.2 pCi/l) is slightly more dangerous than having 20 chest X rays per year; or, the fact that the EPA acceptable level of radon exposure (4 pCi/l) is comparable to having more than 200 chest X rays per year. Given that physicians have stopped asking for annual chest X rays due to exposure concerns, it is not easy to say whether the point of the chart is to show that radon is dangerous or that X rays are safe.

The second booklet is the Surgeon General's Report on Acquired Immune Deficiency Syndrome (Koop, undated) issued by the U.S. Department of Public Health and Human Services. This booklet was written personally by C. Everett Koop to inform the public about AIDS and the steps individuals might take to avoid it.

The language in the AIDS booklet is direct and the recommendations are to the point ("[use] a rubber," "do not have sex with prostitutes," "avoid mouth contact with the penis, vagina, or rectum"). Koop also deals in a straightforward and uncondescending way with the statistical aspects of issues such as blood transfusions ("It is estimated that [blood antibody testing may fail to detect the AIDS virus] less than once in 100,000 donations") and with the uncertainties in the forecasts ("With our present knowledge, scientists predict that 20 to 30 percent of those infected with the AIDS virus will develop ... AIDS within five years").

Although the radon booklet attempts to be helpful and is even solicitous of the lay reader—recall all those little heads—it suffers in comparison with the AIDS booklet in terms both of what it presents and what it leaves out. The radon booklet focuses most of its energy on testing and interpretation of test results. This focus extends even to the recommendations, which deal mostly with reliability (when and how to retest if exposure levels are above 4 pCi/l) and with how soon to take action (within a few years or a few weeks). However, the booklet is very short on recommendations for mitigating the dangers by other than general means like stopping smoking, spending less time in the basement, opening windows, and keeping crawl spaces open. No mention is made of caulking along the edges of basement floors (the cheapest, most common fix for the problem) or installing a sub-slab ventilation system (the most expensive fix). Instead, readers are referred to another booklet.

Missing also from the booklet is the one piece of information that someone would probably find most useful in deciding whether to have a home tested. This is information about regions in the country in which radon contamination has already been found due either to industrial or natural sources. Why this information is omitted is unclear, but it is possible that concerns about property values and industrial liability played some role.

2.2. *What Experts Should Know About People*

One way that psychologists have addressed the question of why experts and lay people disagree about risks has been to focus on potential sources of error in the lay assessments. For example, Slovic, Fischhoff, and Lichtenstein (1980b) point to reliance on the availability heuristic as the reason dramatic risks are overestimated and mundane risks are underestimated (p. 44), insensitivity to the role of inappropriate assumptions in arriving at estimates (p. 47), feelings of personal immunity from common hazards such as automobile accidents (p. 47), and failure to consider potential causes of accidents that are "out of sight" (p. 47).

Another reason that is rarely mentioned, however, is that people may simply not believe what they are told. A case in point can be found in Richard Feynman's (1988) description of his service on the Presidential Commission that investigated the loss of the *Challenger* space shuttle. Feynman (no lover of Washington bureaucracy) agreed to serve on the Commission in hopes that he might be able to offer some special insights on the technical causes of the accident. He discovered, however, that the investigation was likely to turn into a long, time-wasting series of 'presentations' by bureaucrats called to testify before the panel.

Feynman refused to accept this kind of involvement and ran his own investigation by talking directly with engineers. Among the several notable discoveries of his private investigation are two that deserve discussion here.

Of major technical importance was Feynman's discovery that the O-rings in the solid-fuel booster rockets would have failed in the low temperatures that prevailed on the day of the accident. Equally important, however, was his finding that the most knowledgeable engineers at Morton Thiokol (the manufacturer of the rockets) advised against the flight because of their fears of O-ring failure.

Feynman's investigation led him to believe that the engineers understood the hazard involved in the O-ring assembly and appreciated its exacerbation by extreme cold. What dumbfounded him, however, was the mismanagement that shielded higher-level managers from learning about the O-ring hazard by pressuring lower-level managers and technical staff to bias their judgments in a direction that would allow the shuttle to fly on schedule.

Feynman did not conclude that the pressures were explicit, even though he did not think it coincidental that the President's State of the Union Address was to be given that very evening. Instead, Feynman decided that "people in a big system like NASA know what has to be done — without being told" (p. 217). The pressure was on NASA to get the shuttle up for many reasons and no direct pressure was needed from the White House or anyone else to ensure that the goal was achieved as expeditiously as possible.

Feynman's second finding concerned the official probability estimates given by NASA for a shuttle failure. Feynman was utterly amazed when he learned that the official estimate was 1 in 100,000. As he put matters in his Appendix to the Commission's report, "Since 1 part in 100,000 would imply that one could launch a shuttle each day for 300 years expecting to lose only one, we could properly ask, 'What is the cause of management's fantastic faith in the machinery?'" (Feynman, 1988, p. 220).

In talking with engineers involved with the engines, Feynman found that their estimates of failure were nearer to 1 in 200. Nevertheless, management stuck to the 1 in 100,000 figure, reasoning somewhat magically that "since the shuttle is a manned vehicle, the probability of mission success is very necessarily close to 1.0" (Feynman, 1988, p. 222). As Feynman pointed out, however, previous flights had shown numerous troubles and near failures, suggesting that the true probability was probably much higher. In fact, the shuttle was armed with destruct charges just in case it ever went out of control and threatened to crash into a populated area. The official who made the decision to arm the shuttle originally estimated the probability of a failure at 1 in 100 (or one quarter of the known rate of failure in unmanned rockets). He later was pressured to revise his estimate up to 1 in 100,000 and refused to do so. His final estimate of 1 in 1,000 took into account all the special safety precautions that NASA took with manned flights, but still left the likelihood of failure sufficiently high to warrant the installation of destruct devices.

Feynman's findings concerning the engines were initially suppressed (ostensibly by accident) and then edited to near vacuity by an executive officer of the Commission. In the end, Feynman had to threaten to remove his name from the report to have his original Appendix published.

Was Feynman's understanding of the risks involved in the space shuttle faulty? I would say no, although I must report that when I once related

Feynman's remark about 1 in 100,000 being like having only 1 accident in 300 years of daily flight to a risk-research colleague, his response was to point out that Feynman was obviously reasoning fallaciously since there is no guarantee that a low-probability event will not occur early in a long series! Such technical pickiness notwithstanding, I stand with Feynman in finding more than a little reason to distrust that particular probability estimate.

Indeed, all people who are reasonably in touch with events in politics and industry have good reason to distrust probability estimates, particularly when those estimates deal with highly uncertain scenarios of future events or with matters that are politically charged or that involve potentially high profits for individuals or firms. You do not have to be a Nobel laureate to wonder whether the findings of scientists who gather data for cigarette companies on the health effects of smoking are influenced by company wishes. Nor does it require a high degree of paranoia to question whether official statements about public health hazards have been edited for political content. Such political input is apparently routine, as anyone might judge from news items like the *Newsweek* (May 22, 1989) report stating that the testimony of NASA scientist James Hansen on the negative potential of the greenhouse effect had been "edited" by a midlevel federal bureaucrat at the Office of Management and Budget.

If I may borrow Feynman's phrase, it is hard to understand the fantastic faith that most risk researchers have in the technology of risk assessment. And I must agree with Otway (1987) on the necessity of facing the issue of fallible and possibly biased experts, even decision experts. As he put it, "A starting point for opening communications is to acknowledge the limits to expertise and to discuss freely uncertainties, alternative interpretations, peer review, and how research strategies are evolved and funded. It is obviously important to know who funded a particular piece of research [but it is also] reasonable to ask if, despite conscious attempts at objectivity, we have been compromised through sources of past research support, or by accumulated ego investment in a particular position" (p. 128). Otway also suggests that "if we are to change our way of dealing with people, we will first have to reassess how we think about them — and about our science as well" (p. 128). Surely, that is very true of the risk perception area.

One potential direction for reassessment would be to accept as valid the kinds of laboratory tasks that have been studied thus far, but then look beyond apparent anomalies in lay behavior for better understanding of the tasks and of the respondents. For example, one laboratory finding that seems to arouse a high level of righteous indignation among researchers is that most people believe themselves to be safer than the average driver even though, as Svenson, Fischhoff, and MacGregor (1985) loftily exclaim, "it is no more possible for most people to be safer than average than it is for most to have above average intelligence" (p. 119).

Authors typically attribute this particular "error" to optimism stemming from the illusion of control generated as drivers make hundreds and hundreds of trips without accident. But before accepting the optimism interpretation, it is useful to consider that the word *average* has several meanings, at least one of which can describe a situation in which most observations are either below or above average. All that is required is for the distribution to be skewed so that the mean is different from the median.

Might an underlying distribution of this sort be responsible for people's beliefs about their own driving skills? Very likely so. Schwing and Kamerud (1988) have published data showing that fatal auto accidents exhibit a strong time-of-day effect and have a highly skewed frequency distribution, with hourly accident rates differing by a factor of 134 from lowest to highest. Thus, contrary to Svenson et al.'s pronouncement that most people cannot be safer than average, Schwing and Kamerud found that "85% of all travel is safer than average" (p. 133) and they concluded that "It is quite possible ... that average risks apply to only a small fraction of the population at large and to an even smaller fraction of the population surveyed. Indeed, risk researchers might be underestimating the judgmental capabilities of the layman" (p. 133).[5]

The second direction for reassessment would involve reinserting risk judgments into the political and social context in which they occur in the real world. Risk perception is only partially about our technical comprehension of hazards from natural and artificial sources. It is also about politics and consent, economics and competition, morality and culture. Even if our own inclinations do not predispose us to accept or reject some particular risk, our beliefs about the motives of those who try to persuade us may convey all we need or care to know about the activity or technology at issue.

Political, economic, and social aspects of behavior are typically much harder to manipulate in the laboratory than cognitive aspects. But issues of trust and accountability are part of the way people think about public policy, and there is no reason why researchers might not as easily ask people to rate the likelihood that a bureaucrat or scientist will provide candid information about a hazard as to ask them to rate the likelihood of fatal collisions between motor vehicles and trains. Researchers can also ask people to tell them what provisions they would like to have for public oversight of new or hazardous technologies. There are simply whole realms of psychological material concerning trust and consent that ought to be part of risk-perception research.

Notes

1. Conditionalizing on the number of people who fly each year would only make matters worse since the total number of passengers on U.S. airlines far exceeds the population of the United States.

2. For example, the writer states at one point that "every time you take a walk down the street you reduce your life expectancy by an average of 37 days" (p. 31). Were this true, the United States Post Office would seldom need to pay out pensions to mail carriers since, by this measure, they would lose more than 20 years of life expectancy for *each year* they work and would consequently not be expected to survive to retirement age.

3. An alternative interpretation of the "object" of risk perception can be found in Fischhoff, Watson, and Hope (1984). They define objective risk as "the product of scientific research, primarily public health statistics, experimental studies, epidemiological surveys, and probabilistic risk analyses" (p. 124). Subjective risk, on the other hand, refers to "nonexpert perceptions of that *research* embellished by whatever other considerations seize the public mind" (p. 124, emphasis added). Thus, "risk perception" is really "risk research perception."

4. PicoCuries per liter.

5. Factors such as age and drinking habits would almost certainly contribute to similarly skewed accident distributions.

References

Bryson, B. 1988. "Living Dangerously," *Saturday Evening Post*, 260 (September), 30–34.

Christensen-Szalanski, J.J.J., D.E. Beck, C.M. Christensen-Szalanski, and T.D. Koepsell. 1983. Effects of Expertise and Experience on Risk Judgments," *Journal of Applied Psychology* 68, 278–284.

Coombs, C.H., and L. Huang. 1970. "Test of a Portfolio Theory of Risk Preference," *Journal of Experimental Psychology* 85, 23–29.

Coombs, C.H., and P.E. Lehner. 1981. "Evaluation of Two Alternative Models of a Theory of Risk: Are Moments Useful in Assessing Risks?" *Journal of Experimental Psychology: Human Perception and Performance* 7, 1110–1123.

Curley, S.P., J.F. Yates, and R.A. Abrams. 1986. "Psychological Sources of Ambiguity Avoidance," *Organizational Behavior and Human Decision Processes* 38, 230–256.

Einhorn, H.J., and R.M. Hogarth. 1985. "Ambiguity and Uncertainty in Probabilistic Inference," *Psychological Review* 92, 433–461.

Ellsberg, D. 1961. "Risk, Ambiguity, and the Savage Axioms," *Quarterly Journal of Economics* 75, 643–669.

Feynman, Richard P. 1988. *What Do You Care What Other People Think?* New York: Norton.

Fischhoff, B., P. Slovic, and S. Lichtenstein. 1982. "Lay Foibles and Expert Fables in Judgments About Risks," *The American Statistician* 36, 240–255.

Fischhoff, B., S. R. Watson, and C. Hope. 1984. "Defining risks," *Policy Sciences* 17, 123–139.

Koop, C. E. (undated). *Surgeon General's Report on Acquired Immune Deficiency Syndrome.* U.S. Department of Health and Human Services.

Kunreuther, H. 1989. "The Role of Actuaries and Underwriters in Insuring Ambiguous Risks," *Risk Analysis* 9, 319–328.

Lichtenstein, S., R. Gregory, P. Slovic, and W. A. Wagenaar, 1990. "When Lives Are in Your Hands: Dilemmas of the Societal Decision Maker." In R. Hogarth (ed.), *Insights in decision making.* University of Chicago Press, pp. 91–106.

Lichtenstein S., P. Slovic, B. Fischhoff, M. Layman, and B. Combs. 1978. "Judged Frequency of Lethal Events," *Journal of Experimental Psychology: Human Learning and Memory* 4, 551–578.

Lopes, L. L. 1984. "Risk and Distributional Inequality," *Journal of Experimental Psychology: Human Perception and Performance* 10, 465–485.

Luce, R. D. 1980. "Several Possible Measures of Risk," *Theory and Decision* 12, 217–228.

Markowitz, H. M. 1959. *Portfolio selection: Efficient diversification of investments.* New York: Wiley.

Otway, H. 1987. "Experts, Risk Communication, and Democracy," *Risk Analysis* 7, 125–129.

Pollatsek, A., and A. Tversky. 1970. "A Theory of Risk," *Journal of Mathematical Psychology* 7, 540–553.

Schwing, R. C., and D. B. Kamerud. 1988. "The Distribution of Risks: Vehicle Occupant Fatalities and Time of Week," *Risk Analysis* 8, 127–133.

Slovic, P. 1987. "Perception of Risk," *Science* 236, 280–285.

Slovic, P., B. Fischhoff, and S. Lichtenstein. 1980a. "Facts and Fears: Understanding Perceived Risk." In R. C. Schwing & W. A. Albers, Jr., (eds.), *Societal Risk assessment: How safe is safe enough?* New York: Plenum Press, pp. 181–214.

Slovic P., B. Fischhoff, and S. Lichtenstein. 1980b. Risky assumptions. *Psychology Today*, June, 44–48.

Starr, C. 1969. Social benefit versus technological risk. *Science*, 165, 1232–1238.

Svenson, O., B. Fischhoff, and D. MacGregor. 1985. Perceived driving safety and seatbelt usage. *Accident Analysis and Prevention*, 17, 119–133.

U.S. Environmental Protection Agency and U.S. Centers for Disease Control. 1986. "A Citizen's Guide to Radon: What It Is and What to Do About It." Booklet OPA-86-004.

Wildavsky, A. 1988. *Searching for safety.* Studies in Social Philosophy and Policy, No. 10. New Brunswick: Transaction.

4 THE MEDIA AND PUBLIC PERCEPTIONS OF RISK: HOW JOURNALISTS FRAME RISK STORIES

Sharon Dunwoody*

When it comes to risk coverage, it seems that the mass media can do nothing right. They are regularly accused of bias, sensationalism, inaccuracies, indifference, and of being simplistic and polarized. If we believe the wealth of commentary that has spilled across the printed page since such landmark events as Love Canal and Three Mile Island in the late 1970s, then the mass media are — in a word — lousy at conveying appropriate notions of risk to general audiences.

The evaluative din obscures, however, several important gaps in our understanding of risk communication. For example, we know very little about how journalists select and structure risk messages. We know equally little about how individuals use those mediated messages to inform their

* Sharon Dunwoody is Evjue-Bascom professor of journalism and mass communication at the University of Wisconsin-Madison. She also holds an instructional appointment in the Institute for Environmental Studies and is head of the Center for Environmental Communications and Education Studies. She would like to thank Prof. Robert Griffin of Marquette University and Prof. Stephan Russ-Mohl of the Free University of Berlin for their contributions to the conceptualization of journalistic work presented here.

own risk judgments. Such knowledge is crucial in making informed judgments about the quality of media coverage of risky situations. Research is
proceeding apace on the latter issue (see, for example, Dunwoody and
Neuwirth, 1991). The primary aim of this chapter is to examine what we
know about the first issue and to suggest a conceptual map to aid in
further exploration.

How do journalists go about constructing risk stories? The map chosen
here will designate the "frame" as a powerful predictor of risk story
selection and structuring and will suggest that two classes of phenomena
account for much of the variance in reporters' framing efforts: individual
knowledge of information relevant to risk and journalistic occupational
norms. Of the two, the map will suggest that occupational norms are
likely the more powerful and may serve to standardize journalists' responses
to risk across time and space. However, under certain circumstances,
individual journalists will be able to override the normative mechanisms,
producing rather singular coverage. Given these circumstances, the map
suggests that reporters' levels of knowledge about science, mathematics,
and audience perceptions of risk will become significant predictors of
story content.

It is important to emphasize that this proposed map must yet survive
empirical tests. Too little is yet understood about journalists' responses to
risky situations to make one confident that the map accurately tracks the
lay of the land. Still, more generic — and copious — literatures that explore
news-making practices of journalists and sense-making practices of individuals provide useful insights.

1. Studies of Media Coverage of Risk

As in other topic domains, studies of media coverage of scientific and
technological risk have looked more intensively at the products — risk
stories — than at the process of story construction. This means that, with
few exceptions, such studies attempt to explain how coverage comes
about by inference rather than by direct observation.

These analyses of media coverage, in general, detect two large patterns
in stories. The first is that media coverage of risks does not mirror reality,
as defined by the researcher (see, for example, Combs and Slovic, 1979;
Greenberg, Sachsman, Sandman, and Salomone, 1989). The second is
that risk stories contain very little risk information, as defined by science
(see, for example, Sandman, Sachsman, Greenberg, and Gochfeld, 1987;
Singer and Endreny, 1987).

In most cases, discussions of why the patterns exist are speculative, and nearly all of the authors frame such speculation as a level-of-analysis issue. In other words, they implicitly array individual journalists, media organizations, and such extraorganizational concepts as occupation against one another as predictors of patterns of information selection and story structuring. Almost all authors conclude that organizational or occupational variables account for most of the variance. For example, Greenberg et al. (1989) argue that topic choices by network TV news journalists in their study were driven more by standards of newsworthiness (usually defined as an organizational attribute) than by level of risk. Similarly, Singer and Endreny (1987) assert that the poor fit between the amount of media coverage and the level of risk in their content analysis of 15 media outlets could be explained by occupational new judgments:

> A rare hazard is more newsworthy than a common one, other things being equal; a new hazard is more newsworthy than an old one; and a dramatic hazard — one that kills many people at once, suddenly or mysteriously — is more newsworthy than a long-familiar illness (p. 13).

Combs and Slovic (1979), too, speculate that the patterns of risk coverage they see in newspapers may be the product of occupationally tuned thinking. Specifically, they note that journalists may focus on the kinds of risks that "represent sources of societal vulnerability about which people need to be informed so that they can take precautions or institute appropriate controls" (p. 843).

Among these half-dozen studies, only one has explored possible individual-level predictors of risk news making. In a study of environmental risk reporting in New Jersey daily newspapers, Sandman et al. (1987) interviewed reporters at each of the 26 media organizations involved in the project and found that they expressed a need for greater knowledge of a particular chemical or other toxic substance if it were implicated in a breaking story. In fact, when presented with more than 60 types of specific information about such a chemical, a majority of the journalists defined more than two-thirds of the types as "important and urgent" bits of information.

This level-of-analysis approach has contributed much to our understanding of news making. For summaries of work in this area, see Ettema and Whitney (1982, 1987). It has helped to clarify the way in which "knowledge-as practice" is generated across the various strata that influence the news-making process, and indeed suggests that the knowledge provided by some strata are more powerful shapers of journalistic behavior than others. However, it is not a very useful framework for illuminating the process by which an individual journalist makes composition choices when confronted with a risky situation. In other words, while levels of analysis are conceptually appealing at a macro level, when one wishes to explore the locus of power in a process, the more micro world of how an individual makes choices about information selection and composition may be better grounded in concepts that have arisen in the process of studying writing itself. This chapter uses one such concept — the frame — as a basis for its discussion of the reconstruction of risky events as news. I will reintroduce the level-of-analysis "power" component as a factor influencing frame choice.

2. Frame as a Concept

The term *frame* has become very popular among media scholars, so popular that its use has become divorced from any single conceptual definition. At present, it is employed not only by those studying the construction of mediated messages, but also by scholars examining the ways in which such messages are interpreted by audiences. For a discussion of this latter category, see Kellermann and Lim (1989). Within the former category, frames are accorded great weight as predictors of nearly every element of story structure from choice of topic and sources to use of terms and decisions about the inclusion or exclusion of information.

What is a frame? If cognitive theorists are correct, a frame is a schema or heuristic, a knowledge structure that is activated by some stimulus and is then employed by a journalist throughout story construction. Gitlin says as much when he notes that "frames are principles of selection, emphasis, and presentation composed of little tacit theories about what exists, what happens, and what matters" (Gitlin, 1980, p. 6). Similarly, Stocking and Gross argue that journalists' prior knowledge about the world "allows them to organize and make sense of incoming information" (1989, p. 13). Flower and Hayes suggest that any act of writing "is best described as the act of juggling a number of simultaneous constraints" (1980, p. 31). These constraints create a kind of "cognitive strain" with which writers must cope, and one powerful coping strategy, say the researchers, is to "depend on procedures that are so automatized or routine that they don't require conscious processing in Short-Term Memory" (p. 42). Those cognitively economical procedures are frames.

If frames do have a great influence on the selection and structuring of risk stories, then scholars first must specify the frames — the mental maps — that might be activated when journalists are confronted with an event or issue that contains a scientific or technological risk dimension. Second, they must try to locate the explanatory precursors of such maps.

Although frames are not unique to journalism, they are central to journalistic work. Reporters and editors are confronted with countless happenings and issues about which they must make hurried decisions. Under such circumstances, they have developed a host of mental maps that can be activated quickly. For example, within seconds of hearing about an upcoming press conference, an editor can decide what the story is about and whether or not to send a reporter to cover it.

In her influential book, *Making News*, sociologist Gaye Tuchman makes a case for the ubiquity of the news frame in journalistic work (1978). She describes the frame as a way of coping with a glut of information, as a way of imparting meaning to processes "out there," meanings to which both media organizations and the legitimized institutions of society can subscribe. While one might more profitably think in terms of many frames rather than just one, the point of this section is that the typical journalist's arsenal of frames does not contain the frame "risk story" or, more specifically, does not contain a frame that prompts a reporter to think of risk as a scientifically constructed concept.

Journalists may write about risks quite often, but they rarely define their accounts as stories about risk. Instead, they employ a host of other frames to make sense of the information they see. When information is framed as something other than a risk story, it may contain little information about the risk component. On the other hand, if it is framed initially as a risk story, then it may contain a great deal of information about the risk, information determined in large part by the individual journalist's knowledge of the situation and of risk as a scientific and social construction.

To put this another way, journalists may frequently omit details about risk from an account that contains a risk dimension not because they are ignorant but because the information has activated a knowledge structure that does not include risk as an attribute. Secondarily, when an account is framed as a risk story, the types and extent of risk information provided will be heavily influenced by the writer's expertise.

How does one characterize the mental maps used by journalists? I would suggest that 1) frames are largely concept- rather than process-oriented and within the domain of concepts, concrete rather than abstract; and 2) a stimulus activates a knowledge structure *about a thing* rather than about the class of phenomena that the thing represents — or about ways in which tasks are accomplished. Further, the "things" about which journalists are most likely to have developed frames are common ones that audiences also are likely to recognize and define as worthy of attention. Examples from the domain of science reporting include the following:

First, science reporters are familiar with the scientific process and with the notion that research is an on-going series of behaviors with few beginnings and endings. Yet they are generally unwilling to write about work in progress or about the process of research. Instead, they wish to write about research when it achieves a kind of timely closure, when it is being presented at a conference, for example, or published in a journal. Journalists argue, with some justification, that this preference for closure, operationalized here as a hook that is event-oriented and timely, stems from both reader and source needs. It is argued that readers pay more attention to timely material, and scientist-sources urge journalists to put off writing about research until it has successfully negotiated peer review. But another factor may be at work as well. Many science writers do not have an available knowledge structure into which they can place on-going research; they have no frame for such a process. They do have frames, on the other hand, for "research report at a meeting" and "research report from a journal."

Second, in a massive study of media coverage of social science research, Weiss and Singer (1988) found that journalists rarely included in their stories the kinds of details that would illuminate for readers or viewers the theories and methods being employed. Unfamiliarity with research processes is one reason for omission, they suggest. However, they also allude to a problem of framing when they note that "much social science research is not defined as such by reporters or editors. And if a story about, say, attitudes toward nuclear power, or satisfaction with the conditions of work, or differences in sex roles is not seen as involving social science research, then social science criteria for evaluating and reporting such research will not come into play" (1988, p. 257). In other words, Weiss and Singer found little research information — use of researchers as sources, discussion of studies conducted, etc. — in the social science stories they encountered not because such research is unavailable but because the journalists' story frames excluded social science research as a relevant information domain for the stories.

One might also speculate that, even if a frame called "social science research" existed for journalists, it would place a poor second to, for example, the frame "story about two-career couples who live apart." The latter frame would be judged much more familiar and concrete to readers. Yet it could easily preclude any extended discussion of two-career couples *as a research topic.*

The argument that journalists have generated frames to accommodate specific, relevant things in their environment would seem to argue for — rather than against — a risk frame. After all, what could be more specific than a risk estimate, and what could be more relevant to readers than a statement about the likelihood of coming to harm from exposure to some substance or situation? However, such an argument ignores the fact that risks typically enter social consciousness not as formal bits of scientific knowledge proferred in a refereed research report — although some are introduced in such fashion — but rather as the byproducts of occurrences: a train derailment, an accident at a chemical plant, an airplane crash. It is those events that will capture the initial attention of journalists. A toxic spill, for example, might be labeled "an accident story" well before anyone thinks in terms of the risks posed by the chain of events. Even when the concept of risk does surface during coverage of the accident, it may continue to be relegated to a secondary berth in the story. To date, no studies have attempted to characterize the frames utilized by journalists for stories that contain some dimension of risk. However, the dearth of risk information (as defined by science) found in these mediated accounts suggests that, whatever those mental maps may be, they do not readily signal to journalists that a risk situation requiring scientific explanation is present.

Where do these maps come from? Many things in a journalist's world could play a role in constructing frames. The goal here is to tap the most powerful factors, the ones accounting for most of the variance in frame construction. This brings us back to levels of analysis. The conceptual roadmap posited earlier suggests that two levels play powerful roles in framing: occupational and individual levels.

3. Occupational Predictors of Frames

As with many other occupations, in journalism a variety of normative behaviors have evolved to which most members adhere. These norms are drilled into journalists not only in academic settings but also in the workplace. In the United States, a degree in journalism is increasingly a prerequisite for finding a job (Weaver and Wilhoit, 1986), and since academic journalism training is fairly homogeneous across university programs, such training instills a kind of standardized, normative framework in all who become enmeshed in it. Although Becker, Fruit, and Caudill (1987) argue that the impact of university experiences on the professional attitudes of journalism students may be less than expected, if both the academy and the occupation emphasize roughly the same norms, then one could still argue on behalf of a cumulative impact.

Once on the job, journalists are subjected to normative socialization in the newsroom (Breed, 1955). Although some proportion of that socialization may be unique to the particular news setting—journalists very quickly learn that their most important audience member is their editor— the emphasis on occupational norms continues as well. It is on those norms that we will focus here.

Occupational norms in journalism have evolved to meet at least three goals: 1) to maximize service to the reader, 2) to allow products to be constructed efficiently, and 3) to minimize the effects of attacks on the occupation from outside groups. We mention three norms here as examples, with emphasis on how they influence reporters' mental maps.

Norm 1.   Emphasis in story selection on events over processes.   Production processes dominate the lives of journalists. The typical journalist is responsible for helping to produce a daily product—an issue of a newspaper, a television newscast—and all information must thus be evaluated in light of that daily cycle. The editor's question "what do you have for me today?" encourages the writer to compress the world into informational chunks that characterize what is happening now, today.

If a newspaper science writer is covering a days-long scientific meeting, for example, both journalist and editor will assume that the reporter will file at least one story a day. Such an a priori assumption makes no conceptual sense; neither the writer nor the editor has any real insight into the quality of the information to be presented at the meeting. It does, however, make occupational sense, for the editor will realize a return on her travel investment in the form of stories that she can incorporate into a daily news hole that must be filled.

The assumption that the journalist will file daily from the meeting, not surprisingly, pushes the reporter to focus on what happens on a given day. What happens are research presentations and—with luck—press conferences. Both of these occurrences can be rather efficiently framed as research findings "presented today at a scientific meeting." Thus, a relatively timeless, highly amorphous collection of research projects is transformed into a series of discrete stories.

That the emphasis on events is occupationally driven becomes apparent when the occasional media organization changes the occupational parameter most crucial to the norm: production pressures. In one study of journalists' news-making behaviors at a major scientific meeting,

Dunwoody (1979) found that journalists sent to the meeting with explicit instructions to write stories only when something important takes place behaved very differently from those who arrived with the traditional norm intact. The former group wrote fewer and longer stories than did the latter.

This emphasis on events may be one of the most important predictors of nonrisk frames. Risks come to light within a particular community or culture in a variety of ways, and it is the events coincident with such visibility that are likely to play the major role in journalists' framing efforts. For example, when a governmental agency issues a report on radon, the story may be framed as a governmental announcement story, not as a risk story. Similarly, a truck crash that causes a toxic spill may be more likely framed as an accident story than a risk story.

Risk information may very well be present in a story with a nonrisk frame, but it may not be emphasized and, in fact, may play a very secondary role. Consider the truck crash story as an example. The reporter using an accident frame will focus primarily on what happened, when, where, who was injured, and whether the road is now passable. Information about the contents of the truck are by no means trivial but are not central to a crash story. The reporter using a risk frame, on the other hand, may regard the pragmatics of the accident as secondary to the hazards presented by the chemical. Rather than calling the hospital to ascertain the condition of the injured parties, she may call the city emergency response office to find out more about the goo spreading across the highway.

Norm 2. A journalist's task is to inform, not educate.   The interesting thing about this normative distinction, for our purposes, is that it absolves journalists from the obligation to explain things in any depth. Thus, when stories do require attention to risk, reporters may feel no obligation to help readers or viewers understand the risk. Their occupational obligation is to report the story. While the distinction between informing and educating is lost on many people, within journalism it means that a reporter's task is to tell audiences about happenings, not to provide them with the basic knowledge required to understand those happenings. Such basic knowledge, the reporter argues, must be supplied by the educational system and is the responsibility of the reader, not the journalist.

The inform-or-educate distinction is not as cavalier as it sounds. Journalism is writing on the run, and story-length limits generally preclude detailed treatises on any topic. Almost as hurried as the writing is its ingestion; most readers or viewers don't pay close attention to stories.

Journalists are aware that their audience skims rather than reads, so they regard explanatory detail as not only a waste of time but also as potentially dysfunctional. In a world of skimmers, a paragraph full of definitions can be an effective roadblock, and many journalists are not willing to risk such premature death.

A focus on informing rather than educating encourages a journalist to report but not necessarily to explain. Thus, he may include a risk estimate in his story but may feel no obligation — and may not have the space — to help readers understand enough about probability theory to place the estimate in an appropriate perspective. Journalistic frames, in summary, are at best indifferent to and, at worst, actively discourage explanation.

Thus, even though a risk frame may direct a journalist to select bits of information that accurately (to scientists) describe the risk at hand, it may be no more influential than any other type of frame at signaling the journalist to include the kind of explanatory material that will help readers understand that risk.

Norm 3. Journalists must not only convey information but also must attract readers. Audiences don't have to ingest journalistic products. They can (and do) skip over entire stories in newspapers and magazines, turn their attention away from TV news, or switch channels on the radio to avoid a particular story or seek other content. Hence, journalists have always faced the challenges of both luring audiences into their products and keeping them once they start reading or listening.

Journalists utilize a variety of mechanisms as story lures, but one characteristic underlying most of these strategies is concreteness, or specificity. The more concrete the story the better. Thus, a journalist may begin a story about risk taking not with a straightforward assertion but with a vivid narrative:

> You are desperately clinging to a sheer rock face. Heart pounding, short of breath, you look above to a teetering sky. Far below, a dizzying impasto of green and brown — and you are frozen in the knowledge that one slip of the toe will send you hurtling to your death on the ledges below. Sound like your idea of a good time? The scene is nothing short of a nightmare for most, but for some — that spry minority we call rock climbers — this is an ideal Sunday afternoon (Weiss, 1987, p. 57).

As Nisbett and Ross (1980) note, the more concrete, the more memorable. Thus, selecting particular dimensions of a story about which to be specific may also mean that a journalist is enhancing comprehension of those bits, perhaps to the exclusion of comprehension of others.

One common strategy for enhancing concreteness in journalistic stories is the utilization of a personalized narrative. Often found in the lead of a story — although it can occur anywhere in the account — the narrative portrays an individual caught or engaged in the topic at hand; the risk-taking story lead above serves as an example. The aim is to make information so vivid that the reader or viewer gets caught up in the story and, almost by default, attends to the more abstract points.

Typical of such an effort within a risk story was coverage in the early 1980s by a Wisconsin newspaper of a report in the *New England Journal of Medicine* suggesting a link between drinking coffee and pancreatic cancer. To give context to the study and its findings, a reporter visited a local coffee shop to ask the regulars if the news had convinced them to stop drinking coffee. In that instance, the reporter or editor had chosen to frame the story in a way that highlighted local, vivid information that may or may not have assisted in comprehending the risk information (Ryan, Dunwoody, and Tankard, forthcoming).

4. Individual Predictors of Frames

Some studies of journalistic work suggest that occupational norms are by far the strongest predictors of what's news, even for science reporters (Dunwoody, 1979). However, the most cursory comparison of stories about the same topic by journalists from different media organizations suggests that a considerable amount of story variation remains to be explained once occupational factors have been taken into account. Journalists behave in relatively homogeneous ways, thanks to these norms. *Within* occupational boundaries, however, individual journalists will produce accounts that vary — sometimes slightly, sometimes considerably — from those of their colleagues.

Occupational norms and constraints act to corral journalists cognitively in the same way that a fence might enclose a herd of wild mustangs. At first the distraught animals focus on the fence, defining it as the enemy, and avoiding it at all costs. Over time, however, the fence figuratively disappears as a force to be reckoned with and becomes, instead, an assumption. The horses' universe, instead of being truncated by the fence, becomes defined by it.

For journalists, occupational norms constitute the fence. As with the hypothetical mustangs, the journalistic fence acts to prevent dramatic departures from occupationally prescribed behavior. It does not, however, wipe out individual differences. In some cases, an individual journalist may accumulate enough power within a media organization to chop a hole in the fence, to produce products that seem to fly in the face of the norms. This last phenomenon may be very rare, but I will later describe a coverage situation that appears to be, at least in part, an example of the exercise of individual power.

This section, then, will be devoted to the kinds of individual variables that may influence construction of risk stories. Specifically, I will briefly examine the impact of varying levels of scientific knowledge and audience knowledge on reporter behaviors.

4.1. Science Knowledge

Most individuals in the United States apparently know little about science and mathematics, and surveys of precollege and college or university students' intentions to specialize in science or engineering find scant and even declining interest in fields beyond biology and the social sciences (National Science Board, 1989). The typical journalist in the United States is even less likely to have majored in science or math than is the average U.S. citizen, and science and math courses constitute only a tiny fraction of his university courses (Weaver and Wilhoit, 1986). Even science writers in the United States—those likely to have higher levels of science and math training—may have low levels of formal training in these areas. Although no current data exist on the backgrounds of science writers, past surveys have found much variance in these journalists' scientific and mathematical backgrounds, with nonscience majors such as journalism and English dominant (Ryan and Dunwoody, 1975). Science journalists' concerns with knowledge levels are such that one veteran science writer— Victor Cohn of *The Washington Post*—was commissioned to write a basic statistics book for science journalists (Cohn, 1989).

What is meant by low levels of knowledge with respect to risk stories? I will briefly discuss two possible aspects: 1) the variance in specific knowledge of risk and 2) awareness of the rules of evidence in science.

4.1.1. Knowledge of risk and risk analysis. Although no single study has sought to determine the extent to which journalists understand risk as a scientific concept, probability theory, or the processes by which risk estimates are constructed, the scant amount of science and mathematics knowledge apparently culled by journalists from their college educations leads one to suggest that the typical reporter or editor knows little of these things. Such ignorance may have a profound impact on a journalist's decisions about story frame and about what constitutes appropriate information for that story when she is confronted with reporting a risky situation.

Certainly, social scientists who study the risk perceptions of nonscientists generally find that such ignorance leads to a variety of judgments that are at odds with scientific assessments of risk. For example, Slovic (1986) notes that any factor that makes a risk more memorable—vivid media coverage, timeliness of occurrence—can lead individuals greatly to overestimate the likelihood of occurrence of that risk. Likewise, ignorance of mathematics can lull individuals into interpreting a mathematical statement, a priori, as both precise and true. Any risk manager worth her salt will tell you, however, that the typical mathematical risk estimate is neither precise nor is it likely to be accurate—human judgment plays a major role in an estimate's construction.

In each example above, were the ignorant party a journalist wrestling with reporting of a risky situation, knowledge could have a large effect on the type of information conveyed. In the first instance, ignorance of a probabilistic context within which to interpret a dramatic event might lead the journalist to overplay the risk—to frame it as something that is more likely to occur than might otherwise be the case. In the second example, the journalist who knows little of risk assessment processes might simply take the first risk estimate that comes along, define it as true, and not seek any information about its construction or about other risk estimates that might be at variance with it.

4.1.2. Understanding how science determines and evaluates evidence.
The scientific culture has specialized in systematic rather than anecdotal evaluation. To that extent, its tenets run counter to the tendency of human beings to generalize from anecdotal experiences (Nisbett and Ross, 1980). The extent to which a journalist understands scientific processes, then, might be related to his decisions about what constitutes appropriate evidence for cause-and-effect relationships.

For example, if a local farmer calls the newspaper to complain that a pesticide sprayed near his farm caused his family to become ill, the response to that individual may vary dramatically with the ability of a journalist to distinguish between systematic and anecdotal evidence. The reporter who cannot make such a distinction may assume that such a first-person report is ample evidence for the presence of a cause-and-effect relationship, and her story may *assume* rather than *question* such a relationship. The journalist with an understanding of the distinction may still be sympathetic to the testimony of the farmer (after all, the farmer may be right) but will not assume the cause-and-effect relationship; in fact, he may make its determination the primary aim of his information gathering.

Stocking and Gross (1989) explain that all individuals share a strong tendency to define first and then seek confirmatory information, no matter how anecdotal. However, the occupational norms of journalism may make reliance on anecdotal evidence particularly compelling. For example, journalism relies heavily on first-person interviews for its information. Such a strategy has the benefit of allowing the journalist to question sources in ways that enable her to tailor information to her audience. However, this strategy also allows individual comments to have great impact. Thus, a charismatic source who "speaks in quotes" can dominate a story whether or not the person reflects a dominant or aberrant position on an issue.

That problem is exacerbated by journalists' search for vivid, specific information to include in stories. Again, there are benefits to such a strategy, since vivid accounts are more widely read and more likely to be remembered by audiences. However, a search for the concrete can supersede a search for patterns, giving the anecdotal the upper hand once again.

A third norm that can truncate any kind of skilled selection and evaluation of evidence is the pressure for balance in a journalistic account. The exigencies of daily reporting make it very difficult for a journalist to determine which source is telling the truth. Journalists have neither the time nor the expertise, in most cases, to do validity checks. The profession has thus developed a surrogate: if you cannot determine who is telling the truth about an issue, then you must make an effort to include in your story the full variety of available positions. At the very least, then, audiences can know that such positions exist and can work to determine their validity.

Over time, however, the norm has forsaken its original conditional frame. Now many newsrooms assume that the good journalistic account must give approximately equal space or time to the various positions *regardless of the probable validity of any one claim*. In such a world, the anecdotal claims of one camp may be arrayed as co-equal with the more systematic claims of another. Taylor and Condit, for example, analyzed journalistic accounts of a 1980s-court case challenging a Louisiana law requiring creation science to be given equal treatment with evolution in the science classroom. They found that journalists' attempts to provide a balanced accounting of both positions during the trial "produced a journalistic leveling which rhetorically transformed competing discourses into equivalent ones (1988, p. 293)."

4.2. Audience Knowledge

Journalists claim a high level of sensitivity to the needs of their audiences. Yet few journalists know what readers or viewers actually do with information. Within the occupation, understanding audience behaviors has been assigned such low salience that even the most skilled journalists typically rely on idiosyncratic samples of audience members (neighbors, parents, letters to the editor) to assess interest in a topic, willingness to read, etc. (Gans, 1980). Science writers are no different (Dunwoody, 1980). Interestingly, such incomplete data gathering still seems to give working journalists an edge over their editors. At least two studies have found that journalists' assumptions about audience wants and needs coincide more closely with audience reports than do editors' assumptions (Johnson, 1963; Nunn, 1979).

Information about uses of mediated messages is often made available to journalism students via university coursework, particularly in large journalism schools that define scholarly activity as part of their mission. However, it is hard to find evidence that the occupation embraces such information. One can find many more articles in the journalistic trade press expressing concern for students' spelling and grammar preparation than those worrying about these students' grasp of the impact of their message.

If an understanding of audience wants and needs in general is sparse, one can only guess that the typical journalist knows little about how individuals use information to reach judgments about scientific and technological risks. Such ignorance is, of course, not restricted to journalists. Research on the role that information plays in risk judgments is just gathering steam in the United States, suggesting that risk managers and scientists have been operating on nothing more than educated guesses for years.

Still, one would expect to find variance in story structure depending on reporters' assumptions about audience and their knowledge of audience perceptions of risk. I will briefly discuss the likely impact of one common assumption about the audience. I will then list several assumptions that recent research suggests communicators *should* be making about individuals' use of mediated risk messages.

4.2.1. An assumption we all share: The audience knows nothing about risk. As a generalization, journalists assume that the typical reader knows nothing about the topic of the story at hand, whether that topic be U.S. foreign policy, perennial gardening, or local land-use policies. Since audiences only occasionally dip into media stories and tend to comprehend little from them, the assumption has some merit (Robinson and Davis, 1990).

Journalists are particularly quick to embrace the "ignorant audience" assumption with respect to science information, as ignorance of science and mathematics is presumed to be widespread. In fact, in a world where scientists and journalists seem to disagree on nearly every aspect of communicating risk, perhaps the one assumption they hold in common is that the audience knows little about risk. Since a journalist's profession does not reward her for offering explanations, countering such presumed ignorance is problematic.

This problem is handled in two ways: 1) she provides explanation in short superficial bursts that require little space or time and 2) she redefines the task as one not of explaining risk concepts and processes but of explaining the event-oriented context within which her story is embedded. Thus, a journalist faced with writing a story about a new report by the paper industry on dioxin contamination in paper may provide a one-sentence definition of dioxin and, perhaps, a comparison of the likelihood of harm from exposure to dioxin with the likelihood of harm from exposure to another hazard (brief explanation). She may then devote the bulk of her explanatory space to a description of the events that prompted the industry to issue such a report, as well as to earlier events — say, the use of Agent Orange in Vietnam — that placed dioxin on the regulatory agenda. Thus does explanation become redefined as a need for social context.

This subjugation of explanation of concepts and processes to explanation of social context has several advantages: 1) it allows a journalist to write about risk without knowing much herself about it as a scientific and mathematical concept; 2) it provides an account that her scientifically illiterate audience can understand; 3) it provides an event-oriented context that her editor will define as appropriate matter for journalistic attention; and 4) it provides a context that can easily be edited by a third party. Stories are often revised — and shortened — by editors who have no familiarity with the topic at hand, and such individuals will find social context much easier to work with than lengthy explanations of scientific concepts and processes.

Has our journalist provided her audience with the risk information that they are seeking from the mass media? Research to date cannot answer that question easily. However, research does suggest some patterns that should provide a useful context for journalists and scientists confronted with information decisions.

First, the typical audience member has access to numerous channels of information. It is probably incorrect to assume that any given individual obtains all—or even most—of his information about risks from the mass media. Studies of the agenda-setting function of the media suggest that the mass media indeed can play a primary role in alerting us to phenomena about which we are unaware (McCombs, 1981). Once that signaling has taken place, however, individuals may have at their disposal a number of information channels from which to solicit information. An angler who has just learned from his Sunday newspaper that Great Lakes fish may contain toxins can acquire risk knowledge not only by reading newspapers but also by talking to other anglers, getting information in the mail from regulatory agencies, attending meetings or getting newsletters from fishing organizations, and, in some states, even by reading the back of a fishing license.

Second, use of any particular information channel will depend on the cost of accessing that channel, and a judgment of the likelihood that the channel will yield relevant information. Chaffee (1986) argues that one can determine the likelihood that an individual will utilize a particular information channel by comparing the cost (to the individual) of gaining access to the channel with that individual's judgment of the likelihood of gleaning relevant information from the channel.

Costs are not necessarily monetary. Our angler, for example, might not solicit information from state agencies because he has no idea how to contact them. The time or effort required to gather names, phone numbers, and addresses, in other words, is too high for that individual, regardless of any determination of the likely relevance of the information. Similarly, an individual might prefer to discuss the risk of a particular disease with a physician but will not contact such a person because physicians are not routinely available to the general public. Even when, as with full insurance coverage, the cost to the individual is very low, we are unlikely to make a call to a physician to ask a few questions. Not surprisingly, the mass media are some of the most accessible channels available to the general population, although access to any particular medium—say, the *New York Times* or the *Atlantic*—may be constrained by geography or cost.

Even if cost is low, do individuals judge risk information available in the media to be relevant? There is some indication that individuals find certain types of mediated risk information relevant to particular dimensions of risk judgment. Specifically, when confronted with a risky situation to which we have already been alerted, we may preferentially use mediated messages to gather knowledge about the societal impact of the risk. We seem to resist using mediated channels, on the other hand, to inform ourselves of personal risk. To put this another way, we seem to prefer to use the mass media to learn generally about a risk but prefer other information channels to help us decide how worried we personally should be about that risk. For information about our personal level of risk, we generally want to talk to other people (Tyler and Cook, 1984; Dunwoody and Neuwirth, 1991; Mutz, forthcoming).

Thus, it seems likely that individuals will rely on mass media messages to learn about a risk. If those messages eschew information about the risk (the nature of the risky substance, its method of doing harm, individuals' likelihood of being harmed, information about how that estimate was constructed, courses of action to reduce harm) then the stories represent lost opportunities for that individual. Journalists may be omitting from their stories some of the very information that audiences turn to the mass media to find.

5. The Impact of Locus of Power

Earlier in this chapter, I considered attempts to examine newsmaking across levels of analysis as synonymous with efforts to isolate the locus of power for news decision making. Since power is the point of this last section, I return to the levels of analysis considered before—namely, those of the individual journalist and of the organization.

Early studies of journalistic work assumed that power resided at the level of the individual reporter or editor. Researchers went looking for individual-level, idiosyncratic decision making in newsrooms and, not surprisingly, found it (White, 1950). But such analyses were soon overwhelmed by work that concluded, to the contrary, that power lay in the hands of media organizations themselves (Hirsch, 1977). The bulk of research that has examined these two levels still gives an edge to the newsroom. The best predictor of individual reporter behavior, in other words, is the constellation of organizational rules and norms within which a reporter works.

Newsroom hierarchies are exceedingly rigid, as management makes publish/no publish decisions about stories in ways that give reporters little recourse. The typical reporter is relatively powerless in such a setting. If he were to attempt to set aside an occupationally sanctioned frame in favor of his own personal one, for example, in all likelihood the story would be killed. Idiosyncratic behavior in such contexts leads to unpublished reports.

It is difficult to say if news organizations are more or less hierarchical than other work settings. However, some characteristics of newsrooms clearly contribute to the relative powerlessness of their employees. One of the most obvious characteristics is a news organization's reliance on reporters who must be prepared to cover any story. Called general assignment reporters, they constitute the majority of reporters working in newsrooms today (Weaver and Wilhoit, 1986). They have little autonomy in story selection, receiving most of their story assignments from their editors.

Another characteristic — the decentralized nature of the production process — ensures that reporters have little control over what happens to their stories once an editor has accepted them for publication. Editors of various kinds may revise the story — eliminating entire segments, writing a headline, and determining its placement in the newspaper. The computerization of this production process in recent years allows the reporter to see what is happening to her work, but many reporters are still constrained in their ability to intervene as their story changes shape and, sometimes, meaning.

In journalism an individual's ability to accumulate power seems not only desirable but also crucial to long-run well being. Journalists report that autonomy is one of their most cherished occupational goals, although the proportion claiming to have a great deal of autonomy in their work has not changed much in the past 15 years (Weaver and Wilhoit, 1986). Autonomy in journalism is the ability to make your own decisions about story topic, frame, and organization. Most studies of journalists implicitly regard the term *autonomy* to be synonymous with power accumulation.

A journalist can gain power relative to his media organization in a number of ways. One strategy may be to accumulate time in rank, although findings by Weaver and Wilhoit (1986) do not support this route. They report that journalists are currently leaving the profession at an earlier age than they did a generation ago. Moreover, those who intend to leave report dissatisfaction with their level of autonomy as a primary reason for their lack of professional commitment. Another power-accumulation strategy is to acquire prizes and other individual rewards and use them to barter for greater reporting freedom. One national study of journalists found that respondents saw prizes as effective bargaining tools, but the study found no relationship between prize-winning and increased autonomy on the job (Beam, Dunwoody and Kosicki, 1986).

One of the most successful ways to gain autonomy is to become a specialty reporter, a journalist who is responsible for a geographic or content area and is therefore allowed to decide, for the most part, what is news within that domain. Editors typically defer to such selection efforts and give specialty reporters considerable latitude in story structuring as well. Science writers, for example, report very high levels of autonomy and correspondingly high levels of job satisfaction (Dunwoody, 1980).

If an individual journalist accumulates power within a news organization, that individual often may override the occupational norms and frames that govern the shape and content of news products. The result, then, depends heavily on the knowledge that the individual writer brings to the topic. An influential, but scientifically ignorant, journalist can produce a risk story that conveys little scientific information about the risk, while a powerful and scientifically literate writer may do just the opposite.

Given the considerable control that media organizations exercise over their employees, stories that run roughshod over occupational norms are probably even rarer than the powerful journalists who write them. They do exist, however, and I offer, in closing, an example of such work.

We have here a tale of two large newspapers in a single town confronted with the same story about risk. Journalists at each newspaper indeed framed the issue as a risk story. Yet their decisions about story content varied dramatically within that frame, with one newspaper following occupational norms, while the other reflected the intervention of individual reporters.

6. The Milorganite Story

Early in 1987, two former professional football players were confronted with a problem. They and a colleague — all former team members of the San Francisco 49ers — had been diagnosed with Lou Gehrig's disease. The third player had died, but the other two players prompted headlines with their questions about how three players from the same team had come to be afflicted with this rare condition. Formally called amyotrophic lateral sclerosis (ALS), the disease causes nerve cells to die, rendering its victim increasingly unable to move or to function. Death usually occurs between two and ten years after a person gets the disease. It is indeed extremely rare, with incidence pegged at between two and four cases per 100,000 persons. No one knows what causes ALS, although a number of hypotheses have been proffered, among them that ALS may result from exposure to heavy metals, a mysterious virus, or impairment of the immune system.

Could the incidence of ALS in 3 of 45 athletes on a single team be a chance occurrence? The players thought not. In the search for a culprit, they came across Milorganite, a processed sewage sludge sold as fertilizer by the Milwaukee Metropolitan Sewerage District. As had a number of professional football teams, the San Francisco 49ers spread Milorganite on their practice field. The fertilizer, like most treated sewage sludge, contains small amounts of heavy metals and toxins, and that proved to be provocative for many people, including journalists at a Milwaukee newspaper.

The *Milwaukee Sentinel*, a morning daily, quickly picked up on the potential link between Milorganite and Lou Gehrig's disease. In a series of front-page stories it called for a study of the possible link and then began bombarding readers with condemning evidence:

- Reporters examined the death certificates of 155 employees of the Milwaukee Metropolitan Sewerage District and found that two had died of ALS (Collins and Manning, 1987).
- ALS sufferers called the newspaper claiming to have been exposed to Milorganite. For example, the newspaper reported that an equipment salesman with Lou Gehrig's disease called to say that he frequently repaired package-stapling equipment in the Milorganite plant and had used Milorganite on his lawn and garden. In that same article, the newspaper reported that 39 ALS sufferers — including the three football players — had surfaced, all reporting some level of exposure to Milorganite (Collins and Manning, 1987).
- *The Sentinel* checked Milwaukee County death certificates and reported, as preliminary findings, that as many as 115 individuals may have died of ALS in the previous eight years, an incidence of 1.6 deaths per 100,000. That rate, the newspaper noted, was higher than the 0.6 per 100,000 established for the entire state by a previous study (Manning and Collins, 1987).

After several days of such stories, the public was getting wary. The *Milwaukee Sentinel* reported that the Milwaukee Zoo planned to delay further purchases of Milorganite. Officials from parks departments of two Wisconsin counties reported plans to suspend use of Milorganite until its safety could be established. The Green Bay Packers, who annually but some two tons of the fertilizer on Lambeau Field, said they would await more information before using Milorganite again (Manning and Collins, 1987).

Curiously, the other daily newspaper in town avoided any mention of the ALS-Milorganite link during the *Sentinel*'s barrage of front-page stories. Milwaukee is one of the few remaining cities in the United States with two daily newspapers and, although both are owned by the same company, they complete fiercely with one another. Typically, a big story such as this one in one of the newspapers would quickly be matched by the competition. Yet *The Milwaukee Journal* remained silent for days. Then, in a front-page story on February 12, 1987, the *Journal* signaled its position on the issue with the following lead:

> From viruses to heavy metals, pneumatic tools to household pets, more than a dozen possible causes of Lou Gehrig's disease have been investigated by the world's scientists. To date, they have been unable to pin down a definitive cause (Rosenberg, 1987).

Medical reporter Neil Rosenberg went on to discuss the variety of hypothesized causes of ALS, including the potential link between the disease and heavy metals. He also explained the type and amount of metals detected in Milorganite and discussed the kinds of studies that would be necessary to investigate the implied link between Milorganite and ALS.

The following day the *Journal* ran another front-page story, this time debunking the statistical argument raised by the *Sentinel* that the incidence of ALS in Milwaukee County and among sewerage district workers was higher than the state incidence. A statistician who examined the various calculations, reported the *Journal*, concluded that the differences between the district, county, state, and national rates were not statistically significant. The story, written by Rosenberg and environmental reporter Don Behm, also noted that tests of the levels of heavy metals in the blood of employees of the sewerage district showed those levels either at or below the level of heavy metals present in the blood of the general population (Behm and Rosenberg, 1987).

The risk accounts structured by reporters at the two newspapers could not have been more different. The *Sentinel* immediately framed the story as "Milorganite causes Lou Gehrig's disease" and then accumulated both anecdotal and statistical evidence to support that link. The *Journal*, on the other hand, framed the story as "why we cannot forge a causal link between Milorganite and Lou Gehrig's disease" and presented information—some of it identical to the data offered by the *Sentinel*—to bolster that contention.

One must take care when trying to infer behavior from products such as stories. Nonetheless, an interview with one of the reporters involved in the stories supports several conclusions.

The *Sentinel's* response to the alleged link between ALS and Milorganite seems to reflect two things: 1) occupational norms and 2) the work of reporters with little scientific and mathematical preparation in the subject at hand. Occupational norms charge journalists with the responsibility to convey information from credible sources. Thus when former professional football players and scientists suggested that a cluster of three ALS sufferers from a group of 45 did not look like a chance occurrence, the *Sentinel* journalists reported it. When an official of the National Football Leage Alumni Association suggested that Milorganite might be a culprit, the newspaper reported it. When *Sentinel* reporters uncovered evidence that two employees of the Milwaukee Metropolitan Sewerage District had died of Lou Gehrig's disease, they took an additional step. They accepted the argument that Milorganite may cause Lou Gehrig's disease. Stocking and Gross (1989) would argue that the journalists constructed a cause-and-effect story and then proceeded to seek out evidence that confirmed — rather than disconfirmed — their theory. Actually, the anecdotal and statistical evidence summoned by the *Sentinel* to support its causal link did *not* support it. Apparently, however, no one at the *Sentinel* had the scientific or mathematical background to realize it.

The *Milwaukee Journal*'s stories also reflected occupational norms, to the extent that they reported the initial reluctance of football players and others to view the three ALS cases as a chance occurrence, as well as the suggested link between Milorganite and the disease. However, the *Journal* has a staff of science, medical, and environmental reporters with the scientific and mathematical background to question the link. Equally important, the reporters also had enough power in the newsroom to silence the newspaper long enough to evaluate the evidence being compiled by the competing newspaper and to construct a response that reflected a more realistic understanding of the situation. The resulting frame — "no one knows what caused the cases of Lou Gehrig's disease among the football players" — would normally be a difficult one to sell to editors, who lust after impact and certainty. Thus, the delay in — and the nature of — the *Journal* stories speak strongly to the power that individual journalists wielded in that setting.

7. Conclusions

We know precious little about how journalists construct stories regarding scientific and technological risk. The explanation proffered here, while based on a generic body of research on journalistic work, has yet to be substantiated. If it holds up to empirical tests, it will offer scientists a frustrating picture of an occupation guided by rules of information dissemination that have little to do with the nature of the information itself or with the needs of those who purchase the information products. It will also be a picture punctuated by moments of clarity, by instances of stories that reflect a sophisticated understanding of both topic and audience. The question is: How often will this happen, and what variables can maximize the frequency of that occurrence?

Journalists will always behave differently from scientists. A good thing, too. To lose the writer's interest in detail or the ability to build rich tapestries from conversations with one or two individuals would doom us all to media accounts that are both dry and uncompelling. However, successful communication of information about scientific and technological risk must also depend heavily on systematic knowledge gleaned from the scientific culture, and on a greater understanding of how we all go about making personal judgments about what to do when confronted with risky situations. Unfortunately, journalists at present may acquire such knowledge in spite of their occupation rather than because of it.

References

Beam, R. A., S. Dunwoody, and G. M. Kosicki. 1986. "The Relationship of Prize-winning to Prestige and Job Satisfaction." *Journalism Quarterly* 63(4):693–699.

Becker, L. B., J. W. Fruit, and S. L. Caudill. 1987. *The Training and Hiring of Journalists*. Norwood, NJ: Ablex.

Behm, D., and N. D. Rosenberg. 1987. "Milorganite Workers Test Normal for Metals in Blood," *The Milwaukee Journal* 13 (February), 1A, 8A.

Breed, W. 1955. "Social Control in the Newsroom," *Social Forces* 33:326–335.

Chaffee, S. H. 1986. "Mass Media and Interpersonal Channels: Competitive, Convergent, or Complementary?" In G. Gumpert, and R. Cathcart (eds.), *Inter/Media*, 3rd ed. New York: Oxford University Press, 62–80.

Cohn, V. 1989. *News & Numbers*. Ames, IA: Iowa State University Press.

Collins, T., and J. Manning 1987. "Two Linked to Milorganite Plant Died of Lou Gehrig's Disease," *Milwaukee Sentinel*, 10 (February), 1, 13.

Combs, B., and P. Slovic. 1979. "Newspaper Coverage of Causes of Death," *Journalism Quarterly* 56(4):837–843; 849.

Dunwoody, S. 1979. "News-gathering Behaviors of Specialty Reporters: A Two-level Comparison of Mass Media Decision-making," *Newspaper Research Journal* 1(1):29–41.

Dunwoody, S. 1980. "The Science-Writing Inner Club," *Science, Technology, & Human Values* 5:14–22.

Dunwoody, S., and K. Neuwirth. (1991). "Coming to Terms with the Impact of Communication of Scientific and Technological Risks." In L. Wilkins and P. Patterson (eds.), *Risky Business*. Westport, CT: Greenwood Press, 11–30.

Ettema, J. S., and D. C. Whitney. 1982. *Individuals in Mass Media Organizations*.

Newbury Park, CA: Sage.

Ettema, J. S., and D. C. Whitney. 1987. "Professional Mass Communicators." In C. R. Berger and S. H. Chaffee, (eds.), *Handbook of Communication Science*. Newbury Park, CA: Sage, 747–780.

Flower, Linda S., and John R. Hayes. 1980. "The Dynamics of Composing: Making Plans and Juggling Constraints." In L. W. Gregg and E. R. Steinberg (eds.), *Cognitive Processes in Writing*. Hillsdale, NJ: Lawrence Erlbaum, 31–50.

Gans, H. J. 1980. *Deciding What's News*. New York: Random House.

Gitlin, T. 1980. *The Whole World Is Watching*. Berkeley, CA: University of California Press.

Greenberg, M. R., D. B. Sachsman, P. M. Sandman, and K. L. Salomone. 1989. "Risk, Drama and Geography in Coverage of Environmental Risk by Network TV." *Journalism Quarterly* 66(2):267–276.

Hirsch, P. M. 1977. "Occupational, Organizational and Institutional Models in Mass Media Research: Toward an Integrated Framework. In P. M. Hirsch, P. V. Miller, and F. G. Kline, (eds.), *Strategies for Communication Research*. Newbury Park, CA: Sage, 13–42.

Johnson, K. 1963. "Dimensions of Judgment of Science News Stories." *Journalism Quarterly* 40:315–322.

Kellermann, K., and Tae-Seop Lim. 1989. "Inference-generating Knowledge Structures in Message Processing." In J. J. Bradac, (ed.), *Message Effects in Communication Science*. Newbury Park, CA: Sage, 102–128.

Manning, J., and T. Collins. 1987. "Health Official Orders Study of Gehrig's Deaths in City." *Milwaukee Sentinel*, 11 (February), 1, 14.

McCombs, M. E. 1981. "The Agenda-setting Approach." In D. D. Nimmo, and K. R. Sanders, (eds.), *Handbook of Political Communication*. Newbury Park, CA: Sage, 121–140.

Mutz, D. C. (forthcoming). "Mass Media and the Depoliticization of Personal Experience," *American Journal of Political Science*.

National Science Board. 1989. *Science & Engineering Indicators–1990*. Washington, DC: U.S. Government Printing Office.

Nisbett, R., and L. Ross. 1980. *Human Inference: Strategies and Shortcomings of Social Judgment*. Englewood Cliffs, NJ: Prentice-Hall.

Nunn, C. Z. 1979. "Readership and Coverage of Science and Technology in Newspapers," *Journalism Quarterly* 56(1):27–30.

Robinson, J. P. and D. K. Davis. 1990. "Television News and the Informed Public: An Information-processing Approach," *Journal of Communication* 40(3):106–119.

Rosenberg, N. D. 1987. "Experts Can't Find ALS Cause." *The Milwaukee Journal* 12 (February), 1A, 9A.

Ryan, M., and S. Dunwoody. 1975. "Academic and Professional Training Patterns of Science Writers." *Journalism Quarterly* 52(2):239–246; 290.

Ryan, M., S. Dunwoody, and J. Tankard. 1990. "Risk Information for Public

Consumption: Print Media Coverage of Two Risky Situations." forthcoming. *Health Education Quarterly*.

Sandman, P.M., D.B. Sachsman, M.R. Greenberg, and M. Gochfeld. 1987. *Environmental Risk and the Press*. New Brunswick, NJ: Transaction Books.

Singer, E., and P. Endreny. 1987. "Reporting Hazards: Their Benefits and Costs." *Journal of Communication* 37(3):10−26.

Slovic, P. 1986. "Informing and Educating the Public About Risk." *Risk Analysis* 6(4):403−415.

Stocking, S.H., and P.H. Gross. 1989. *How Do Journalists Think?* Bloomington, IN: ERIC Clearinghouse on Reading and Communication Skills.

Taylor, C.A., and C.M. Condit. 1988. "Objectivity and Elites: A Creation Science Trial." *Critical Studies in Mass Communication* 5:293−312.

Tuchman, G. 1978. *Making News*. New York: The Free Press.

Tyler, T.R., and F.A. Cook. 1984. "The Mass Media and Judgments of Risk: Distinguishing Impact on Personal and Societal Level Judgments." *Journal of Personality and Social Psychology* 47:693−708.

Weaver, D.H., and G.C. Wilhoit. 1986. *The American Journalist*. Bloomington, IN: Indiana University Press.

Weiss, C.H., and E. Singer. 1988. *Reporting of Social Science in the National Media*. New York: Russell Sage Foundation.

Weiss, R. 1987. "How Dare We? Scientists Seek the Sources of Risk-taking Behavior." *Science News* 132:57−59.

White, D.M. 1950. "The Gatekeeper: A Case Study in the Selection of News." *Journalism Quarterly* 27:383−396.

5 THE POLICY RESPONSE TO RISK AND RISK PERCEPTIONS

Kathleen Segerson*

Virtually every human activity involves a certain amount of risk, from walking downstairs and crossing the street to eating and breathing. Thus, the goal of a risk-free environment is meaningless, unless individuals are willing to cease all activity. We can, however, learn to manage risks more effectively. While some risk management is best conducted by individuals without the involvement of governments, other types of risks require a clear public-policy response.

Effective risk management has three possible goals: 1) to reduce risks by reducing the probabilities or the negative impacts of adverse events, 2) to spread risks across a given group so that no one individual faces the prospect of suffering from those events without some offsetting payment, and 3) to allocate appropriately the responsibility for bearing the costs generated by the risk. Risk management strategies can be targeted toward any one goal by itself or some combination of these goals.

The first goal, risk reduction, involves changing behavior that affects risks before the adverse events occur or it involves taking steps to mitigate or contain those effects once the event has occurred. In either case, the objective is to reduce the risks that individuals face, and the effectiveness

* Kathleen Segerson is in the Department of Economics, University of Connecticut.

of the risk management strategy can be viewed in terms of its efficiency in reducing risks. The second and third goals are sometimes lumped together under the rubric of victim compensation, but there is an important distinction between them. Achieving the second goal, risk spreading, often requires the existence of some mechanism by which contingent payments will be made to victims to offset losses when they occur. As with risk reduction, it can be judged on an efficiency basis. In particular, efficient risk spreading can be achieved regardless of whether the contingent payments come from an insurance policy that the victim has purchased or from direct compensation payments from the party responsible for the risk. The third goal, however, cannot be judged on an efficiency basis. A determination of the appropriate party to pay for the risk, either through lump-sum or contingent payments, cannot be made on the basis of efficiency. It depends instead on the entitlement system that one believes in (see chapter 1).

This chapter provides an overview of public policy responses to a specific type of risks, namely, environmental risks. We focus on the first two goals of risk management, risk reduction and risk spreading. In doing so, we recognize that in many cases a reallocation of the costs of risk (the third goal) may be one (perhaps *the*) primary concern. In such cases, victim compensation *by a third party* — rather than through the purchase of first-party insurance — may be the primary goal of a risk management policy and in the text we note the potential for alternative policies to achieve this goal. However, since distributional issues are discussed in chapter 1, our primary emphasis is on the efficiency rather than the distributional implications of alternative approaches to risk management.

We begin by examining the conditions under which there might be a role for the government in environmental risk management. Depending upon the nature of the risk, the government's role can range from simply providing information to one of trying to reduce or spread risks. Delineating possible roles for the government in environmental risk management provides a basis for evaluating what the goals of specific public policies might be. We then discuss some characteristics of environmental risks that make policy formation particularly challenging in this context. Finally, we discuss alternative public policy approaches to risk management. The focus is on general approaches that can be used rather than the actual implementation of specific approaches. The goal throughout is to provide an overall framework for the analysis of environmental risk-management policies. This framework should be useful in analyzing specific policies, such as those discussed in the case studies provided in the following chapters.

1. The Role of the Government in Environmental Risk Management

In theory, the presence of uncertainty poses no problem in the efficient operation of a market economy. Economic theory suggests that, in the absence of market imperfections, individual producers and consumers acting in their own self-interest through markets will make efficient production and consumption decisions. While this result is generally developed under assumptions of perfect certainty, in theory it can be extended to the presence of uncertainty (risk) by allowing some of the "goods" that are bought and sold to be "contingent contracts."[1] Extending the model of producer/consumer interactions to allow for the purchase and sale of contingent contracts permits the standard efficiency results regarding competitive markets to be extended to the case of uncertainty regarding future states of the world (see Arrow, 1984).

As with the standard model under certainty, however, if markets are missing or imperfect, then the resulting allocation will not be efficient. Markets will generally be missing if there is no opportunity for buyers and sellers to interact, due to high transaction costs or temporal separation (Bromley, 1989). Standard market imperfections include the existence of public goods, externalities, and imperfect information. Any one of these can provide a rationale for government involvement to attain efficiency. The need for such involvement is likely to be particularly strong when environmental risks exist, since the nature of those risks suggests that standard markets will not be well suited to dealing with them.

In this section, we discuss three different types of environmental risks, distinguished by the degree to which the effects of a risky activity are internalized to the person engaging in the activity.[2] For each type of risk, we suggest possible roles for the government in the management of those risks. In each case, the intent is to increase efficiency by creating a market where one did not previously exist or correcting an existing market imperfection.

1.1. Internalized Risks

Some of the risks people face are those they impose upon themselves, perhaps unknowingly.[3] These risks are often created by natural phenomena. Examples include the increased risk of skin cancer from prolonged exposure to the sun, the health risks from naturally occurring radon gas in homes (see chapter 3), and the risks from living in hurricane- or flood-prone areas. These risks can be termed *internalized risks*, since the person undertaking the activity that generates the risk (sunbathing, living in a house with high radon levels, or living in a flood zone) is also the person facing that risk. Thus, the risks are internal to the decision maker.

One might be tempted to argue that, when risks are internalized, there is no role for the government in risk management. It will be said that individuals are capable of comparing the benefits that would be derived from a risky activity with its costs (including any risks) and, on the basis of this comparison, deciding for themselves whether or not to undertake the activity. Even in the case of internalized risks, however, there are several rationales for government involvement in risk management. These can relate either to the generation of information regarding those risks, or to a more active role in reducing those risks.

1.1.1. Economies of scale. Because of set-up costs for laboratories and specialization of both personnel and equipment, economies of scale[4] are likely to be important in the generation of risk-related information.[5] Scale economies can also exist in the prevention of — or response to — internalized risks. While the existence of economies of scale does not necessitate government involvement in risk management, such economies may increase its likelihood. Since government agencies are generally large organizations, they have the ability to realize scale economies. Thus, it may be more efficient to have certain activities, such as risk-related research and development, conducted by large government organizations rather than by a number of small private research firms.

1.1.2. Public goods. The existence of public goods relating to risk management may also justify government involvement in the management of internalized risks.[6] Since private benefits are less than social benefits,[7] it is well known that the private sector will produce too little (if any) of a public good. In such cases, government provision of the public good can improve overall efficiency.

Information regarding environmental risks is a public good when there is some commonality among the risks faced by different individuals. For example, if individuals within a certain group face similar risks, then providing information about the risks faced by one member of the group provides useful information to other members of the group as well. This information has the characteristics of a public good.

Likewise, public goods can arise in risk prevention or response. If a reduction in risk for one person simultaneously reduces risks for others, then the risk reduction can be viewed as a public good. For example, construction of a dam would reduce the risk of flooding for all those who live downstream in the floodplain.

1.1.3. Imperfect information. A third rationale for government involvement in the management of internalized risks is imperfect information. In many cases, individuals have insufficient information to assess correctly the risks associated with a given activity. Imperfect information could result from 1) lack of access or exposure to available information or 2) an inability to understand or evaluate the information. Lack of information is particularly likely for risks that may not be readily apparent. In addition, even if the information is known to individuals, they may not be able to understand its implications fully and thus use it in their decision-making processes. Information regarding low probability−high consequence (LP-HC) events may be particularly difficult to evaluate.

In the presence of imperfect information regarding risks, a central agency may be in a better position to assess trade-offs regarding those risks than are the individuals who face them, especially if the risks are fairly homogeneous across the population. In fact, consumers may want the decisions regarding adequate safety to be made by "experts," who presumably have a better knowledge and understanding of the magnitudes of the risks.[8] Thus, the government may regulate allowable indoor radon levels or prohibit construction in flood plains on the basis of imperfect information.

1.1.4. Risk spreading. Government involvement in management of internalized risks might also be justified on the basis of risk spreading. If individuals are risk averse, efficiency will be increased by spreading risks over many individuals to reduce the amount borne by any single person.

The most common technique for risk spreading is the purchase of insurance.[9] However, for some types of risk, private first-party insurance is not available. This is most likely when probabilities cannot be accurately estimated or risks cannot be adequately spread. Private sector risk spreading is difficult for risks with large, concentrated effects, such as earthquakes, floods, and other natural disasters. If the group of potentially affected individuals is small relative to the magnitude of the potential damages, then the premiums necessary to induce private provision of insurance would be prohibitively high. In other words, those at risk would generally be unable to purchase the insurance. Thus, for such disasters, the standard market is not likely to be effective in spreading risks.

Risk spreading can, however, be facilitated through government-provided insurance or through disaster relief. This government-sponsored insurance program can operate as with private insurance programs — individuals buy the insurance in advance to be eligible for benefits. Alternatively, benefits may be available to all victims without prior arrangement as with disaster relief programs. In either case, since expected compensation is not limited by premium payments, premiums need not be tied to expected losses. Funds can come from other sources, and risks can thus be spread across taxpayers rather than just across the individuals at risk.

1.1.5. Paternalism. A final rationale for government involvement in the management of internalized risks is paternalism, which in this context holds that there are certain risks that people should not be allowed to impose on themselves, even if they want to take those risks. Under this view, the government should 'protect people from themselves' by, for example, mandating the use of certain equipment aimed at risk reduction or prohibiting certain risky activities. This view presupposes that people sometimes do not know what is good for them or are unable to make decisions that are in their own best interests because of influences such as short-sightedness and peer pressure. Examples here might include mandatory seat-belt laws or laws requiring motorcyclists to wear helmets. Thus, government involvement in risk management is justified on the basis of imperfections in private decision making.

1.2. Market-Based Risks

A second category of risks concerns those associated with consumption of purchased goods or provision of paid services in which the person purchasing the good or supplying the service bears the associated risks. Examples include the risks resulting from consumption or use of risky products or from provision of labor in high-risk jobs. Thus, both food safety and occupational safety (see chapter 8) are examples of market-based risks.

Economic theory suggests that, in a perfectly competitive product market, the equilibrium market price of a good will equal both the marginal benefit the consumer receives from consumption of the good (net of any costs resulting from consumption) and the marginal cost the producer incurs from producing the good. Likewise, in a perfectly competitive input market, the equilibrium input price will equal both the marginal benefit the user of the input receives from that use and the marginal cost the supplier incurs from supplying it (opportunity cost plus any associated risks). Thus, with perfectly competitive markets, market-based risks are similar to the internalized risks discussed previously in that both the generator of the risk and the person who faces it will consider that risk in making private production or consumption decisions.[10]

Because market-based risks are similar to internalized risks, the possible roles for the government in the management of internalized risks apply as well to market-based risks. The relative importance of the various roles may differ however. For example, the existence of imperfect information regarding product- or job-based risks could provide a rationale for government risk management. The case may be particularly strong when risks vary across producers of a given product (or across employers) and consumers (employees) have no way of readily observing these risk differentials. In this case, market prices will not accurately reflect those differentials, and as a result the risks will not be fully internalized.[11] Thus, there may be a role for the government either in providing information regarding average risk and risk differentials, or in ensuring adequate protection from unobservable risks.

1.3. Externalized Risks

A third type of risks, externalized risks, are those risks faced by one individual (whom we will call the victim) as a result of the production or consumption activities of another individual or firm (whom we will call the injurer), where the victim and the injurer do not interact directly through a market for the risky activity.[12] Thus, the risks being generated by the activity are external to the agent making decisions regarding that activity. A risk externality exists.

Risk externalities can be either unilateral or bilateral. Unilateral externalities exist if the victim's expected losses or damages depend only on the actions of the injurer. That is, unilateral risks are those instances in which the victim's own actions or decisions do not influence the magnitudes of the risks faced. With bilateral externalities, the victim's expected damages depend on actions or decisions of both the injurer and the victim. Most externalities are bilateral to some degree, although the extent to which the victim can take steps to reduce risks varies considerably. For example, while the probability of a chemical spill is generally determined by the actions of the injurer (a firm or its employees), potential victims can reduce the risks of exposure by moving away from the plant. Likewise, a potential victim can reduce the risks associated with groundwater contamination by switching to bottled water. In contrast, there is virtually nothing that an individual can do to reduce the risks associated with nuclear war.

To the extent that externalized risks are bilateral, a certain portion of the risk—that which can be influenced by the victim—can be viewed as internalized, since individuals can compare the cost of risk avoidance with its benefits in their decision-making process. Thus, the previous discussion regarding the role of the government in the management of internalized risks can be applied to victim decisions regarding externalized risks.

However, because there is no market relationship between the injurer and the victim, the risks faced by the victim will not be reflected in market prices. Thus, an alternative means of promoting efficient injurer decisions must be found. This suggests two additional possible roles for the government in risk management: 1) to establish and enforce property rights where none now exist or 2) to control, directly or indirectly, the levels of risk-related activities.

1.3.1.   Enforcement of property rights.   According to the Coase theorem, if property rights are well defined and bargaining between the injurer and the victim is possible, then the two parties can reach a mutually satisfactory agreement regarding the injurer's activity level through bargaining with side payments (Coase, 1960).[13] Furthermore, if both parties are risk neutral and the income effects of the payments are small, then the resulting outcome will be efficient and independent of the party who holds the initial property rights. The role of the government in this case would simply be to establish and enforce the property rights so that bargaining can proceed.

Although Coase's theorem is an interesting theoretical result, in practice most cases of environmental risk will not be conducive to the type of bargaining required for the results to hold. First, environmental risks are often widely dispersed, and it is well-known that when external effects are dispersed across a large population, transaction costs generally make Coasian bargaining impossible because of the high costs. Secondly, damages are often probabilistic in the sense that exposure increases the probability of contracting a given disease, such as cancer. In such cases, it is generally difficult to prove with certainty that an end result—a specific cancer case—was caused by a given environmental risk—exposure to a particular toxic substance. Thus, if damages are defined in terms of end results rather than exposure,[14] the injurer who should be a party to the bargaining may not be able to be easily identified. Finally, the long latency periods associated with many environmental risks also make bargaining difficult or impossible. For example, Coasian bargaining is impossible in the case of external effects that cross generations, since there are no mechanisms for current generations to bargain with future generations (see, for example, Bromley, 1989).

1.3.2. Internalizing risk externalities. In the absence of Coasian-type bargaining, the resulting decisions about undertaking externality-generating activities will be inefficient since injurers will consider only the private benefits and private costs of undertaking that activity. This provides a further justification for an active government role in risk management. In particular, the government can take steps to ensure that private decisions regarding risky activities will reflect consideration of the external risks imposed on others.

Although we list this as the last rationale for government involvement in risk management, it is among the most obvious and the most important. Many of the environmental risks that make headlines, and are of primary concern to citizens and policy makers alike, require this type of government response. These include the risks associated with 1) surface water pollution and groundwater contamination, 2) hazardous and solid waste disposal (see chapter 7), 3) air pollution and acid rain, 4) global warming and ozone depletion, and 5) biotechnology (see chapter 6).

2. The Nature of Environmental Risk Management

The above rationales for government involvement in risk management are the conventional market failures used to justify many public policies. In this sense, we might view the formation of environmental risk management policies as just another example of public policy formation. There are, however, several dimensions of environmental risk that make the formation of policy in this context particularly challenging. I will review some of these.

2.1. The Psychology of Risk

The formation of public policy regarding environmental risk falls under the economic heading of decision making under uncertainty. Choices must be made now, but the future effects of those choice are uncertain. Economists have traditionally relied on the expected utility model to explain how individuals make decisions under uncertainty, assuming that choices are made to maximize the mathematical expectation of the random utility level resulting from a given choice (Schoemaker, 1982). Under this theory, choices are determined solely by the probabilities of different outcomes given a specific choice, the final outcomes themselves, and the individual's risk preferences (how risk-averse or risk-loving the individual is).

For many years now psychologists have recognized that individual perceptions of, and responses to, risk are complex processes involving a number of psychological factors (see chapter 3). Thus, it is not surprising that the simple expected utility model embraced by many economists fails to predict some forms of individual behavior under uncertainty that have been repeatedly observed (Schoemaker, 1982; Kahneman and Tversky, 1979; Machina, 1987). In response to the poor predictive power of the model, economists are beginning to revise theories so as to incorporate some of the psychological factors that appear to be important in describing actual behavior. These factors include subjective probabilities, regret or disappointment, complexity, ambivalence, and the use of reference points (Opaluch and Segerson, 1989; and chapter 3).

The theory of decision making under uncertainty focuses on individual decision making, where the interest is primarily in predicting how decisions are actually made. The realm of policy making under uncertainty, however, cannot escape the normative question of how decisions *should* be made under uncertainty. In fact, the original appeal of the expected utility theory was based as much on the belief that it defined rational choices as on its predictive power (Machina, 1989).

In light of recent empirical evidence, we may readily accept the role of psychological factors in determining actual individual decisions. However, the appropriate role for these factors in public policy formation is less clear (Weinstein and Quinn, 1983). For example, should policy decisions incorporate possible feelings of regret/rejoicing or disappointment/elation? If these are legitimate psychological feelings experienced by individuals, then perhaps policy makers should reflect these anticipated feelings in policy decisions.[15] However, the dependence of individual choice on the framing of questions is more troublesome. Framing differences suggest that changes in the presentation of options, without any change in substance, can affect individual decisions — primarily through changes in reference points.[16] While these may be legitimate psychological responses for individuals, it is not clear that we want public decisions to be susceptible to such "trickery."[17] In addition, such susceptibility provides an opportunity for manipulation by those presenting the policy options.

There is insufficient space here to explore fully the role of psychological factors in decision making and their implications for the design of risk management policies. However, we should at least recognize that the formation of such policies, both as it actually occurs and as we think it should occur, is likely to be more complex because of these factors.

2.2. The Composite Nature of Risk

A second issue that complicates environmental risk management decisions is the composite nature of many of those risks. Although in theory we generally talk about exposure to risk as a single event, in practice most cases involve a sequence of events and thus a sequence of risks, each of which has its own conditional probabilities (Crouch and Wilson, 1981). The total risk is a composite of these individual risks.

The composite nature of many environmental risks means that they are often difficult to measure, since all of the individual risk components must first be measured and then combined into a single risk assessment. It also means, however, that there are several points at which the government could intervene to reduce or manage those risks.[18] For example, public response to the risks of landfills can occur at any one or more of the steps between initial construction and ultimate damages. Risk management policies could focus on prevention of leaks through regulation of construction and design, or on prevention of exposure to contamination if a leak occurs through monitoring and containment or cleanup. Alternatively, policies might focus on response to actual contamination of drinking water through installation of filters or provision of bottled water, or simply compensation of victims if damages occur. Thus, there is a continuum of possible intervention points.

In practice, any given risk management policy may involve a number of intervention points. The design of the overall policy thus requires a coordination and balancing of the different possibilities to avoid redundancy yet ensure sufficient control. For example, decisions must be made about the appropriate stringency of landfill construction specifications versus the proper amount of monitoring once construction is complete. Such comparisons are inherently more difficult to make than comparisons across, for example, alternative construction specifications. Thus, the composite nature of many environmental risks provides greater opportunities for intervention, but at the same time complicates the policy formation process.

2.3. Learning and the Value of Flexibility

Public risk management decisions are also complicated by the possibility of obtaining improved information over time. In many cases, at least some of the conditional probabilities associated with different stages of a given risk will be unknown. For example, we may be able to estimate fairly accurately the probability that a landfill will leak given its construction and content. Similarly, we may be able to assess the probability that a certain pesticide will leach into the groundwater given the properties of the pesticide and the soil and geological characteristics of the site where it is applied. However, given our current limited knowledge of human dose-response relationships, particularly at low dosages, it might currently be much more difficult to estimate the probability that an individual who drinks water containing low levels of a contaminant from a landfill or pesticide will develop cancer as a result.

There is, of course, the hope that our understanding of these relationships will improve over time so that information about the health risks of drinking contaminated water will improve. The possibility of improved information — learning — over time means that there is some value to flexibility so as to be able to adjust as new information becomes available. This flexibility must be recognized as a distinct benefit and hence objective of policy design. A policy that would otherwise be more costly may still be preferred if it provides greater opportunities to adjust to new information.

For example, having product registration that automatically expires at a certain time unless renewed may be more costly than a system of one-time approval, because of higher administrative costs. However, on the basis of flexibility, the former option may be preferred. If there is uncertainty about the health effects of a given substance, it is desirable to be able to remove it from the market if new information reveals that it is hazardous. Because of the differences in presumed rights, this may be easier under a system of required continual renewal than under a one-time approval system.[19] If the value of this flexibility outweighs the increased administrative costs, then the periodic renewal system may be preferred.

Because many environmental risks involve uncertain probabilities and thus offer the possibility of learning over time, the formation of environmental risk management policies must explicitly recognize the value of flexibility. This, however, complicates the policy process since tradeoffs between flexibility and current costs will often have to be made. Since flexibility has a value prior to learning, while policy decisions are generally evaluated ex post, such tradeoffs may be politically difficult.

For example, the flexibility given by a continual product registration renewal system has value when the ultimate effects of the product are still unknown. Thus, prior to having full information about the product, the continual renewal system may be preferred. However, once full information becomes available, we might wish that we had chosen the one-time approval system. If full information reveals that the substance is truly harmless, then choice of the continual renewal system would have resulted in unnecessary administrative costs. From an ex post perspective, the choice would be viewed as wrong. To the extent that politicians respond to these possible ex post evaluations—and that such policies are judged particularly harshly for choices deemed to be wrong ex post—the need to choose between increased flexibility and increased current costs will provide an additional challenge in the formation of risk management policies.

2.4. Irreversibility

Finally, for many environmental risks, the possible negative impacts are irreversible in the sense that they cannot be undone by subsequent actions. This is clearly true for an individual who suffers health effects leading to diseases for which there is no cure. On a broader scale, it is true—within a relevant time frame—for some of the possible ecological effects of deforestation, global warming, ozone depletion, and biotechnology.

The possibility of irreversible effects makes current policy decisions particularly important, since recovery from bad decisions is not possible. In other words, we must live with the consequences of current policy choices without the possibility of future rectification. In general, the benefits of risk reduction are likely to be greater if the possible negative effects of a risky activity are irreversible than they would be if those effects could be offset, or reversed, by subsequent actions.[20] For example, the benefits of reducing chlorofluorocarbons (CFCs) are greater given the irreversibility of ozone depletion than they would be if we could simply correct the problem by manufacturing stratospheric ozone once we found that we had gone too far. Such additional benefits due to the irreversibility of negative effects should be explicitly considered in policy formation.

3. Alternative Policy Approaches

Having highlighted possible reasons for public risk management policies and some of the difficulties inherent in this type of policy formation, I turn now to a discussion of specific types of policy approaches that can be used to manage environmental risks.

3.1. Privatization of Risk Reduction

With the move toward government deregulation in the 1980s, there arose increasing reliance on private action in markets to allocate resources. In the context of environmental risk management, this approach suggests that risk reduction ought to be conducted primarily by private individuals or firms, with the government playing a relatively passive role, perhaps simply providing information about risks and ways to reduce them.[21]

The appropriateness of this approach to risk management depends upon the nature of the risk involved. Government provision of risk-related information is clearly appropriate if generation of the information is a public good. As noted above, risk-related information is likely to have public-good characteristics for many environmental risks, since individuals within given groups will tend to face similar risks. In addition, reliance on private actions to reduce risks may also be appropriate for certain types of risks.

This first requires that risk reduction be a private good—that reducing the risk for one individual would not also reduce the risks faced by others. For example, reducing the level of radon gas in one house does not reduce risks for people living in other houses. Second, it requires that victims be able to reduce the level of risk they face, or insure against it. For the case of internalized risks, this simply requires that the risk be controllable by individual actions such as installation of radon filters. For market-based risks, it requires that the victim be free to 1) reduce consumption of the good in the case of unsafe products or 2) reduce the provision of his/her service in the case of workplace safety. Finally, for externalized risks, it requires that the risk be a bilateral one, and that the victims be the "least-cost" avoiders.

Note, however, that while being the least-cost avoider in cases of bilateral care suggests that victims should be the ones to undertake steps to reduce risks, it does not necessarily mean that they should be the ones to pay for the costs of those steps. For example, in some cases of groundwater contamination, the least-cost risk reduction approach may be the installation of filters in affected households or use of bottled water.[22] Efficiency thus requires such responses, but it does not require that the associated costs necessarily be borne by households. Instead, these costs could be borne by polluters, by providing filters free of charge to affected households. However, unless polluters voluntarily provide filters,[23] implementation of this version of the 'polluter-pays-principle' would not be possible if the government relies solely on the private incentives to reduce risks.

The privatization of risk reduction is, however, consistent with a somewhat more active role for the government. While still leaving decisions regarding risk reduction to affected individuals, the government could encourage certain steps by providing economic incentives for individuals to undertake certain steps. For example, in cases of high risk, the government could subsidize expenditures related to risk detection such as well testing or monitoring. Similarly, the government could aid in the purchase of risk-reduction equipment such as carbon filters or well replacements.[24] The ultimate responsibility for reducing risks would still lie with the affected individuals, but the cost would be reduced. Such a cost-sharing scheme is warranted under the privatization approach if limited financial resources prevent affected parties from undertaking the risk-reduction steps that society deems appropriate.

3.2. Ex Ante Economic Incentives for Risk Generators

One way to influence the behavior of risk generators is through the use of ex ante economic incentives. There is a considerable literature on the use of incentives to control environmental externalities, both in theory and in practice. Among the instruments usually proposed are Pigovian taxes, refundable deposits, and tradeable emission permits. These instruments can, in theory, be used to reduce polluting activities, including those with uncertain effects. The advantages of using incentives rather than a command-and-control approach are well known.[25] In particular, incentives would allow risk generators greater flexibility in choosing the means used to reduce risk, and thus are likely to be more cost effective.

The potential for the use of ex ante economic incentives to manage risks depends, however, on the type of risk involved (Stewart, 1988). For example, deposits on hazardous waste materials such as automobile batteries encourage proper disposal,[26] and waste disposal fees encourage recycling and waste reduction. Thus, both of these incentive mechanisms could reduce the environmental risks of waste disposal. Likewise, Pigovian taxes on point emissions of air or water pollutants encourage emission reductions, which reduce the risks from polluted air or water. Similar taxes on combustion of fossil fuels or use of chlorofluorocarbons could reduce the risks of global warming or ozone depletion. Since these emissions or uses are continual and predictable, they are amenable to such taxation.

The same is not true, however, for risks that are discrete and stochastic (accidents). Examples include chemical spills or releases, unintended

releases of genetically engineered materials, and outbreaks of food contamination. Since these events occur infrequently and unexpectedly, they
are not amenable to Pigovian-type taxation. While we could try to tax the
underlying behavior that can lead to accidents, in many cases these
actions will also be discrete. In addition, they are often difficult to monitor,
thereby making per unit taxation difficult. Thus, there appears to be
limited potential for using standard ex ante incentive mechanisms for
managing accident-type risks.

When accidents are covered by insurance, however, some economic
incentive to reduce risks can be created through the use of experience
rating.[27] A primary function of experience rating is to reduce the moral
hazard problem generally associated with insurance. Experience rating
has been used in workers' compensation programs to encourage large
employers to increase workplace safety. While evidence on effectiveness
is mixed, experience rating remains, in theory, an effective means to
reduce the costs of accidents.[28]

3.3. Regulation of Risk-Related Activities

In terms of control policies, the direct antithesis of the use of economic
incentives is the use of regulation, under which behavior is mandated
rather than encouraged through pricing policies.[29] Regulation can be
directed toward prevention by reducing the probability of an accident, or
toward response by reducing the magnitude of damages if an accident
should occur.[30] For example, regulation of landfill construction and operation is designed to reduce the risk of contamination by reducing the
probability of leaching (see chapter 7), and regulation of the workplace
environment is intended to reduce the probability of work-related accidents
(see chapter 8).[31] Alternatively, regulations can be used to mandate the
steps that must be taken when an accident occurs so as to contain the
resulting damages.

While regulation has been used in many areas of public policy, its
application to the control of environmental risks has a particularly challenging component, namely, the setting of safety goals. When designing
regulations or economic incentives to reduce the probability of damages,
we must determine (either explicitly or implicitly) the target probability
that is being sought. In other words, how much of a reduction in the
associated probability is desired? Once this target probability has been
determined, it can be translated into regulations or incentives designed to
ensure that it is met. This translation may be direct, as with regulations

designed to reduce the probability of accidents. Alternatively, an inter-mediate step may be involved. For example, when damages take the form of health effects resulting from exposure to toxic substances, target prob-abilities — often defined in terms of additional cancer deaths — are first translated into allowable ambient concentrations. Policies are then designed to ensure that these 'maximum contaminant levels' are not exceeded.

The appropriate criteria to use in setting safety goals have been the focus of much discussion among both researchers and policy makers (Lave, 1990). Several alternatives have been proposed. They differ in terms of the extent to which the benefits of the risk-generating activity are considered in setting the goal, and in whether the risk is treated as known or unknown. One approach is to set the target level at the lowest feasible level without regard for the benefits of the associated activity. Under this approach, substances that pose *any* threat would be banned. This is the approach embodied in the well-known Delaney Clause which bans the addition of known human carcinogens to foods. Alternatively, a risk-benefit — or a cost-benefit — approach could be used under which the benefits of an activity are compared to the risks that it generates. Here, those risks are measured either in physical (risk-benefit) or monetary (cost-benefit) terms. The balancing of risks and benefits can be either explicit or implicit. In either case, such balancing leads to a target level of acceptable risk.

In setting safety goals, the risk associated with a given activity or contamination level is typically treated as known. Alternatively, we could recognize that there is uncertainty about the risk itself. Lichtenberg and Zilberman (1988)[32] have proposed an approach for explicitly incorporating this uncertainty into policy design. They suggest that policy instruments be chosen to minimize costs subject to a constraint that the associated risks fall within a given margin of safety. Here, one would state that the probability that the risk — say the chance of getting cancer — exceeds a given standard such as one in a million is less than some threshold, say 5 percent. This approach allows policy makers to make trade-offs between costs, safety goals (standards), and margins of safety when choosing among alternative regulations.

For the regulatory approach to be an appropriate means of risk manage-ment, the risk must have several characteristics (Shavell, 1984). For example, the actions that determine the level of the risk must be observable at reasonable cost. If they are not, then monitoring is not possible and violations of the regulations cannot be detected. Clearly, this would make the regulations ineffective. Second, those actions should be somewhat standardized. Since it is generally impractical to specify different behavior for each person or firm, regulations must apply to groups of individuals or firms. The more homogeneous the group is, the more appropriate will be the application of a single standard for the entire group. Third, the regulatory body should have better information about the risk than those whose actions generate it, and thus be in a better position to determine the most cost-effective means of risk reduction.

While the above characteristics provide the possibility for cost-effective regulation, the main argument in favor of regulation is generally that, if complied with, its effects are more certain than those of indirect economic incentives. If the costs of deviating from the anticipated target levels are very high, then the uncertainty about the behavioral response to incentives may create unacceptable risks. Thus, even if not completely cost effective, regulation may be appropriate for environmental risks when it is better to be safe than sorry.

3.4. Legal Liability for Damages

An alternative to the use of regulation is reliance on legal liability (Shavell, 1984). While liability clearly has no role to play in the management of internalized risks, it has been used to control market-based and externalized risks. For example, *product liability* deals with the risks associated with purchased products. Likewise, prior to the introduction of workers' compensation programs, work-related accidents were governed by the law of torts. Tort law also covers damage associated with externalized risks.

Liability for damages that result from a given activity is generally thought to serve two purposes. First, it provides an incentive for risk-generators to undertake risk-reducing activities, thereby reducing the probability or magnitude of resulting damages in the future. For example, liability for damages resulting from oil spills encourages oil companies to take steps to reduce the likelihood of future spills. Second, liability compensates victims who have suffered damages, thereby protecting them from the negative effects of the actions of others. Again, with oil spills, parties who suffer losses as a result of a spill can be compensated for those losses. As noted previously, this latter purpose may have either risk spreading or a different allocation of the costs of an activity as its underlying goal.

The effectiveness of liability in reducing risks and providing compensation depends, however, on both the legal rule applied and the nature of the risk. In fact, in some cases there may be a trade-off between the incentive and the compensation goals of liability. For example, in cases of bilateral care, where both injurers and victims can take steps to reduce risks, a strict liability rule will ensure compensation and correct incentives for injurers. However, such a rule will not provide victims with an incentive to take steps to reduce risks.[33] Using a negligence rule instead provides correct incentives for both injurers and victims[34] but does not provide compensation if the injurer is nonnegligent. Likewise, in cases of joint torts where several injurers' actions contribute to a single, indivisible injury, a rule that assigns to each injurer his/her incremental effect on damages will ensure that all injurers face correct incentives. However, this rule will not, in general, provide victims with exact compensation.[35] Joint and several liability is a more effective means of ensuring exact compensation in joint tort cases, but it does not generally provide correct incentives.[36]

A main difference between the use of liability and regulation is that liability allows those whose actions generate risks to decide on the most appropriate way to reduce those risks. In this sense, the ex ante effect of liability is similar to that of economic incentives.[37] As with ex ante economic incentives, this can improve efficiency if the characteristics of risky activities vary considerably. In such cases, cost-effective decisions vary as well and hence risk generators have better information than regulators about risk-reduction options. However, liability also has an advantage when the actions that can be undertaken to reduce risks are not easily observable and thus not easily subject to monitoring and compliance verification (Segerson, 1986). While it may be easy to monitor compliance with improved specifications for construction of landfills, the care that is taken in handling wastes is more difficult to observe. However, even in the absence of regulation, legal liability for resulting damages would still provide an incentive for such unobservable care.

The incentive effects of liability are, however, directly related to the probability that a risk generator will actually be held liable for the full amount of damages that result from his/her actions.[38] While that probability may be fairly high for some types of risks, many environmental risks have characteristics that work to reduce that probability. For example, with damages resulting from exposure to toxic substances, the manifestation of the damages may not appear for many years, by which time the injurer may be judgment-proof. Additionally, it may be difficult to prove that a given illness or death was attributable to that exposure, thereby making proof that a given party was in fact responsible difficult to establish.[39] Finally, if many people are affected, the total amount of damages may exceed the assets of the firm (and its liability coverage), thereby making it impossible to recover the full amount of damages even under a successful suit.[40] All of these factor reduces the incentive effects of liability by reducing the probability that the responsible party will be successfully sued for the full amount of damages. Of course, lack of a successful suit also means that victims will not be compensated. Thus, for environmental risks with these characteristics, reliance on liability may be ineffective for both incentive and compensation goals.

The difficulties caused by long latency periods and uncertainty over causation have led some to suggest that damages (and thus liability) be defined by exposure rather than manifestation of effects (Landes and Posner, 1984; Robinson, 1985). In cases of unintended releases or spills of toxic substances, the injurer would be liable at the time of exposure to all of those exposed. This would be in contrast to being liable in the distant future to those who, presumably as a result of exposure, ultimately contract diseases.[41] Since liability for exposure would be more immediate, it would generally increase the probability that a responsible party would be successfully sued. This aspect would provide greater incentives for risk reduction.[42] However, the compensation role of the liability would be changed considerably.

Defining damages in terms of *exposure* rather than *effect* incorporates the losses experienced by those who are exposed to — but do not ultimately contract — the disease. Such losses clearly exist prior to learning whether or not you will be one of those who contracts the disease. These losses can also be said to exist after knowing you will not be affected because of the anxiety and fear suffered during the interim period of uncertainty. In this sense, it is appropriate to compensate even those who do not ultimately contract the disease (Robinson, 1985). However, it is not clear that victims are, in fact, better off under such a system. The number of people compensated would be much larger, but the award per person would be much smaller. If compensation is defined correctly, then under the expected utility hypothesis — and from an ex ante perspective — exposed individuals should be indifferent between compensation for exposure and compensation for effects.[43] However, under alternative behavioral assumptions this may not be true. For example, if individuals experience regret over lost opportunities — as hypothesized by Loomes and Sugden (1982) — they may prefer compensation for effects. This would allow them to avoid the feelings of remorse they would expect to experience if they ultimately contracted the disease but had settled for a relatively small payment based on an ex ante assessment of the damages from exposure.[44] Thus, while liability based on exposure rather than effect may increase risk-reduction incentives for injurers, it may be a less satisfactory means of managing risks through compensation.

3.5. *Victim Compensation Funds and Other Forms of Insurance*

Legal liability is one means of securing compensation for damages from risks, but other possibilities exist as well—victim compensation funds for instance.[45] A recent example is the establishment of a fund for asbestos victims. Other examples include workers' compensation funds and the black lung program. Such funds are sometimes used in lieu of compensation through legal liability, since they can reduce transaction costs in cases where a large number of very similar suits arise (Elliott, 1985).

Victim compensation funds are essentially a form of third-party insurance for victims.[46] The advantages and disadvantages of using insurance as a risk-management tool are well known (Arrow, 1971). While insurance facilitates risk spreading, it can dull risk-reduction incentives for both injurers and victims.[47] In addition, insurance is more effective in compensating for monetary than nonmonetary damages.[48] Finally, some risks are more amenable to insurance coverage than others. For example, accident-type risks in which the event and its effects are sudden—such as workplace accidents or natural disasters—are more easily covered than effects that occur gradually or have a long latency period. Even in the case of long latency periods, an insurance approach may be possible if the cause-effect relationship can be readily established. This would be the case with black lung disease, asbestosis, or mesothelioma. However, for diseases with multiple causes, such as cancer, identifying a pool of eligible 'victims' would be very difficult, since it is generally not possible to determine whether a given cancer case is due, for example, to work-related exposure to toxic substances or other causes.[49] Thus, while provision of insurance is a standard risk-management tool, in the context of environmental risks its applicability may be limited to certain types of risks.

4. Summary and Conclusions

Environmental risks can be categorized into three types: 1) internalized risks such as radon (chapter 3) in which decisions regarding risk reduction are made by the individual who faces the risk, 2) market-based risks such as those associated with food safety and workplace health and safety (chapter 8) in which there is a market relationship between the risk generator and the victim, and 3) externalized risks such as those associated with biotechnology (chapter 6), waste disposal (chapter 7), and air or water pollution. Here the risk generator and the victim do not interact through standard markets.

For each of these types of risks there is a possible role for the government in risk management based on standard market imperfections such as the existence of public goods, imperfect information, and externalities. In this sense, public policies designed to manage environmental risks are similar to other forms of government involvement in market economies. However, the nature of environmental risks renders the design of appropriate policies more difficult than it is in typical cases of market imperfections. The psychological response to risk is complex, at both the individual and the societal levels. In addition, the risks themselves are complex, often being a composite or succession of many risks. While this provides an opportunity for managing risks at various points in the decision chain, it also complicates the decision-making process. Finally, if there is the possibility of improved information over time or if some potential losses are irreversible, the value of flexibility and the implications of irreversibility must be explicitly acknowledged.

There are, of course, a number of approaches available for managing environmental risks. Each approach has advantages and disadvantages.

Privatizing risk management in the spirit of the 1980s deregulation provides victims with incentives to reduce risks but does not provide compensation unless private insurance for environmental risks is available. Additionally, except in cases of purely internalized risks, private risk management does not provide proper risk-reduction incentives for injurers.

Ex ante economic incentives — such as taxes and deposits — are potentially useful for risks emanating from predictable, observable actions and have the usual advantages in this context. However, their use in the control of accident-type risks such as oil spills is limited because of the infrequent nature of these events. In addition, incentive mechanisms do not generally provide victim compensation.

With regulation the amount of risk reduction is more certain since risk-related activities are controlled directly rather than indirectly. However, regulations are often not cost-effective. In addition, they cannot be used to control unobservable actions that affect risks, and regulation does not provide victim compensation.

Legal liability is intended to provide both incentives for cost-effective risk reduction as well as victim compensation, although these two goals often conflict. In addition, liability may not achieve either goal effectively for risks with long latency periods, particularly if the resulting damage could have arisen from multiple causes.

Victim compensation funds and other forms of third-party insurance are designed to facilitate compensation and reduce transaction costs, but they are only useful for risks that are amenable to insurance coverage. In addition, the presence of insurance can decrease risk-reduction incentives for both injurers and victims.

Clearly, in designing an appropriate risk management policy, it is essential that the nature of the risk — internalized, market-based, or externalized — be identified and that the goal of the policy be specified. The alternative approaches vary in their ability to achieve efficient risk reduction, efficient risk spreading, and an appropriate allocation of the costs of risk-generating activities, with some policies achieving one goal at the expense of another. No single approach dominates for all types of risks and all goals.

Finally, because risk management has multiple goals that cannot generally be achieved with a single policy instrument, it is likely that the appropriate policy requires a combination of approaches, with that combination determined by the nature of the specific risk and the policy goals. For those risks related to accidental releases such as chemical spills or unintended releases of genetically engineered materials in which victim incentives are relatively unimportant and it is better to be safe than sorry, a strong regulatory approach coupled with liability or a fund to provide compensation may be appropriate. Alternatively, for risks from continual low-level exposure to pesticide residues in foods, or to air or water pollutants in which victim compensation is not practical because of the large number of victims and the difficulty of proving causation, a combination of regulation and economic incentives could be used. While the details will vary with specific risks, the goal in each case is to combine the available policy tools so that they most effectively address the concerns that give rise to the need for a public policy response.

Notes

1. A contingent contract is an agreement to deliver or receive a certain quantity of a good at a specified time in the future if and only if a certain state of the world exists at that time. The most common example is an insurance contract, under which the insurer agrees to pay in the future an amount $L (less any deductible) if and only if the purchaser has suffered a loss of $L at that time.

2. The taxonomy used here follows closely that used in Shavell (1980), although his focus is on the use of liability to control different types of accidents.

3. In the risk management literature, a distinction is often made between "voluntary" and "involuntary" risk. Under this distinction, an internalized risk would be an example of a voluntary risk.

4.   Economies of scale exist when the average or per unit cost of producing a given good or service decreases as the quantity produced increases. This can result from input specialization or from the presence of fixed costs, which must be incurred regardless of the amount of output produced. When economies of scale exist, then for any two output levels q_1 and q_2,

$$C(q_1) + C(q_2) > C(q_1 + q_2),$$

where $C(q)$ is the total cost of producing q units of output. In other words, if the total amount to be produced is $q_1 + q_2$, it is cheaper (and thus more efficient) for a single agent or organization to produce the entire amount (incurring a cost of $C(q_1 + q_2)$) than for the total to be produced by two different agents, each producing an amount q_i ($i = 1,2$) and incurring a cost of $C(q_i)$.

5.   This information can relate either to the magnitude of the risk (such as the probability or likely impact of an adverse event) or to methods of risk reduction (through risk prevention or response).

6.   Public goods are goods that exhibit two characteristics, nonrivalry and nonexcludability. Nonrivalry exists when one person's consumption or use of the good does not diminish the amount available for others to consume or use, while nonexcludability means that it is not possible (at reasonable cost) to prevent an individual from enjoying or consuming the good. Clean air is a classic example of a public good, since the amount of clean air that one person enjoys does not diminish the amount available for others to enjoy, and individuals cannot be easily excluded from enjoying the benefits of clean air.

7.   In making decisions regarding production, individuals or private firms compare private benefits to private costs. Efficiency, on the other hand, requires that social benefits be compared to social costs. With public goods, social benefits will exceed private benefits. Because of nonrivalry, many people will benefit from production of the good. However, because of nonexcludability, they will not have to pay for those benefits. Thus, private producers will not consider those benefits in their decision-making process and as a result will face insufficient incentives to produce the good.

8.   There is, of course, an important dynamic element to government involvement of this kind. If the government has historically assumed the role of risk manager for internalized risks, then individuals will come to rely on the government to protect them. For example, they will come to assume that, if a given product is on the market, it must have been deemed safe by the appropriate experts. Thus, to fulfill consumer expectations, adequate protection will require that the government continue in this role. If, on the other hand, the government has historically left risk management to the individual, then individuals will take more care to consider the risks in making decisions regarding risky activities. The fact that a product is on the market will not be viewed as evidence of an underlying expert judgment that the product is safe.

9.   Insurance allows an individual to trade a risky situation (uncertainty regarding future losses) for a relatively certain one (payment of a given premium with compensation if losses occur). In this way, the risks are spread among the group of individuals purchasing the insurance. If individuals are risk averse, purchasing actuarily fair insurance should make them better off.

10.   For example, when making consumption decisions, the consumer will weigh both the cost (price) of a risky product and the corresponding risk against the benefits gained by consumption. In this sense, the consumer decisions for risky products will be similar to those for naturally risky activities, i.e., the risk will be internalized for the consumer. Furthermore, the reduced demand for a product because of its risks will reduce its market price and thus

cause those risks to be reflected in the decisions of producers of the product as well. Similar arguments could be made in the context of high-risk jobs. Employees will compare the benefits of employment (wages) to the costs (opportunity costs and risks) in their labor supply decisions. Likewise, employers will consider the increased wages they must pay as a result of increased risks. Thus, the market relationship between the two parties will cause the risks to be internalized by both. In this sense, market-based risks are another example of voluntary risks. The voluntary nature of the risk requires, however, that consumers and employees have full information about the risks they are imposing on themselves. For a further discussion, see Shavell (1980) and the text.

11.   See, for example, Smith (1979) and Dickens (1984) on whether risks are internalized in the labor market through risk premiums in wages.

12.   Externalized risks are examples of involuntary risks.

13.   In particular, if the marginal benefit of the activity exceeds its marginal cost (including risk-related costs), the injurer will have an incentive to offer to the victim (and the victim will have an incentive to accept) a payment greater than the marginal cost but less than the marginal benefit in exchange for an allowed increase in the activity level. Alternatively, if the marginal cost exceeds the marginal benefit, the victim will have an incentive to offer to the injurer (and the injurer will have an incentive to accept) a payment greater than the marginal benefit but less than the marginal cost to induce a reduction in the activity level.

14.   Some people have argued that damages occur at the time of exposure, even if an individual never actually contracts the disease. In this case, bargaining would take place over exposure, and the responsible party could be more readily identified.

15.   For an example of the implications of incorporating feelings such as regret in policy decisions, see the discussion of alternative compensation mechanisms.

16.   For example, changing the reference point so that changes appear to be gains rather than losses has a significant effect on choices. See Kahneman and Tversky (1979) and Tversky and Kahneman (1981) for a general discussion of this phenomenon and Bromley (1989) and Knetsch (1990) for discussions in the context of environmental policy.

17.   There is, of course, considerable anecdotal evidence that how policies are framed is very important in determining their political acceptability. For example, the notion of tradeable pollution permits was politically less saleable than the equivalent notion of tradeable emission reduction credits, and the change in terminology is believed to have been an important factor in winning approval of the current trading programs.

18.   The distinction that is sometimes made between risk prevention and response suggests that there are only two possible points of intervention, before and after. However, for composite risks, it is possible to have prevention or response for each stage. In addition, response at one stage may simply be (attempted) prevention of the next stage. Thus, in the context of composite risks, the dichotomous distinction between prevention and response is not very meaningful. Nonetheless, for expository convenience, we use it when no confusion is likely to result.

19.   Under the one-time approval system, once approved the manufacturer presumes that he has the right to produce the product indefinitely and a subsequent ban on production is viewed as a reduction in his rights. Under the continual renewal system, he presumes that he has the right to produce it for the specified period and failure to renew the registration cannot be viewed as a reduction in that right. Thus, it seems likely that the political battles over failure to renew registration would be less severe than those over banning a previously approved product, thereby improving the prospects for responding expeditiously to any new information about the health risks of the product.

20. See Miller and Lad (1984) and Viscusi (1988) for discussions of the conditions under which this conclusion holds.

21. See Ippolito (1981) for a model of how individuals respond to risk-related information, and Viscusi, Magat, and Huber (1986) for empirical evidence on the efficacy of this approach.

22. Raucher (1986) presents some case studies of prevention versus response in the context of groundwater contamination. See, however, Smith and Desvousges (1988) for some qualifications of Raucher's results.

23. There are, of course, examples where polluters have voluntarily done so. For example, Union Carbide (Rhone-Poulenc) has a policy of providing filters to households with detected levels of the agricultural pesticide aldicarb that exceed federal standards.

24. For example, the state of Wisconsin has a well replacement program under which it will pay 80 percent of the cost of replacing a qualifying contaminated well.

25. For a recent survey of the advantages of using economic incentive mechanisms to control environmental pollution, see Stewart (1988).

26. See Russell (1988) for a discussion of the potential for and limitations of using economic incentives to encourage proper disposal of hazardous wastes.

27. With experience rating, insurance premiums are based on the insured's past history with respect to accidents. This approach is commonly used in automobile insurance.

28. In some sense, experience rating is closer to a liability approach than an ex ante incentive approach. As with liability, the injurer's costs are determined by whether or not an accident occurs. With experience rating, however, in the event of an accident, the injurer's payment goes to the insurance company (in the form of higher future premiums) rather than the victim.

29. Much work has been done on comparing the use of prices (ex ante economic incentives) and regulation as alternative means to control externalities under uncertainty. The seminal article is Weitzman (1974). See also Stewart (1988) for a comparison of the two approaches.

30. See Portney (1990) for a detailed description of the use of regulation in controlling environmental risks.

31. Of course, the intention of regulations and their actual effects may differ, depending on (among other things) enforcement and compliance. See Portney (1990) for discussions of the effectiveness of some existing environmental regulations and chapter 8 for the case of regulations to improve workplace safety.

32. See Lichtenberg, Zilberman, and Bogen (1989) for an application of this approach to groundwater contamination.

33. See Shavell (1987) for an excellent overview of the theoretical literature establishing this and other related results.

34. A negligence rule provides the correct incentives for injurers in the short run but not necessarily in the long run. See Polinsky (1980).

35. Under such a rule, the sum of payments by all injurers can be less than, equal to, or greater than total damages suffered by victims, depending on the synergisms that exist. See Miceli and Segerson (forthcoming) for a detailed discussion.

36. See Miceli and Segerson (forthcoming) for a general discussion and Tietenberg (1989) for a discussion in the context of liability imposed under the Comprehensive Emergency Response, Compensation and Liability (CERCLA) Act.

37. See Segerson (1990) for a comparison of liability and ex ante economic incentives, in particular Pigovian taxes.

38. Under a negligence rule, this refers to the probability he will be held liable when he has acted negligently.

39. A related issue regarding proof of causation arises when a victim is unable to identify which of several possible injurers was in fact responsible for the damages suffered. The now classic example is the DES case, where long lag times between the sale of the product and the manifestation of damages made it virtually impossible for affected women to identify the specific manufacturer of the responsible product. Several rules that would maintain correct injurer incentives in such cases have been proposed. See, for example, Shavell (1985) and Marino (1988).

40. For example, the damages due to exposure to asbestos fibers have clearly exceeded the assets of the producers of asbestos, forcing some into bankruptcy proceedings. Even with sufficient assets, however, injurers may not pay the full amount of damages because of the way awards are determined in practice. See Dewees (1986).

41. While the definition of *exposure* may appear to be clear cut, it is not always unambiguous. For example, one might argue that exposure to increased risk has occurred long before an actual release of a toxic chemical, perhaps at the time that the plant that produces it was built, because of the *possibility* of a release. This alternative definition is, of course, consistent with the notion of compensating communities for some types of "locally unwanted land uses (LULUs)," even if no releases have actually occurred. See chapter 7.

42. This presumes that exposed individuals will file suit. If the expected compensation for exposure is small, the payoff net of legal fees may be negative, thereby eliminating incentives to sue. One possible solution to this problem is the use of class action suits.

43. This can be shown in the following way. Let $U(y,H)$ be an individual's von Neuman-Morgenstern utility function, where y is wealth and H is health. Let y_0 be the initial wealth level, and let $H = 0$ correspond to a state of having contracted the disease while $H = 1$ corresponds to not contracting it. Without any exposure, expected utility is given by $U(y_0,1)$. Let p be the probability of contracting the disease, conditional on exposure. Then the correct ex ante compensation, C_a, is defined by

$$U(y_0,1) = pU(y_0 + C_a,0) + (1 - p)U(y_0 + C_a,1),$$

implying that expected utility under ex ante compensation is $U(y_0,1)$. Likewise, the correct ex post compensation, C_p, is defined by

$$U(y_0,1) = U(y_0 + C_p,0).$$

Ex ante expected utility under ex post compensation is then

$$pU(y_0 + C_p,0) + (1 - p)U(y_0,1),$$

which by definition of C_p reduces to $U(y_0,1)$. Thus, expected utility is the same under the two types of compensation, namely, $U(y_0,1)$, the reference level of utility.

44. Carson (1985) has proposed an interesting solution to this problem, namely, that part of the award granted to victims of exposure be in the form of an insurance policy to cover future damages if the victim ultimately contracts the disease. Such an approach effectively provides ex ante (at the time of exposure) for ex post compensation.

45. See Trauberman (1981) and Elliott (1985) for discussions of the use of victim compensation funds for environmental risks.

46. In this sense, they are similar to federal flood insurance and other disaster relief programs that are available for internalized risks. There is a difference, of course, in who finances the compensation, but all of these programs provide some form of compensation for victims that does not require a legal suit.

47. For discussions of the effect of insurance on victim incentives, see Ehrenberg (1988) for the case of workers' compensation and Lewis and Nickerson (1989) for federal disaster relief programs.

48.   A basic premise of many economic analyses is that any nonmonetary damage can be translated into an equivalent monetary damage through the concepts of willingness-to-pay and willingness-to-accept. However, in trade-offs between health and dollars, the notion of indifference that underlies these concepts seems inappropriate. At best, individuals might feel ambivalent about these trade-offs. See Opaluch and Segerson (1989) for a discussion of some of the implications of feelings of ambivalence.

49.   In such cases, an insurance approach is still possible if victims are not required to prove causation. Such a program would have to be very broad-based, thereby eliminating any risk reduction incentives. An example is Social Security Disability Insurance. See Trauberman (1981).

References

Arrow, Kenneth J. 1971. *Essays in the Theory of Risk-Bearing*. Chicago, Markham Publishing.

Arrow, Kenneth J. 1984. *The Economics of Information*. Cambridge, Mass.: Harvard University Press.

Bromley, Daniel W. 1989. "Entitlements, Missing Markets and Environmental Uncertainty," *Journal of Environmental Economics and Management* 17(2), 181–194.

Carson, Brent. 1985. "Increased Risk of Disease From Hazardous Waste: A Proposal for Judicial Relief." *Washington Law Review* 60, 635–652.

Coase, Ronald H. 1960. "The Problem of Social Cost," *Journal of Law and Economics* 3, 1–44.

Crouch, E., and R. Wilson. 1981. "Regulation of Carcinogens," *Risk Analysis* 1, 47–57.

Dewees, Donald N. 1986. "Economic Incentives for Controlling Industrial Disease: The Asbestos Case," *Journal of Legal Studies* 15, 289–319.

Dickens, William T. 1984. "Differences Between Risk Premiums in Union and Nonunion Wages and the Case for Occupational Safety Regulation," *American Economic Review* 74(2), 320–323.

Ehrenberg, Ronald G. 1988. "Workers' Compensation, Wages, and the Risk of Injury." In Burton, John F., Jr. (ed.), *New Perspectives in Workers' Compensation*, Ithaca, New York: ILR Press, Cornell University.

Elliott, E. Donald. 1985. "Why Courts? Comment on Robinson," *Journal of Legal Studies* 14, 799–805.

Ippolito, Pauline M. 1981. "Information and the Life Cycle Consumption of Hazardous Goods," *Economic Inquiry* 19, 529–558.

Kahneman, Daniel, and Amos Tversky. 1979. "Prospect Theory: An Analysis of Decisions Under Risk," *Econometrica* 47(2), 263–291.

Knetsch, Jack L. 1990. "Environmental Policy Implications of Disparities between Willingness to Pay and Compensation Demanded Measures of Value," *Journal of Environmental Economics and Management* 18(3), 227–237.

Landes, William M., and Richard A. Posner. 1984. "Tort Law as a Regulatory

Regime for Catastrophic Personal Injuries," *Journal of Legal Studies* 13, 417–434.

Lave, Lester B. 1990. "How Safe Is Safe Enough? Setting Safety Goals," St. Louis: Center for the Study of American Business, Washington University, 96 (January).

Lewis, Tracy, and David Nickerson. 1989. "Self-Insurance against Natural Disasters," *Journal of Environmental Economics and Management* 16(3), 209–223.

Lichtenberg, Eric, and David Zilberman. (1988). "Efficient Regulation of Environmental Health Risks," *Quarterly Journal of Economics*. 103(1), 167–178.

Lichtenberg, Eric, David Zilberman, and Kenneth T. Bogen. 1989. "Regulating Environmental Health Risks Under Uncertainty: Groundwater Contamination in California," *Journal of Environmental Economics and Management* 17, 22–34.

Loomis, Graham, and Robert Sugden. 1982. "Regret Theory: An Alternative Theory of Rational Choice Under Uncertainty," *Economic Journal* 92, 805–824.

Machina, Mark J. 1987. "Choice Under Uncertainty: Problems Solved and Unsolved," *Journal of Economic Perspectives* 1(1), 121–154.

Machina, Mark J. 1989. "Dynamic Consistency and Non-Expected Utility Models of Choice Under Uncertainty," *Journal of Economic Literature* 27(4), 1622–1668.

Marino, Anthony M. 1991. "Market Share Liability and Economic Efficiency," *Southern Economic Journal* 57(3), 667–675.

Miceli, Thomas J., and Kathleen Segerson. (forthcoming). "Joint Liability in Torts: Marginal vs. Non-Marginal Efficiency Effects," *International Review of Law and Economics*.

Miller, Jon R., and Frank Lad. 1984. "Flexibility, Learning and Irreversibility in Environmental Decisions: A Bayesian Approach," *Journal of Environmental Economics and Management* 11, 161–172.

Opaluch, James J., and Kathleen Segerson. 1989. "Rational Roots of 'Irrational' Behavior: New Theories of Economic Decision-Making," *Northeast Journal of Agricultural and Resource Economics* 18(2), 81–95.

Polinsky, A. Mitchell. 1980. "Strict Liability vs. Negligence in a Market Setting," *American Economic Review Papers and Proceedings* 70(2), 363–367.

Portney, Paul R. 1990. *Public Policies for Environmental Protection.* Washington, D.C.: Resources for the Future.

Raucher, Robert L. 1986. "The Benefits and Costs of Policies Related to Groundwater Contamination," *Land Economics* 62(1), 33–45.

Robinson, Glen O. 1985. "Probabilistic Causation and Compensation for Tortious Risk," *Journal of Legal Studies* 14, 779–805.

Russell, Clifford S. 1988. "Economic Incentives in the Management of Hazardous Wastes," *Columbia Journal of Environmental Law* 13(2), 257–274.

Schoemaker, Paul J. H. 1982. "The Expected Utility Model: Its Variants, Purposes, Evidence and Limitations," *Journal of Economic Literature*, 20, 529–563.

Segerson, Kathleen. 1986. 'Risk Sharing in the Design of Environmental Policy,' *American Journal of Agricultural Economics* 68(5), 1261–1265.

Segerson, Kathleen. 1990. "Institutional 'Markets': The Role of Liability in Allocating Environmental Resources," Department of Economics Working Paper, University of Connecticut.

Shavell, Steven. 1980. "Strict Liability Versus Negligence," *Journal of Legal Studies* 9(1), 1–25.

Shavell, Steven. 1984. "Liability for Harm vs. Regulation of Safety," *Journal of Legal Studies* 13, 357–374.

Shavell, Steven. 1985. "Uncertainty Over Causation and the Determination of Civil Liability," *Journal of Law and Economics* 28, 587–609.

Shavell, Steven. 1987. *Economic Analysis of Accident Law*, Cambridge, Ma.: Harvard University Press.

Smith, Robert S. 1979. "Compensating Wage Differentials and Public Policy: A Review," *Industrial and Labor Relations Review* 32, 339–352.

Smith, V. Kerry, and William H. Desvousges. 1988. "The Valuation of Environmental Risks and Hazardous Waste Policy," *Land Economics* 64(3), 211–219.

Stewart, Richard B. 1988. "Controlling Environmental Risks Through Economic Incentives," *Columbia Journal of Environmental Law* 13(2), 153–169.

Tietenberg, Tom H. 1989. "Indivisible Toxic Torts: The Economics of Joint and Several Liability," *Land Economics* 65(4), 305–319.

Trauberman, Jeffrey. 1981. "Compensating Victims of Toxic Substances Pollution: An Analysis of Existing Federal Statutes," *Harvard Environmental Law Review* 5(1), 1–29.

Tversky, Amos, and Daniel Kahneman. 1981. "The Framing of Decisions and the Psychology of Choice," *Science* 211, 453–458.

Viscusi, W. Kip. 1988. "Irreversible Environmental Investments with Uncertain Benefit Levels," *Journal of Environmental Economics and Management* 15(2), 147–157.

Viscusi, W. Kip, W. A. Magat, and J. Huber. 1986. "Informational Regulation of Consumer Health Risks: An Empirical Evaluation of Hazard Warnings," *Rand Journal of Economics* 17, 351–365.

Weinstein, Milton C., and Robert J. Quinn. 1983. "Psychological Considerations in Valuing Health Risk Reductions," *Natural Resources Journal* 23(3), 659–673.

Weitzman, Martin L. 1974. "Prices vs. Quantities," *Review of Economic Studies* 41(4), 477–491.

Worrall, John D. 1983. *Safety and the Work Force: Incentives and Disincentives in Workers' Compensation*. Ithaca, New York: ILR Press.

6 DECISION MAKING ABOUT BIOTECHNOLOGY: THE COSTS OF LEARNING FROM ERROR

E.J. Woodhouse*
Patrick W. Hamlett

One of the main obstacles to the use of science and engineering for human betterment is that new technological endeavors quickly develop economic, political, and intellectual momentum. As a result, these technologies then resist improvement, even when serious environmental or social impacts become apparent. The time to make mid-course corrections, therefore, is early in the life cycle before momentum becomes irresistible (Winner, 1977, 1986; Morone and Woodhouse, 1989). Among the most significant new technical endeavors for the foreseeable future are those in the field of molecular genetics — popularly referred to as biotechnology. This chapter attempts to assess whether early commercialization of this technology is proceeding sensibly or whether changes may be desirable. The analysis relies on a framework developed by decision theorists for evaluating the regulation of toxic chemicals, nuclear power, and other environmentally hazardous technologies (Collingridge, 1980, 1983; Morone and Woodhouse, 1986).

* E.J. Woodhouse is in the Department of Science and Technology Studies, Rensselear Polytechnic Institute, and Patrick W. Hamlet is in the Division of Multidisciplinary Studies, North Carolina State University.

1. Economic Risks

The range of potential uses for biotechnology is immense, involving products worth hundreds of billions of dollars. Boosters in the biomedical community foresee new and improved vaccines, antiviral medicines, and artificially synthesized hormones (e.g., human-growth hormone). Also possible are artificial enzymes such as insulin, blood proteins, natural painkillers, and cancer-fighting agents. The market for genetic testing already is growing rapidly (Nelkin and Tancredi, 1989).

Production of bulk pharmaceuticals such as vitamins and antibiotics could be radically changed through the introduction of molecular genetics. The potential effects on the organic chemical industry are equally profound. Glucose isomerase and other enzymes can replace feed stocks currently derived from expensive and unreliable petroleum sources. Genetic engineering may help construct microorganisms useful in treating sewage, accelerating decomposition of garbage in landfills, and disposing of agricultural wastes. As a by-product, these activities could provide a cheap source for methane gas, currently a $12 billion industry.

The most promising application of molecular genetics may be in farming and forestry. The goals are "to reduce chemical, energy, or labor inputs," while improving "yield potential, resistance to diseases, pests, and environmental stresses" (Flavell et al., 1986, p. 200). For example, propagating plants from the growing tips of roots or stems usually eliminates viruses that presently cause large losses in yield for potato and cassava crops throughout the world. Moreover, as biomass becomes a more important source of energy, bioengineered microorganisms could help make the breakdown of cellulose less costly.

Because new technology often serves as a resource in economic competition, biotechnology may be used to further the interests of some nations, businesses, and individuals at the expense of others. What strategies are being used to protect against competition from other nations' businesses? Are there strategies to protect especially vulnerable groups who could be immiserated by the impending changes?

Due to flexible financial markets and potentially huge profits, venture capitalists "have been falling all over themselves to get into the neuroscience field" (Nelkin and Tancredi, 1989, p. 34). Large corporations like Monsanto and duPont also have invested heavily in molecular genetics. Altogether, the industry has attracted an estimated $1.5 billion per year during the 1980s (OTA, 1988a). In the United States, federal and state governments have made deliberate efforts to encourage commercialization. New York State has given approximately $30 million to Cornell University to set up a biotechnology research center (Worthington and Black, 1986). The federal nature of American government tends to motivate multiple governmental units to help encourage university-industry collaboration. After all, no state wants to lose out to others in the competition for jobs and tax revenues. While this probably works better for the universities and businesses than for the citizenry, perhaps it contributes to the new industry's diversity. With some 400 separate companies pursuing opportunities from pharmaceuticals to agricultural products, if one line of investigation fails to pay off, others would still be available to protect what is perceived to be the American stake.

Moreover, the normal operations of the business world promote learning from experience in new competitive industries. Investors monitor the technical and financial health of both start-up biotechnology firms and the larger chemical and pharmaceutical companies. Large numbers of knowledgeable observers with a stake in the outcome are in a position to signal their displeasure if managers do not adjust quickly to new information. However, no comparable incentives prevail in those aspects of biotechnology policy where governments must act.

In sum, while no one yet knows for sure how biotechnology will affect global economic competition, or what products will be most important, the strategies employed by the United States to date have been sensible means of protecting against the possibility of being outmaneuvered by international rivals. Japan, France, Germany, and most other affluent nations have been pursuing similar paths, although none with quite the diversity of the United States. It remains to be seen, of course, which nations prove best at marketing genetically engineered products.

Farmers represent one group that could be affected negatively by biotechnology. There are millions of small farmers in Europe, Japan, and the United States, and hundreds of millions throughout the world. The first threat biotechnology poses to their way of life comes from bovine somatotropin (bST), an animal growth hormone. Cows produce somatotropin, or bovine growth hormone (bGH), naturally in minute amounts in the pituitary gland. Biotechnology firms now have learned to mass-produce the hormone and injections of bST are thought to increase milk output per cow by as much as 10 percent (Tangley, 1986).

The bST technology is dominated by four of the largest American chemical and pharmaceutical companies. All expect bST to become a major profit maker. As a representative of American Cyanamid said, "It's not just bST. We're laying the groundwork for a whole series of products" (Rauch, 1987, p. 818). Because the market for bST will not be large enough to support all four firms, the first usable bST approved by the Food and Drug Administration will represent a major gain for one of these companies—and a big loss for the others.

Environmental groups have filed suit in federal court to block use of bGH, and have testified before congressional committees investigating the hormone's safety. The Wisconsin Family Farm Defense Fund, the Humane Society, and others are attempting to turn dairy farmers against the technology, claiming excessive production will lower prices and "probably accelerate the trend toward fewer and larger farms" (Kalter, 1985, p. 131). Critics also dispute the industry's claims that bGH is harmless and leaves no residues in the milk. This has led to at least one episode in which California dairies hastily pulled off the market milk from test herds using bGH, and tried to get assurances from the chemical companies that such tainted milk would not again enter the milk supply. As one member of the California Milk Advisory Board said, "The word *hormone* scares people; psychologically, the consumer is not ready for that" (Rauch, 1987, p. 820). To counteract these tactics, the biotechnology companies have hired public relations consultants, commissioned opinion surveys, and cooperated in information campaigns aimed at the diverse participants in dairy policy making (Browne and Hamm, 1988).

This is likely to be the first of many changes in agricultural technology that will be promoted by agribusiness concerns. Such technology nicely illustrates a technological treadmill on which farmers have been trapped for most of this century. The first farmers to innovate will generally benefit for a time from lower costs and higher yields. As others adopt the innovation,

> an increased supply of product depresses prices and sets the stage for another round of innovation. Those who fail or are unable to adopt new technologies suffer economic loss; marginal producers are continually forced out of business, and their operations are absorbed by more successful operators (Kloppenburg, 1984, p. 296).

Effects also will be felt in the poorer nations (Kenney and Buttel, 1985). Although imports from Third World nations constitute a small percentage of overall food consumption in the affluent nations, commodities such as coffee, sugar, bananas, and spices are vital to the livelihood of millions of near-subsistence farmers. Molecular genetics may provide alternatives for many such imports; use of immobilized enzymes to convert corn biomass into high fructose corn syrup, for example, cut U.S. sugar imports by almost 75 percent in the early 1980s (Stewart, 1983). Gum arabic, tapped from gum trees and used in textiles and many other products, has been the major source of cash income for farmers in western Sudan; a French company now is attempting to culture the tissue in laboratories (Conservation Foundation, 1988). Firms are beginning the in-vitro manufacturing of substances that traditionally had been imported, including saffron and other spices, fragrances, mint oil, quinine, and various fruit-based flavors (Wheat, 1986).

More generally, there are prospects for combining new techniques of cell culturing with older methods of growing bacteria for use in fermentation processes. This could presage a partial shift of agriculture from fields to factories (Goodman et al., 1987). Few cooks would prefer cucumber essence to actual cucumbers, but foods consumed in highly processed forms might well come to be cultured rather than grown in traditional ways. While agribusiness presumably will diversify into these new technologies, traditional farmers — even large ones — probably cannot. The new high-technology methods might provide equal enjoyment at reduced cost; or there may be a diminution in quality, as with the not-very-tasty modern tomato. Whatever the other effects, producers of ordinary agricultural commodities will suffer if their markets are captured by higher-technology methods. The world's fishermen face a similar threat from genetically based aquaculture.

In sum, this new technology constitutes a problem as well as an opportunity. Those who have the funds, organization, and other resources to use biotechnology to advance their own ends will probably do well from it. But not everyone will. And the most vulnerable groups are essentially unprotected, especially in the poorer nations (Buttel et al., 1985).

2.   Environmental Risks of Biotechnology

In addition to the economic benefits and costs of biotechnology, there are potential environmental risks as well. Informed policy will require careful consideration of these potential risks at a cost which will not jeopardize the commercialization of valuable products. Such assessment may proceed along the following lines.

2.1.   The Low-Cost Framework

Good decision making generally is thought to be achieved primarily via accurate analysis of options and pitfalls at the outset of a new endeavor. While highly plausible, this common-sense idea turns out to offer a misleading guide for complex social choices (Lindblom, 1959). For technical innovation in particular, many studies show that technological systems evolve in unforeseeable ways (Drucker, 1973). Satisfactory direction of technology therefore requires decision makers to adjust adroitly in the face of evolving problems and opportunities.

If it is quite inevitable that significant unanticipated consequences will arise, and therefore some form of trial-and-error choice is necessary, the main question is whether errors will come at high financial and human cost. Low-cost learning can never be guaranteed in complex sociotechnical endeavors. Yet studies of decision making find that the odds of unacceptably costly errors can be greatly reduced by a combination of four components:

- Early, vigorous review from diverse points of view designed to debate the goals, potential pitfalls, and strategies to be pursued.
- Built-in flexibility to delay accumulation of technological momentum, and also to make it feasible to alter directions in light of experience.
- Initial precautions to guard against egregious errors during the first several decades when a technological system is likely to have the highest uncertainty, and the greatest potential for inadvertent harm.
- Active monitoring of feedback, and other ways of accelerating learning from experience.

These four dimensions reduce to two general considerations. The first requirement stems from the "intelligence of democracy" (Lindblom, 1965). Large technological systems affect myriad people in diverse ways, and no small group of insiders will have sufficient insight (or concern) to protect enough of the competing interests. If lack of early debate allows a technology to evolve in ways that conflict with significant social needs, correcting the imbalance at a later stage can be very costly. With civilian nuclear power, debate did not occur until after investment of a hundred billion dollars in giant reactors with the potential for catastrophic meltdowns. If policy makers had realized that the public would not accept even a small risk of such a catastrophe, they may have pushed for the development of small — "inherently safe" — reactors. Such reactors have proven to be technically and economically feasible. This would have reassured millions of people, and perhaps could have prevented the industry's demise (Morone and Woodhouse, 1989).

A second key to successful decision making is that new endeavors must be flexible enough to allow for substantial adjustment on the basis of experience. While this appears simple, technological systems quickly develop considerable inertia (Hughes, 1983). Consider, for a moment, how few years it took for television to become invulnerable to thoughtful redirection. British decision theorist David Collingridge identifies four elements contributing to inflexibility (Collingridge, 1980; 1983):

- *Lead time*: a long period between initiating a technology and getting convincing feedback about its inadequacies routinely interferes with error correction. It took about 25 years for the ecological effects of DDT to become widely recognized.
- *Infrastructure*: If a new technology depends on huge manufacturing facilities, complicated supply networks, and other supporting facilities, change will be expensive.
- *Unit size*: Large-scale endeavors, such as nuclear power plants, are generally harder to modify than smaller-scale efforts.
- *Timing of payment*: If costs are primarily borne in advance, as in building a huge power plant, then learning from experience cannot occur in time to prevent high-cost mistakes.

These aspects of inflexibility obviously can reinforce each other, as when large unit size requires high capital investment for big infrastructure facilities, and the long delay during planning, construction, and diffusion allows errors to accumulate for an extended period before they are detected. Inertia thereby develops in organizational routines, interest group expectations, and policy networks. Such powerful forces are likely to resist change even when evidence of a serious problem eventually becomes available. All told, the more flexible a new technology, the better the prospects for revision on the basis of experience.

With early debate and flexibility, ordinary trial-and-error processes might be sufficient to refine a technological system incrementally on the basis of experience. However, for some major new technologies the costs of error could be too severe to bear; and there rarely is *enough* debate or flexibility. Thus, it generally makes sense to use a more sophisticated form of trial-and-error, employing several common-sense strategies to protect against unacceptably costly mistakes and to accelerate the learning process:

- Even in highly uncertain endeavors it is possible at or near the outset to foresee and protect against some of the worst risks. Containment shells around nuclear reactors are an example.
- Because it is impossible to know the likelihood or severity of hypothetical risks from a new technology, it makes sense to err on the side of caution by putting the burden of proof on advocates.
- Costs and inertia from delayed feedback can be minimized by speeding up receipt of negative feedback (via laboratory testing) instead of waiting for it to arise naturally.
- Well designed trial-and-error processes are not purely reactive but

prepare for error correction, as by establishing procedures for careful monitorng of initial trials to refine key uncertainties.

Taken together, and coupled with efforts to maintain maximum flexibility, these strategies offer the prospect not of avoiding errors altogether, but of low-cost learning from the errors that inevitably will occur (Woodhouse, 1988).

2.2. Application to Biotechnology

When Stanford biochemist Paul Berg proposed in 1971 to use new recombinant DNA techniques to transfer genetic material between microorganisms, some scientists feared that genetically altered bacteria might escape from the lab and colonize in humans or the environment, possibly creating serious health problems. They argued that close examination of the risks should precede experimentation. Berg cancelled his plans, but others went ahead. By 1974 concern had mounted to the point that a National Academy of Sciences committee called for a temporary moratorium on many types of rDNA experiments, and all researchers in the field voluntarily complied. These controversies are documented elsewhere (Krimsky, 1982; Morone and Woodhouse, 1986; Wright, 1986; Zilinskas and Zimmerman, 1986).

To assess the potential risks involved in these activities, more than a hundred microbiologists and other scientists from many nations convened for four days in 1975 at Asilomar, California. The group ratified the moratorium on risky experiments, set safety requirements, and endorsed earlier calls for a Recombinant DNA Advisory Committee within the National Institutes of Health. Such a committee was appointed soon thereafter, and in 1976 the NIH promulgated formal guidelines.

Several classes of experiments initially were banned: 1) deliberate releases to the environment, 2) larger experiments using more than 10 liters of culture, and 3) most research on pathogens and toxins. Permissible research was classified according to the level of the estimated hazard, with the riskiest work to be performed only in labs with air locks, systems for decontaminating air, autoclaves, shower rooms, and other safeguards for preventing the escape of microorganisms. In case such containment efforts did not entirely succeed, certain experiments could use only enfeebled bacteria that would not survive outside the perfect temperature and growth media provided by the lab.

Such precautions enabled research to go forward while important uncertainties were clarified: 1) could an organism escape from a laboratory and colonize in a human? 2) could disease-causing organisms be trans-mitted, as via an infected laboratory worker passing the infection on to others? and 3) could a dangerous organism unwittingly be created? Some scientists thought from the outset that the answer to all these questions was no, but a majority wanted further evidence. They got it through the typical scientific process: by feeding billions of *E. coli* to volunteers and finding that the organisms all died in a few days and none were passed out in the stool. Viruses were inserted into *E. coli* and administered to laboratory animals, and the results suggested that the recombinant pro-cedures generally made the viruses less rather than more dangerous. While some critics questioned the adequacy of the testing, most observers found the results reassuring (see Krimsky, 1982). As experience and testing accumulated, the original precautions were eased step by step.

This process conformed closely with the requirements for low-cost learning. Rather than waiting until actual problems arose, researchers and regulators acted early to protect against potential risks. They estab-lished a variety of initial precautions, including a ban on experiments considered too risky. Moreover, they erred on the side of caution by making the guidelines stricter than most really believed necessary: enfeeble-ment as well as physical containment. In addition, there was an active process for narrowing uncertainties and learning from experience: priorities were set, large numbers of experiments quickly provided additional infor-mation, and both the Recombinant Advisory Committee and numerous conferences continuously evaluated emerging data.

The technology's introduction also fit the requirements for flexibility. Capital investment was low, with most research funds initially repro-grammed from other ongoing research projects. Businesses were not yet pressuring regulators, so there was somewhat less political pressure than usual. Existing labs and instruments sufficed for many experiments. More-over, even new infrastructure such as P4 containment laboratories could be developed in piecemeal fashion at a few universities each year. The units of analysis — bacteria and viruses — obviously were small ones and because of their quick replication, feedback accumulated very rapidly to refine uncertainties. In sum, the decisions were relatively inexpensive and reversible during the early period while uncertainty was highest.

Of course, scientific organizations are fairly well suited to the sort of testing-while-learning process used in rDNA regulation in the 1970s. It would be more difficult to apply the approach in broader political settings with more competing interests and less orientation toward rea-soned inquiry. Additionally, there certainly was plenty of self-interested political activity even within the scientific community (Wright, 1986).

Still, as molecular genetics moves from the laboratory into commercial use, the early rDNA experience sets a standard toward which subsequent risk-protection efforts can aspire. Unfortunately, the more recent experience is less reassuring.

Exploring the possible uses of biotechnology obviously requires releasing organisms into the environment. We turn now to a consideration of the extent to which the development of biotechnology has followed the low-cost learning process outlined above.

Despite early concerns, most government officials and citizens seem to approve of moving ahead fairly rapidly with commercialization of biotech-nology (OTA, 1988b). Very few scientists are calling for caution and restraint. The issue is not very high on the agendas of environmental groups, and the public concern of the mid-1970s has not returned. A few knowledgeable observers are worried about the rapid pace, however, suggesting that "genetic engineering is in grave danger of becoming an imprudent technology" (Wheale and McNally, 1988, p. 274). To determine whether this small minority can safely be ignored, it makes sense to examine the extent to which strategies for low-cost learning are presently being applied.

First, has there been early and diverse debate about the hazards of environmental release? The 1970s obviously initiated such debate, but it abated well before businesses were ready to release new organisms into the environment. The first major battle over environmental release occurred in 1983–1984, when University of California scientists Steven Lindow and Nickolas Panopoulos received permission from NIH's Recombinant Advisory Committee to field test a bacteria genetically altered to resist frost damage. Environmental groups led by Jeremy Rifkin brought suit in federal court, seeking to block field testing of the new microorganism on the grounds that NIH had violated the National Environmental Policy Act. This followed from the fact that an environ-mental impact statement had not been prepared.

Most researchers in the area believed that release of bacteria virtually identical to those already in the environment provided no significant risk, while promising substantial benefit in reducing crop losses of $1–3 million annually (Pendorff, 1985). Critics argued that the risks were beyond the ability of contemporary science to assess. Moreover, they argued that if the microorganism's safety could not be guaranteed, no release into the environment should be allowed. On May 16, 1984, federal judge John Sirica granted an injunction stopping the experiment, thereby sending shock waves through the scientific community. Yet, according to the ruling, private businesses not relying on federal funds could proceed with their experiments because no federal legislation applied to their activities. The Environmental Protection Agency soon approved an "ice-minus" experiment proposed by a private biotechnology company, Advanced Genetic Sciences, Inc. This experiment quickly became embroiled in lawsuits filed by environmental groups using several different legal strategies. Experiments on frost resistance ultimately have gone ahead, although additional regulatory and legal challenges are mounted to new proposals each year. Thus the courts have offered some recourse to those opposing rapid release of bioengineered organisms, but there has not been widespread political debate akin to the nuclear power controversy.

To what extent has this scrutiny resulted in precautions to guard against the serious consequences feared by some observers? Here the record is mixed. In 1984–1985, a Cabinet-level working group attempted to determine whether new legislation might be needed to regulate biotechnology. The group developed a Coordinated Framework for Regulation of Biotechnology that sought to resolve agency jurisdiction problems and enhance coordination by dividing regulatory responsibility among *existing* agencies (OSTP, 1984):

- Federally sponsored university research continues under the NIH Guidelines.
- The Occupational Safety and Health Administration (OSHA) regulates bioengineered products used in manufacturing.
- The EPA regulates genetically altered microorganisms under the Toxic Substances Control Act (TSCA) and the Federal Insecticide, Fungicide, and Rodenticide Act (FIFRA).
- The Department of Agriculture administers animal biologics, such as gene-altered animal vaccines, diseases, plant materials, and plant pests.
- The Federal Drug Administration (FDA) is responsible for animal drugs and human health care products derived through genetic engineering techniques.

This complex array of agency responsibilities appears, to some observers, to be "a patchwork of conflicting regulatory policies" (Pendorff, 1985, p. 921). Both businesses and university researchers complained about the new regime, but when plans took shape for creating a powerful new board to oversee and coordinate the whole process, the existing system seemed to represent the lesser evil to those who were being regulated (Vandenbergh, 1986). While the regulatory framework was being put together several flagrant procedural violations occurred, including unauthorized field tests by Monsanto, by Genetic Sciences, and by a Montana State University researcher who declared his deed to be "an act of civil disobedience" (Lemonick, 1987, p. 67). All provided fuel for the critics. As Jeremy Rifkin put it, such actions send "a message to the world that the industry is not to be trusted with the responsibility of policing itself" (Wenzel, 1986, p. 306). Researchers and businesses now apparently have learned to live with the regulations, although they complain that EPA is bending over backward to be sensitive to public concern — which the rest of us might find at least mildly reassuring.

Shortcomings in the regulatory framework are not difficult to identify, however. The Toxic Substances Control Act (TSCA), for example, was enacted in 1976 before biotechnology commercialization became an issue. According to TSCA, a manufacturer or any chemical substance must notify EPA prior to manufacturing. EPA interprets this as including genetically engineered organisms. Under the act, a Premanufacture Notice (PMN) must identify each new product and provide any health or environmental data in the manufacturer's possession. EPA has 90 days to study the PMN and reach a decision on whether to require further testing, regulate the product, or permit unregulated usage. Although EPA can delay introduction of the new chemical until further tests are completed, critics consider this short screening time unrealistic for wholly new organisms. They fear EPA will cut corners in the review process, and that EPA clearance for a new microorganism will "create the undesirable presumption" that it is safe (Harlow, 1986, p. 567). Altogether, "biotechnology companies eager to recapture their research investments through the commercialization of bioengineered products are pressing understaffed regulatory agencies to permit the release of microorganisms ... into the environment" (Vandenbergh, 1986, p. 1592).

In contrast to the vague requirements of TSCA, Levin and Harwell propose a four-step process for dealing with genetically engineered organisms, which would actively promote low-cost learning. They propose the following:

> An assessment before the deliberate release of a new organism of the fate and transport of genetic information, and of possible effects on the biota and on system processes in the affected environment; monitoring after the release of the introduced organism of its fate, transport and effects; a plan for containment of the introduced organism within predefined geographical limits; and contingency plans for mitigation in case of undesirable side effects (Levin and Harwell, 1985, pp. 63–64).

A necessary first step would be to require fully documented identification and description of each microorganism considered for commercial use, including extra-chromosomal elements such as plasmids and phages, through which portions of the bacterial chromosome may be transported into other organisms. Additionally, regulators might require each type of microorganism from each firm to carry a specific genetic marker distinguishing it from other strains of the same organism. Once marked, regulatory authorities would be able to trace an organism to its commercial source, and hold the manufacturer responsible for problems that arise.

Monitoring the organism after its utilization in large-scale production also could be more cautious. Testing prior to release is difficult for some types of organism — and may not reveal much, since detecting subtle environmental impacts may require going beyond safely contained laboratory experiments. However, field testing the organism could pose the very unacceptable risks which the testing procedure is intended to probe. Thus, as Thomas McGarity concludes:

> Testing protocols for large-scale-release biotechnologies will have to be especially innovative. The most appropriate approach may be to use a sequential process similar to that used for drugs, in which drugs must first be evaluated in test systems and then in limited real-world situations. Laboratory experiments could attempt to characterize a microorganism's possible disease mechanisms before testing begins. In another attempt to reduce the probability of infection, a crippled version of the same microorganism could be used in the greenhouse during the first tests and later in the outside environment (McGarity, 1985, p. 46).

Another shortcoming is that regulations to date have not established precautions governing biogenetic wastes. A first step would be to prevent escape wherever possible.

> For biological waste to be treated effectively, all equipment which comes into contact with it should be autoclaved or steam-sterilized after each use ... In the industrial disposal of conventional biological waste, a margin of between 6 and 7 percent non-sterility is accepted. If this margin is accepted for the disposal of biogenetic waste, then a substantial quantity of novel organisms will be released into the environment (Wheale and McNalley, 1988, p. 144).

For this reason, the Natural Resources Defense Council maintains that 100 percent sterility should be mandated for waste discharge from industries using DNA techniques (Vogel, 1985). Among other steps, this presumably would require new procedures for testing contamination of equipment used in large-scale operations, along with keeping records of those tests.

No matter how wise "the regulatory guidelines and enforcement procedures, in large-scale biotechnology production, recovery and downstream processing, it is impossible to avoid leakages of microbial agents (Wheale and McNally, 1988, p. 129). Since escape cannot be prevented entirely, erring on the side of caution would require eliminating, reducing, or mitigating the consequences of such events. No such strategies presently exist, and it is not clear what they could be.

Planning for containment and mitigation can be very complex, since microorganisms readily exchange genetic material. Gene transfer among microbes is sufficiently extensive that "the whole kingdom of procaryotes has access to a common gene pool and is thus capable of large evolutionary jumps" (Wheale and McNally, 1988, p. 156). Of course, enfeebled organisms such as *E. Coli* K-12 can be used. However, in field applications the organism has to survive long enough to perform its designated tasks. Moreover, successful enfeeblement hinges in part on unpredictable interactions between the organism and the environment. Thus, "a great deal of research is needed before we can confidently accept a company's claim that a genetically modified organism will be confined to its appropriate place in the environment" (McGarity, 1985, p. 46). On the other hand, biotechnology proponents point out that gene transfer is a nonissue in ordinary efforts to control infectious diseases from *known* pathogens, so why should it be given a high priority in engineering organisms that don't start out as pathogens?

Some biotechnology companies are believed to be conducting research and field testing in Third World countries with lax regulations and low public awareness. While there are standardized protocols for handling microorganisms in affluent nations — along with professional norms and regulatory structures to enforce them — safety precautions cannot be enforced in countries where state regulatory agencies have grossly inadequate expertise and personnel. Of course any commercial products will ultimately have to be approved before they can be sold. Meanwhile, deliberate release of genetically altered organisms in the Third World conceivably could produce consequences in precisely those areas least able to respond effectively. So the lack of global agreements for regulating biotechnology is an obvious weakness in the current decision-making process.

There are consequences for domestic regulation as well. Since chemical, pharmaceutical, and bioengineering firms can point to the rapid progress available to manufacturers who test overseas, they may argue that American firms will be able to compete in international markets if and only if safety regulations in the U.S. are relaxed. The biotechnology industry and its allies have been successful in altering the terms of the debate, shifting public concerns and the political agenda away from safety, toward the issue of international competition (Plein, 1989). Those same companies actively petition Congress and the regulatory agencies for exemptions for various kinds of genetically engineered organisms. If there is an AIDS vaccine attributable to relaxed regulations overseas, there is sure to arise a drumbeat of complaints against excessive safety precautions. This may be inevitable, but it suggests that those who want to err on the side of caution need to push for institutionalization of a regulatory schema before political and economic pressures sweep away thoughts of caution.

3. Conclusion

Several issues merit emphasis. Economic and environmental issues hardly constitute the full range of risks posed by biotechnology. New capacities in human genetics perhaps top the list of those slighted in our analysis. Medical diagnostic testing arguably is in the process of placing unwise capacities in the hands of governments and businesses to discriminate among people on the basis of genetic makeup (Nelkin and Tancredi, 1989). The human genome project, intended to map the entire genetic structure of the species, has a troubling Brave-New-Worldesque aura (Suzuki and Knudtson, 1989).

Second, it is worth recalling that deliberate damage caused by humans using successful technologies has usually constituted a larger threat than anything done by accident. Native grasses and flowers were deliberately displaced by manmade hybrids of corn and wheat, forests were clear-cut, and many large wild animals were hunted to virtual (or actual) extinction, while domesticated ones flourish. The hybrids did not escape from containment and prove 'more biologically fit.' As philosopher Mark Sagoff points out, these changes stemmed from the hybrid's *appeal* to humans (Sagoff, 1989). There is reason to expect a repetition of that phenomenon as genetically engineered animals and plants become available. If we want to protect the natural environment from deliberate, successful releases of new organisms, the time to enact appropriate legal protections clearly is before lucrative new opportunities become available.

Third, whatever the risk from microorganisms for civilian purposes, *intentional* deployment of lethal pathogens could pose a far greater threat. The gruesome possibility of biological warfare predates the development of molecular genetics. A long list of toxins and other biological agents have been studied for their military potential, including anthrax, plague, and the AIDs virus (Wheale and McNally, 1988, 190–195). Few scientists or policy makers therefore have paid much attention to any additional threat from bio-engineered organisms (Piller, 1988). However, as molecular genetics becomes a 'black-box' technology that can be done with a personal computer and inexpensive lab equipment, there is a nontrivial risk that it will appeal to terrorist groups. Biotechnology may provide a way around an important barrier to bioterrorism, the fact that in their natural forms, many biological agents are not very destructive and are hard to diffuse.

While biological agents have not yet been used by terrorists, that hardly implies much about the future. It is almost a cliche that biologial weapons could be "the poor man's atomic bomb," because they can be produced relatively quickly and inexpensively, and without extremely high-powered scientific expertise. Political motives might actually make them weapons of choice.

> Terrorism is theater and as such depends on the use of audacious behavior to create a dramatic effect which will be amplified by the mass media. Given the revulsion to biological weapons . . . the simple threat of their use could provide a credible mechanism of coercion. (And) as public sensitivity toward violence becomes more blunted, terrorists may seek increasingly demonstrative acts of terror in order to command the attention of the media (Wiegele and Oots, 1989, 8–9).

A few observers suggest that it may eventually become possible to design biowarfare agents specifically targeted toward particular ethnic groups, enabling genocidal campaigns rivaling the holocaust (Wiegele and Oots, 1989).

Turning from substantive to procedural worries, there is an uncomfortable correspondence between the nearly unbridled enthusiasm for biotechnology and previous cases of overoptimism about the social effects of technology. Virtually every new technology is introduced with glowing promises about its benefits. While many of these turn out to be partially fulfilled, major technological systems also change the fabric of society in unexpected and sometimes unfortunate ways. The ebbing of skepticism about biotechnology in the 1980s is particularly reminiscent of the unfortunate cycle of concern about ozone depletion. Intense debate in the mid-1970s led several nations to ban aerosol fluorocarbons, but then scientific evidence temporarily became more reassuring, and the media's issue-attention cycle turned to other issues. By the time the ozone hole over Antarctica was confirmed in the mid-1980s, there had been an extra decade of escalating worldwide releases of fluorocarbons and other ozone-depleting chemicals.

In sum, compared with previous technological controversies, biotechnology has shown some improvement along each of the dimensions required for low-cost learning from experience: early debate, flexible structuring, initial precautions, and accelerated learning. However, current protections against environmental releases of commercial biotechnology do not conform to these theoretical requirements nearly as well as did the regulations originally adopted for recombinant DNA research in the 1970s. No strategies are being used to promote social justice in distributing the costs and benefits of this new technology. Bioterrorism is scarcely mentioned as a threat, even in the research literature. No authoritative forum is addressing the issue of whether humans are prepared to make wise use of new medical diagnostics and interventions that molecular genetics is making possible.

Altogether, despite early scrutiny of biotechnology's risks, despite several decades of bad experience with rapidly deployed technologies like nuclear power and fluorocarbons, despite development of a widespread environmental consciousness, thinking and behavior toward technology nevertheless remains rather childlike. We run toward the shiny object in the street, instead of stopping to look both ways for oncoming dangers. Thus, biotechnology commercialization conforms fairly closely with the normal pattern of technological politics: proceed rapidly with research and commercialization of new technical potentials, and hope they will translate into human betterment despite massive technological momentum. Need it be said that hope is a poor substitute for strategy?

References

Berardi, Gigi and Charles Geisler. 1984. *The Social Consequences and Challenges of Agricultural Technologies*. Boulder CO: Westview Press.

Browne, William P., and Larry G. Hamm. 1988. "Political Choice and Social Values: The Case of bGH," *Policy Studies Journal* 17: 181–192.

Busch, Lawrence, and William B. Lacy. 1983. *Science, Agriculture, and the Politics of Research*. Boulder CO: Westview.

Buttel, Frederick H. et al. 1985. "From Green Revolution to Biorevolution: Some Observations on the Changing Technological Bases of Economic Transformation in the Third World," *Economic Development and Cultural Change* 34(1): 31–55.

Collingridge, David. 1980. *The Social Control of Technology*. New York: St. Martin's Press.

Collingridge, David. 1983. *Technology in the Policy Process: The Control of Nuclear Power*. New York: St. Martin's Press.

Conservation Foundation Letter. 1988. "Biotechnologies Are Tricky to Manage in the Third World." 6: 1–8.

Daly, Peter. 1985. *The Biotechnology Business: A Strategic Analysis*. London: Rowman, Allanheld.

Drucker, Peter F. 1973. "New Technology: Predicting Its Impact" *The New York Times*, April 8. Reprinted in *Technology and the Future*. Albert H. Teich, (ed.), 4th ed. New York: St. Martin's Press.

Fiksel, Joseph. 1986. *Biotechnology Risk Assessment*. New York: Pergamon.

Flavell, R. B., et al. 1986. Plants and Agriculture. pp. 199–221 in Silver 1986.

Goodman, David, Bernardo Sorj, and John Wilkinson. 1987. *From Farming to Biotechnology: A Theory of Agro-Industrial Development*. Oxford: Basil Blackwell.

Gore, Sen. Albert, Jr. 1987. "Gene Revolution's Progress Must Be Aimed Toward Helping Small Individual Farmers," *Genetic Engineering News* 7 (May), 4.

Hacking, Andrew J. 1986. *Economic Aspects of Biotechnology*. London: Cambridge University Press.

Hanson, Betsy, and Dorothy Nelkin. 1989. "Public Responses to Genetic Engineering," *Society* November/December, p. 77.

Harlow, Ruth E. 1986. "The EPA and Biotechnology Regulation: Coping with Scientific Uncertainty," *The Yale Law Journal* 95: 553–576.

House Committee on Science and Technology. 1986. *Issues in the Federal Regulation of Biotechnology*. Washington, D.C.: USGPO.

Hughes, Thomas Parke. 1983. *Networks of Power*. Baltimore: Johns Hopkins.

Kalter, Robert J. 1985. "The New Biotech Agriculture: Unforeseen Economic Consequences, *Issues in Science and Technology* Fall, 125–133.

Kenney, Martin, and Frederick H. Buttel. 1985. "Biotechnology: Prospects and Dilemmas for Third World Development," *Development and Change* 16: 70–89.

Klausner, Arthur. 1985. "Food from the Sea," *Bio/Technology*, January: 26–32.

Kloppenburg, Jack R. 1988. *First the Seed: The Political Economy of Plant Biotechnology*. London: Cambridge University Press.

Kloppenburg, Jack, Jr. 1984. "The Social Impacts of Biogenetic Technology in Agriculture: Past and Future." In Gigi Berardi and Charles Geisler, (eds.), *The Social Consequences and Challenges of Agricultural Technologies*.

Krimsky, Sheldon. 1982. *Genetic Alchemy: The Social History of the Recombinant DNA Controversy*. Cambridge, MA: The MIT Press.

Lemonick, Michael, D. 1987. "Montana State's Troublesome Elms," *Time Magazine*, September 14, p. 67.

Levin, Simon A., and Mark A. Harwell. 1985. "Environmental Risks and Genetically Engineered Organisms." In Sandra Panem, (ed.), *Biotechnology: Implications for Public Policy*. Washington, D.C.: The Brookings Institution.

Lindblom, Charles E. 1959. "The Science of 'Muddling Through,'" *Public Administration Review* 19: 79–88.

Lindblom, Charles E. 1965. *The Intelligence of Democracy*. New York: Free Press.

McGarity, Thomas O. 1985. "Regulating Biotechnology," *Issues in Science and Technology* 1(3): 40–56.

Morone, Joseph, and Edward J. Woodhouse. 1986. *Averting Catastrophe: Strategies for Regulating Risky Technologies*. Berkeley: University of California Press.

Morone, Joseph, and Edward J. Woodhouse. 1989. *The Demise of Nuclear Energy? Lessons for Democratic Control of Technology*. New Haven, CT: Yale University Press.

National Research Council. 1987. *Agricultural Biotechnology: Strategies for National Competitiveness.* Washington, D.C.: National Academy Press.

Nelkin, Dorothy, and Laurence Tancredi. 1989. *Dangerous Diagnostics: The Social Power of Biological Information.* New York: Basic Books.

Office of Science and Technology Policy. 1984. "Proposal for a Coordinated Framework for Regulation of Biotechnology," *Federal Register* 49 (December 31), pp. 50,856–50,907.

Office of Technology Assessment. 1988a. *U.S. Investment in Biotechnology.* Washington, D.C.: U.S. Congress, Office of Technology Assessment.

Office of Technology Assessment. 1988b. *Public Responses to Biotechnology.* Washington. D.C.: U.S. Congress, Office of Technology Assessment.

Office of Technology Assessment. 1986. *Technology, Public Policy, and the Changing Structure of American Agriculture.* OTA-F-285, Washington D.C.: U.S. Congress, Office of Technology Assessment.

Orsenigo, Luigi. 1989. *The Emergence of Biotechnology: Institutions and Markets.* New York: St. Martin's Press.

Pendorff, Stephan. 1985. "Regulating the Environmental Release of Genetically Engineered Organisms: *Foundation on Economic Trends v. Heckler*," *Florida State University Law Review* 12: 891–921.

Piller, Charles. 1988. *Gene Wars: Military Control Over the New Genetic Technologies.* London: Beech Tree Books.

Plein, L. Christopher. 1989. *The Emergence of the Pro-Biotechnology Coalition: Issue Development and the Agenda Setting Process.* Atlanta, Georgia: American Political Science Association.

Rauch, Jonathan. 1987. "Drug on the Market," *National Journal*, April 4, pp. 818–821.

Robertson, F. Dale. 1988. "Rise to the Future: The Forest Service Fisheries Program," *Fisheries* (May-June) 13(3): 22–23.

Sagoff, Mark. 1989. *On Making Nature Safe for Biotechnology.* Unpublished manuscript, University of Maryland.

Senate Committee on Environment and Public Works. 1986. *Releasing Genetically Engineered Organisms into the Enviroment.* Washington, D.C.: USGPO.

Silver, S. 1986. *Biotechnology: Potentials and Limitations.* New York: Springer-Verlag.

Stewart, G. G. 1983. "Impact of Biotechnology on the Food and Beverage Sector." In *BIOTECH 83.* Northwood UK: On line Publications Ltd.

Sussman, Max. 1988. *The Release of Genetically-Engineered Micro-organisms.* New York: Academic Press.

Suzuki, David, and Peter Knudtson. 1989. *Genetics: The Clash Between the New Genetics and Human Values.* Cambridge, MA: Harvard University Press.

Tangley, Laura. 1986. "Biotechnology on the Farm," *BioScience* 36(9): 590–593.

Vandenbergh, Michael P. 1986. "The Rutabaga That Ate Pittsburgh: Federal Regulation of Free Release Biotechnology," *Virginia Law Review* 72: 1529–1568.

Vogel, S. 1985. "Biogenetic Waste: A Federal and Local Problem," *GeneWATCH*, 2(4): 7–9.

Wenzel, Lauren. 1986. "Congress Enters Biotech Regulatory Arena," *BioScience*, 36(5): 305–306.

Wheale, Peter R., and Ruth M. McNally. 1988. *Genetic Engineering: Catastrophe or Utopia?* New York: St. Martin's Press.

Wheat, David. 1986. "Strategies for Commercialization of Biotechnology in the Food Industry." In S. K. Harlander and T. P. Labuza, (eds). *Biotechnology in Food Processing*. Park Ridge, NJ: Noyes Publications.

Wiegele, Thomas C., and Kent Layne Oots. 1989. "Biotechnology and Terrorism: Characteristics of Organizations Likely to Employ Biological Weapons." Presented at the American Political Science Association meeting, Atlanta, August 31, 1989.

Winner, Langdon. 1977. *Autonomous Technology: Technics-out-of-control as a Theme in Political Thought*. Cambridge, MA: MIT Press.

Winner, Langdon. 1986. *The Whale and the Reactor: The Search for Limits in an Age of High Technology*. Chicago: University of Chicago Press.

Woodhouse, Edward J. 1988. "Sophisticated Trial-and-Error in Decision Making about Risk." In Michael E. Kraft and Norman J. Vig, (eds.), *Technology and Politics*. Durham: Duke University Press.

Worthington, Richard, and Michael Black. 1986. The Center for Industrial Innovation at RPI: Critical Reflections on New York State's Economic Recovery. In Morton Schoolman and Alvin Magid, editors. *The Reindustrialization of New York*. Albany, NY: SUNY Press.

Wright, Susan. 1986. "Molecular Biology or Molecular Politics? The Production of Scientific Consensus on the Hazards of Recombinant DNA Technology," *Social Studies of Science* 16: 593–620.

Yoxen, Edward. 1984. *The Gene Business: Who Should Control Biotechnology*. New York: Harper and Row.

Zilinskas, Raymond A., and Burke K. Zimmerman. 1986. *The Gene-Splicing Wars: Reflections on the Recombinant DNA Controversy*. New York: Macmillan.

7 GAINING ACCEPTANCE FOR NOXIOUS FACILITIES WITH ECONOMIC INCENTIVES

Howard Kunreuther*
Douglas Easterling

In recent years considerable controversy has surrounded efforts to site prisons, AIDS treatment centers, and every form of waste disposal facility. While these facilities benefit the majority of the public, they also impose some burden on residents living near the site. Familiar terms such as NIMBY (Not in My Backyard) and LULU (Locally Unwanted Land Use) permeate the media, indicating the strong resistance shown by communities targeted to host these facilities (Popper, 1983). This public opposition is often effective in thwarting projects. For example, since 1980 not a single major new hazardous waste disposal facility has been sited anywhere in the United States, and the outlook does not appear any brighter in the immediate future (Weidenbaum, 1989). The key questions addressed in this chapter are 1) why there is such resistance to siting facilities and 2) whether there are ways that policy makers can reduce the level of resistance to such facilities. The following three examples provide concrete illustrations of the challenges we face in finding locations for siting facilities:

---

* Howard Kunreuther is Riklis Professor in the Practice of Creative Management and Director of the Risk and Decision Processes Center, and Douglas Easterling is with the Risk and Decision Processing Center, Wharton School, University of Pennsylvania.

1.1. Solid-Waste Facilities

With many communities adopting mandatory recycling laws, there is a need for solid-waste processing centers to handle newspapers, metal, glass, and plastic. Although the idea of recycling is immensely popular, few people appear to want a solid-waste facility in their neighborhood.

1.2. Incinerators

Many experts argue that other than waste reduction, incineration represents one of the more promising solutions for dealing with hazardous chemical wastes (Sweet, Ross, and Velde, 1985). Indeed, the federal Resource Conservation and Recovery Act (RCRA) contains provisions designed to increase the role of incineration. While many industrial firms would like to build incinerators to treat their waste, they often find it difficult to convince local citizens and public officials to accept such a facility.

1.3. High-Level Radioactive Waste Repository

One of the major environmental dilemmas currently facing the United States is how and where to store high-level radioactive wastes that have been generated by the nation's commercial and military reactors. In 1982, Congress instituted what it considered to be a fair siting procedure, the Nuclear Waste Policy Act (NWPA), to locate two repositories, one in the eastern United States and one in the western United States. For each repository, the Department of Energy would simultaneously study the three most suitable sites to determine which one best met a complex set of geologic and hydrologic safety criteria.

This siting policy has been badly compromised in practice (Merkhofer and Keeney, 1987; Carter, 1987, 1989; Shapiro, 1988). In 1986, the Reagan administration abandoned the plan to build the eastern repository to avoid political opposition from densely populated states to the repository program. In 1987 Congress amended NWPA to authorize studies at only at a single site. Yucca Mountain in Nevada was designated largely because it was anticipated that this would minimize public dissent; Nevada was by far the least populated of the three states in contention, and many residents of the southern part of the state are already employed by the federal government on nuclear projects such as weapons testing.

In spite of this seemingly auspicious set of circumstances, Nevadans strongly resisted having the repository in their state, prompting the Nevada legislature to outlaw the disposal of high-level nuclear waste within the state, and the state attorney general to file suit against the federal government to block work at Yucca Mountain. The intense public scrutiny accompanying the repository program has also had the effect of forcing Department of Energy (DOE) Secretary James Watkins in November 1989 to reevaluate the studies that the DOE was relying on to determine the suitability of the Yucca Mountain site, thus postponing the building of the repository.

The common thread connecting these three examples is that the facility in question is perceived by the public as imposing an unwanted burden — health risk, economic loss, negative environmental impact, psychological cost — on nearby residents. Such perceptions make it extremely difficult to obtain the local acceptance, or tolerance, that is required to build the facility. Yet at the same time, the public generally recognizes that these facilities must be built to dispose of residential and industrial waste.

We will discuss the factors important in locating a facility, and will propose a siting procedure that may facilitate this contentious process. Particular emphasis will be placed on the role of incentives in the form of compensation or benefits to the host community, and also the conditions under which trade-offs between risk and benefits appear to be appropriate.

In analyzing the siting problem, we draw on two surveys of public attitudes toward a high-level nuclear waste (HLNW) repository. The results of these surveys suggest that a repository will be perceived as acceptably safe only if the *siting process* instills trust and public confidence. Compensation packages alone are not likely to allay public concerns. Although an HLNW repository differs from other noxious facilities such as a solid-waste processing plant or an incinerator, the findings from our surveys are informative for these other siting contexts as well.

2. Public Opposition to Facilities

The central issue associated with siting a new facility can be stated rather simply. A community or state is asked to host a facility that benefits the region as a whole, but which fails to provide positive net benefits to the residents living in the vicinity of the facility. For example, one of the difficulties in finding a home for solid-waste processing centers, incinerators, and repositories is that few if any direct benefits (e.g., employment opportunities) accrue to the host community. At the same time, these facilities are perceived to entail major health and environmental risks. This provokes intense public opposition.

A task force recently established in Ontario to facilitate the siting of a low-level radioactive waste facility in the province concluded that social and political issues are pivotal and much more difficult to resolve than technical issues. In discussing the siting problem with citizens, municipal officials, regulators, and public interest groups, the task force learned that opposition to facilities is due to 1) lack of trust of government and experts, 2) high perceived risk and fear of stigma of the facility, 3) desire for control by citizens in the community over what happens to the facility, and 4) a perceived inequity between those who benefit and those who live near the facility and who hence bear most of its costs (Rennick and Greyell, 1990).

For most waste-disposal facilities, the crucial determinant of public opposition is the high level of perceived risk associated with the handling and storage of hazardous and radioactive materials. For an incinerator, the major public concerns include the emission of carcinogenic heavy metals into the air and the concentration of heavy metals in the bottom ash. A radioactive waste repository presents a potential cancer risk from the leaching of wastes into the groundwater or from an accidental release during the transport of the spent fuel rods from reactors to the facility.

The risks associated with these facilities are viewed as high, at least in part because of the novelty of the technology. When one decides whether or not to take a particular job, a historical record is normally available to allow an assessment of the health and safety risks of that employment. In contrast, with new technological facilities, such as a waste incinerator, there is little or no historical experience to estimate the probability and consequences of a release of toxic substances. Uncertainty regarding the size of the risk is further compounded by discrepancies—sometimes of more than an order of magnitude—in the risk assessments reported by "experts." Faced with this uncertainty, residents may feel justified in assuming that the facility's risks are very high.

The public's perception of risk is not fully explained by traditional factors of probabilities and loss magnitudes. Instead, risk severity depends on subjective features such as the voluntariness of exposure, familiarity, catastrophic potential, and dread (Fischhoff, Slovic, Lichtenstein, Read, and Combs, 1978; Slovic, 1987). The perceived risks associated with nuclear facilities—commercial nuclear reactors, nuclear weapons production plants, radioactive waste repositories—are especially severe, since these facilities occupy highly negative positions on factors such as dread. Mufson (1982) has argued further that nuclear technologies are rejected because they are inextricably linked with nuclear warfare and thus viewed as immoral.

Public attitudes toward waste disposal facilities (especially for nuclear) wastes) are also influenced by the perceived impact on future generations. MacLean (1983) notes that the degree to which a geologic repository is acceptable depends both on one's assumptions regarding the long-term impacts of the available alternatives and on one's sense of moral obligation to those individuals who do not have a voice in the decision-making process. Similarly, Kneese et al. (1983) show that a benefit-cost analysis of the potential siting of a radioactive waste repository in New Mexico will be crucially affected by the choice of a discount rate. That is, much will hinge on the degree of consideration given to the welfare of future generations.

Citizens in communities selected to host disposal facilities also express concern regarding the economic impacts. A major source of anxiety for local residents is the possibility that the facility will reduce property values. Such declines have occurred with some, but certainly not all, noxious facilities (Metz, Morey, and Lowry, 1990). In a particularly extensive analysis of this question, McClelland, Schulze, and Hurd (1990) found evidence of depressed property values in the vicinity of an abandoned hazardous waste dump, with the level of loss strongly related to the degree of perceived risk characterizing the neighborhood. Higher levels of perceived risk, and thus greater reductions in property value, were observed in areas afflicted by "risk cues" (odors).

Economic effects may spread widely for nuclear waste facilities, possibly categorizing an entire region as a wasteland or unhealthy place (Slovic, et al., 1989). For example, agricultural communities in eastern Washington state were concerned that the establishment of a nuclear-waste repository at Hanford would be seen as leading to the contamination of fruits and wines grown in the area, thereby causing a decline in the economy (Dunlap and Baxter, 1988). Other studies have raised the possibility that the stigma of a nuclear waste repository could negatively affect tourism (Kunreuther, Easterling, and Kleindorfer, 1988; Slovic, et al. 1989; Easterling and Kunreuther, 1990).

While these negatives would in themselves provide sufficient cause for public opposition, they also tend to be exacerbated by geographic inequity. The benefits of radioactive waste repositories accrue to individuals throughout a wide area, primarily to the consumers of nuclear power. However, the costs attendant to disposal are generally concentrated in communities near the disposal facility and along transportation corridors (Kasperson and Rubin, 1983). Thus, residents of a host community object not only that they will be made worse off, but also that this incursion is unfair.

Any disposal facility provides local residents with an incentive to register opposition. However, the intensity of this opposition will undoubtedly vary as a function of the type of facility. A survey of diverse populations (e.g., urban residents, environmentalists, chemical and nuclear engineers) by Lindell and Earle (1983) found a wide disparity in individuals' willingness to live nearby such facilities. The general public was much less tolerant (i.e., willing to live within 10 miles) of waste disposal facilities than of nonnuclear power plants or oil refineries. For example, 68 percent of urban residents were willing to live or work within 10 miles of a natural gas power plant, compared to 24 percent for a toxic chemical disposal facility, and only 15 percent for a nuclear waste disposal facility.

3. Perceived Risk of a High-Level Nuclear Waste Repository

3.1. Surveys

Our own research can provide a more in-depth portrait of the public's attitudes toward living near nuclear waste disposal facilities. We conducted two telephone surveys of the public's attitudes toward the siting of a high-level nuclear waste repository. The first of these surveys queried 1,001 Nevada residents, with a deliberate oversampling of residents in two rural counties near the proposed Yucca Mountain site. The second survey was conducted on a national sample of 1,201 individuals from states other than Nevada, Alaska, and Hawaii. Because of the modest response rates (approximately 37 percent), and the oversampling aspect of the Nevada survey, the distribution of attitudes reported by these samples may not correspond exactly to opinion in the general population. Still, we believe the results are instructive.

The two surveys were conducted in the spring of 1987 at a time when there were still three candidates for the first repository—Hanford, Washington; Deaf Smith, Texas; and Yucca Mountain, Nevada. The Nevada survey elicited respondents' attitudes toward the possibility of locating a repository at Yucca Mountain, while the national survey asked respondents how they would view the location of a hypothetical repository either 50 or 100 miles from their home. Respondents were randomly assigned to one of these two distance conditions.

3.2. Level of Risk

A series of questions probed the nature of risk perceptions associated with a HLNW repository. These risk perceptions included not only accident probabilities and consequences, but also the more subjective features of controllability and dread. The responses to these questions are shown for the Nevada sample in table 7.1. The national sample has very similar data.

From table 7.1, it is clear that this sample has a very pessimistic view of the safety of the proposed repository. Two of the queried events — wastes leaking into groundwater and accidental release during transport — are each regarded as very likely by over one-third of the sample. Each of these two events is regarded as at least somewhat likely by approximately three-fourths of the sample. The other two events considered in the survey, accidents at the repository and sabotage, were deemed slightly less likely. However, these questions taken as a whole suggest that Nevada residents believe that releases of radiation into the environment are certainly plausible, with the perceived probability much higher than is assumed by the federal government's experts.

Table 7.1 also indicates how seriously the consequences of an accidental release are regarded. Almost three-fourths of the sample either agree or strongly agree that an accident at the repository would result in certain death, while approximately 80 percent agree or strongly agree that an accident could kill many people at once.

The subjective nature of the repository risk is illustrated by the last two items in table 7.1. The vast majority of the Nevada sample (86 percent) believe that the risks cannot be controlled by those living near the repository. Similarly, there is a strong consensus (74 percent) that the risks associated with the facility would invoke dread on the part of nearby residents.

In light of these perceptions, it is not surprising that respondents appraise the risk of a repository to be serious in an overall sense. These more general evaluations are shown in table 7.2. Items included here indicate the perceived severity of the risk not only to the respondent, but also to others who would be affected by the repository — other residents of the state and future generations.

The perceived severity of the personal risk was gauged by having respondents rate (on a scale from 1 to 10) the seriousness of the risk to themselves from the repository and a number of other hazards. As shown in table 7.2, respondents indicated that a repository at Yucca Mountain would

Table 7.1. Perceived Risk from a Repository at Yucca Mountain
Nevada Sample (n = 1001)

	Likelihood of Accidents and Exposure				
	Very Unlikely	Somewhat Unlikely	Don't Know	Somewhat Likely	Very Likely
An accident at the repository	14%	23%	2%	38%	23%
Radiation released during transport of wastes	6%	14%	2%	44%	35%
Wastes leaking into groundwater	10%	15%	2%	34%	38%
Terrorist sabotage at the repository	15%	27%	3%	32%	24%
	Consequences of a Repository Accident				
	Strongly Disagree	Disagree	Don't Know	Agree	Strongly Agree
Certain Death	3%	20%	3%	50%	24%
Kill many people at once	3%	16%	3%	53%	26%
	Other Indicators of Risk				
	Strongly Disagree	Disagree	Don't Know	Agree	Strongly Agree
Persons living nearby could control risk	21%	65%	2%	12%	1%
Repository would be dreaded by residents	2%	20%	5%	54%	20%

pose more serious risks than any they were currently facing. It is interesting to note that technological hazards that may cause cancer (i.e., the repository, exposure to hazardous chemicals, nuclear testing, and nuclear power) are regarded as more serious than the more common hazards involving accidental injury and death.

Table 7.2 also demonstrates that the respondents consider the risks posed by the repository to be serious on a societal level. Although the repository will generate employment during its construction, these benefits do not offset the perceived risks; only 27 percent of the sample agrees or strongly agrees that nearby residents would accrue more benefits than risk. In terms of the temporal dimension, the vast majority of the sample (77 percent) believes the risks to future generations will be serious.

Table 7.2. Appraisals of Seriousness of Repository Risk to Self and Others
Nevada Sample

Seriousness of Risk to Self [1-to-10 scale]				*Mean*
Repository at Yucca Mountain				5.6
Exposure to hazardous chemicals				5.2
Nuclear weapons testing				4.7
Nuclear power plants				4.3
Accident at work				4.1
Accident at home				3.9

	Seriousness of Risk to Others				
	Strongly Disagree	*Disagree*	*Don't Know*	*Agree*	*Strongly Agree*
Benefits would outweigh risks to nearby residents	14%	50%	8%	24%	3%
Poses serious risks to future generations	3%	25%	6%	41%	26%

3.3. Relation of Risk to Voting Behavior

In addition to assessing the public's perceptions of the repository risk, we also wanted to test how important perceived risk might be in dictating the public's opposition to the repository. To do this, respondents indicated how they would vote if a referendum were held on where to locate the repository: 1) at Yucca Mountain, 2) at Hanford, 3) at Deaf Smith, or 4) none of these. The interesting question is what perceptions characterize those who are accepting of a local repository (i.e., those Nevadans who are willing to vote in favor of Yucca Mountain). We thus divided the sample into those who voted for Yucca Mountain (24 percent of the sample) and those who provided one of the other responses.[1]

A logistic regression analysis was used to assess the relationship between perceived risk and willingness to vote for Yucca Mountain. Here we used the three risk appraisal items shown in table 7.2; 1) risk to self, 2) risk versus benefits to nearby residents, and 3) risk to future generations. In this way, we could test whether opposition to the repository depended solely upon the impact to oneself or, alternatively, whether broader social welfare considerations determined opposition.

The analysis found all three risk indicators to be highly significant independent predictors of the vote item. In particular, perceived risk to self, taken alone, could not explain the observed vote responses; many of those who saw little or no risk to themselves voted against Yucca Mountain. This behavior can be easily explained once individuals' perceptions of the societal risk were taken into account; a positive vote generally required perceptions of safety to oneself, to nearby residents, and to future generations.

The independent nature of the effects is apparent from figure 7.1, which shows the proportion of votes in favor of Yucca Mountain as a function of risk to self and risk to future generations.[2] This figure demonstrates that perceptions of risk to future generations reduces acceptance, controlling for the level of perceived risk to oneself. For example, when there is no perceived risk to self, there is a 56 point difference between those who perceive the risk to future generations to be serious (28%), and those who view it as not serious (84%).

3.4. Concern for Future Generations

These data suggest that individuals do not discount the future consequences of nuclear waste storage (the risks are expected to endure for up to 10,000 years). Svenson and Karlsson's study of nuclear waste disposal also found that many individuals were reluctant to discount future projected losses. One reason for this may be the irreversible features associated with storing high-level radioactive waste in the repository.

It is interesting to contrast the public opposition shown to a repository with the largely lackluster response to the radon problem. That is, the public reacts aggressively to the radiation risks from nuclear waste, but seems 'accepting' of the arguably much higher level of radiation risk associated with radon exposure. This cavalier attitude towards radon is manifest in the fact that relatively few residents at potential risk have their homes tested for radon. The lack of response to radon is intriguing because this risk also poses a threat to future generations of children living in the home. Some of the discrepancy between these two sources of risk obviously stems from differences in the etiology of the risk: individuals cannot blame others for creating the radon risk since the causes are natural (Weinstein, Sandman, and Klotz, 1987). However, it might also be the case that homeowners will resist testing for radon even if they recognize that the gas could cause serious risk to their children; the effects of radon may be erroneously viewed as a *fait accompli*. That is, an

% Vote for Yucca
   Mountain

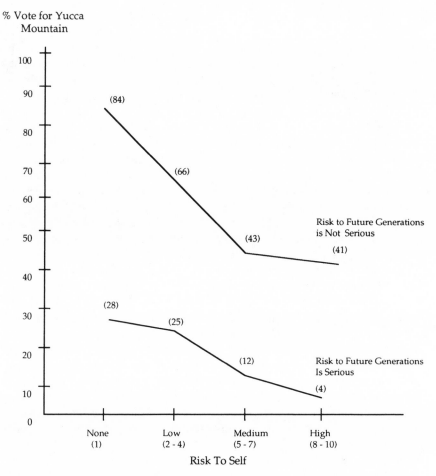

Figure 7.1.   Effect of risk to future generations and risk to self on willingness to vote in favor of Yucca Mountain site.

individual living in a radon-contaminated home may believe that whatever ill effects will occur are already determined, so that testing would serve only to provoke fear and guilt. In contrast, individuals are more motivated to respond to a HLNW repository because they see the potential to prevent the initial imposition of risk upon their descendants.

4. Sharing Benefits to Reduce Local Opposition

The previous analysis indicates that residents oppose noxious facilities in their immediate neighborhood because of the perceived costs—especially the potential health risks. One might argue that these facilities could be rendered acceptable if the costs were somehow offset by a benefits package. Such a package could take different forms: 1) reductions in the taxes paid by local residents, 2) grants to municipalities to provide better schools, new parks, or improved health and social services, or 3) in-kind compensation such as a special emergency response unit placed at the community's disposal. These benefits could be financed by taxing the beneficiaries or by levying specific charges such as tipping fees on those using the facility.

For a benefits package to produce a positive outcome, the stakeholders with veto power must receive benefits that leave them better off with the facility than under the *status quo*. This suggests that importance of tailoring the package to the specific impacts that will occur. For example, residents who think that their area might be stigmatized by the facility will undoubtedly be concerned with losses to property values. Hence, some plan to guarantee the home values in the community is essential to overcome opposition. Champion International Corporation recently established a program to protect the property values of residents within two miles of an industrial landfill it is siting. The company monitors changes in the sale prices in the county over a ten-year period and pays residents if there are any adverse changes in the property value due to the presence of the landfill (Ewing, 1990).

To construct an appropriate benefits package it is necessary to determine the 'cost' that the facility imposes on the key stakeholders; for a benefits package to be effective, it must offset the costs incurred by these individuals. Here, we first present a simple economic model that specifies how benefits balance off against a facility's inherent risks, and then provide an empirical assessment of the costs that a high-level nuclear waste repository would impose on local residents.

4.1. Economic Model

A simple two-period expected utility model developed in Kunreuther and Easterling (1990) provides a framework for examining the relationship between benefits and risks for a representative individual residing in a community that is a candidate for a facility such as a radioactive waste repository.[3] In constructing our model, we first simplify the task by assuming that the facility's negative impact can be represented in the form of a single risk, R.[4] R denotes the risk that a given individual thinks he or she would face if the facility were built. For relatively benign facilities, such as landfills, R might be the risk that one's property values will decline. In contrast, for facilities such as radioactive waste repositories, R might be the risk of wastes contaminating the groundwater and producing cancer. R is defined in terms of the probability (p) that the negative event will occur and the size of the loss (L) the individual suffers if the event occurs. The values of p and L reflect the person's perceived risk associated with the facility rather than the estimates of scientific experts.

The model divides the lifetime of the facility into two periods — period 1, in which the facility is built and the person receives some benefit B, and period 2 in which the facility operates (with risk R). The question addressed by the model is "What level of benefit, B^*, makes the individual just as well off with the facility as he or she would be under the *status quo*?" In other words, we want to determine a B^* that just offsets the costs an individual associates with the facility. To determine B^*, consider an individual who faces the choice either to maintain the *status quo* or to accept the facility with its attendant risks and benefits. Each of these two options will have some utility to the decision maker. For simplicity, but without loss of generality, we assume that the utility associated with having the facility in one's community is given by the following two-period additive utility function:

$$U(\mathbf{y}, \mathbf{F}) = U_1(y_1, F_1) + U_2(y_2, F_2) \qquad [1]$$

In this equation, y_t denotes the individual's income in period t (either 1 or 2) and F_t denotes the consequences of the facility during period t. The vectors $\mathbf{y}$ and $\mathbf{F}$ are defined as simply $\mathbf{y} = (y_1, y_2)$ and $\mathbf{F} = (F_1, F_2)$. For each period t, U_t represents a von Neumann-Morgenstern utility function.

The individual faces a choice between: (1) maintaining the *status quo* (where $F_1 = 0$ and $F_2 = 0$); and (2) having the facility which provides a benefits package B during period 1, and imposes the risk (p, L) during period 2. The expected utility associated with the status quo is thus

$$U^0(\mathbf{y}, \mathbf{F}) = U_1(y_1, 0) + U_2(y_2, 0) \qquad [2]$$

while the expected utility associated with having the facility is

$$U^1(\mathbf{y}, \mathbf{F}) = U_1(y_1, B) + (1 - p)U_2(y_2, 0) + pU_2(y_2, L) \qquad [3]$$

The individual's preference between the status quo and having the facility is determined by the comparison between $U^0(\mathbf{y}, \mathbf{F})$ and $U^1(\mathbf{y}, \mathbf{F})$. This choice of whether to accept a facility is conceptually similar to a worker's decision of whether to accept a new job that entails an increased level of health risk, but provides higher pay. Fighter pilots, garbage collectors, and employees who work with hazardous materials are told that if they undertake a particular job, a portion of their wages reflects the special risks that they undertake.

The expected utility model allows one to specify the level of benefits $B*$ where an individual is indifferent between the status quo and having the facility in his or her immediate locale. In particular, $B*$ is defined as the level of benefits where the utility associated with the facility is equal to the utility of the status quo:

$$U_1(y_1,0) + U_2(y_2,0) = U_1(y_1,B*) + (1 - p)U_2(y_2,0) + pU_2(y_2,L)$$
[4]

If we rearrange terms, we obtain the following equation:

$$U_1(y_1,B*) - U_1(y_1,0) = -p[U_2(y_2,L) - U_2(y_2,0)]$$
[5]

This equation allows us to define $B*$ more precisely. $B*$ produces an improvement in utility during period 1 that just offsets the expected loss from the facility during period 2. Because of the highly subjective nature of the utility functions, and the estimates of p and L, the level of $B*$ that will produce indifference for a given individual must be determined empirically.

4.2. Benefit Packages for a Repository

The repository surveys explored the effect that alternative benefit packages would have on the willingness of residents to vote in favor of having a repository nearby. The first type of benefit we tested was in the form of an annual rebate on the respondent's federal income tax. This rebate could be either $1,000 per year, $3,000 per year, or $5,000 per year, depending on the experimental condition to which the respondent was assigned. In the survey of Nevada residents, respondents were told that rebates would accompany a repository at Yucca Mountain:

Suppose after thorough study, the federal government decided to put a high-level nuclear waste repository at Yucca Mountain in Nevada. This repository would be built according to federal safety standards. Suppose also that you could receive a [either $1,000/$3,000/$5,000] rebate or credit on your federal income taxes each year for 20 years. Would you vote to locate the repository at Yucca Mountain?[5]

In the national survey, rebates were associated with a hypothetical repository located near the respondent. Specifically, "at Yucca Mountain in Nevada" was replaced with "in a geologically safe place" either 50 miles or 100 miles away from the respondent's home—distance was manipulated experimentally. By design, only half of each sample was asked this question on rebates; the remainder answered an alternative question on valuation (discussed below).

The key research question concerns whether the offer of rebates would increase the proportion of respondents willing to vote in favor of a local repository. In other words, do large annual payments—at least $1,000 per year—offset the perceived risks of the repository for those who are otherwise opposed to having the facility nearby?

Results from this section of the questionnaire, which are presented in table 7.3, indicate that rebates of this size yield little if any increase in the acceptability of a repository. Table 7.3 shows that roughly 29 percent of each sample reported they would vote in favor of a repository with rebates. There were no significant differences either between survey or as a function of rebate level. More importantly, there was no significant difference in the Nevada sample between the proportion who voted for Yucca Mountain with rebates and the proportion voting for Yucca Mountain in a simple referendum where no benefits were specified (27 percent).[6]

These data suggest that the opponents of a repository—those who would vote against the Yucca Mountain site in a simple referendum—regard the facility's impact as not simply negative, but as severe. The rebate offers are relatively generous, but still failed to reduce opposition to the repository. This result indicates the extent to which opponents, who constitute a clear majority of the sample, perceive a repository as imposing risk to the health of current and future generations, environmental disruption, and economic dislocation. It may also suggest an unwillingness to trade off risks to other individuals in exchange for income for the respondents.

4.3. An Alternative Assessment of Repository Costs

In designing a benefits package to offset the losses of a repository, it is important to determine whether the costs associated with the facility are as high as implied by the responses to the rebate questions. For example, it is possible that respondents refused the rebate because they believed

Table 7.3. Willingness to Vote in Favor of a Nearby Repository in Return for Tax Rebates

	NEVADA SAMPLE Size of Annual Rebate			
Vote Response	$1,000	$3,000	$5,000	Overall
In Favor of Yucca Mtn	26%	30%	30%	29%*
Opposed to Yucca Mtn	68%	63%	65%	66%
Don't Know	5%	7%	5%	6%
	(n = 170)	(n = 162)	(n = 166)	(n = 498)

	NATIONAL SAMPLE Size of Annual Rebate			
Vote Response	$1,000	$3,000	$5,000	Overall
In Favor of Local Repository	29%	27%	29%	29%
Opposed to Local Repository	66%	69%	66%	67%
Don't Know	4%	4%	4%	4%
	(n = 204)	(n = 205)	(n = 194)	(n = 603)**

* Among these 498 respondents, 27% voted in favor of Yucca Mountain when no rebates were specified.
** Three other respondents in this survey refused to provide an answer.

that such behavior would extract more lucrative packages from the federal government. To obtain a more balanced indication of the actual costs imposed by a repository, we included in the survey a second question concerning the trade-off between money and the prospect of having a repository nearby.

Here, respondents were told to assume that a decision had tentatively been made to build a repository at a nearby location — at Yucca Mountain in the case of the Nevada sample, at a geologically safe place either 50 or 100 miles away in the case of the national sample. The choice then facing the respondents was whether they would pay a surcharge to their federal income taxes over the next 20 years in order to have the repository built at a more distant site.[7] As with the rebate question, respondents were assigned one of three different dollar amounts; they would need to pay either $100 per year, $500 per year, or $2,000 per year.[8]

In more formal terms, the rebate question measures the perceived cost of a repository using a "willingness-to-accept" (WTA) approach, while the extra-tax question employs a "willingness-to-pay" (WTP) approach. Under the WTA question, the respondent begins by assuming that he or she is living in a world without a repository, and indicates the amount of money that would have to accompany the repository to leave him or her at the same level of welfare; in this case, the dollar amount represents the cost imposed by the facility. Under the WTP question, the respondent begins with the repository scheduled to be built nearby and identifies an 'equivalent' world in which he or she is free of the repository and possesses less wealth; the amount he or she is willing to give up represents the benefit of avoiding the facility.

Under standard economic theory, the cost assigned to the repository under a WTA approach — the amount needed to offset a new repository — should be similar to the cost assigned under a WTP approach — the amount one is willing to pay to move a proposed repository. These values should differ only as a function of the 'income effect.' In the present case, this means that we should expect to see somewhat higher dollar values assigned to a repository in the WTA condition than in the WTP condition. The extent of the income effect will depend on the personal cost of the repository relative to an individual's total wealth: if individuals report WTP amounts that constitute only a small portion of their annual income, then the income effect should be minor (Willig, 1976).

4.4. Comparing WTA and WTP Reservation Prices

The major empirical task in this analysis of repository costs is to use the responses we observe to the WTA and WTP questions to obtain a distribution of underlying reservation prices associated with the repository. Each respondent was assigned a range of possible reservation prices based on his or her pattern of response to the initial and follow-up questions. For example, a respondent who votes against a repository in return for a rebate of $5,000 but votes in favor if given $10,000 has an implicit reservation price of between $5,000 and $10,000 per year. Likewise, with the WTP questions, a respondent who is unwilling to pay either $100 or $50 per year to avoid the planned repository has an implicit reservation price of less than $50.

For any given experimental condition defined by the type of question — WTA vs. WTP — and the dollar amount specified in the initial question (X), respondents were classified into the following seven price ranges: 1) less than $X/2, 2) exactly $X/2, 3) greater than $X/2 but less than $X, 4) exactly $X, 5) greater than $X and less than $2X, 6) exactly $2X, and 7) greater than $2X. The important question addressed with these data is how the reservation prices induced by the WTP items compare to those induced by the WTA (rebate) question. To test whether the values are comparable, we have plotted the cumulative frequency distribution for each of the six experimental conditions in figure 7.2 (Nevada sample) and figure 7.3 (national sample).

For each condition — either WTA or WTP, and a starting dollar amount, X — this graph indicates three points of cumulative distribution: 1) the proportion of the sample whose reservation price is $X/2 or less, 2) the proportion at $X or less, and 3) the proportion at $2X or less. For example, figure 7.2 shows that of those respondents in the Nevada sample who were asked the willingness-to-pay questions with a starting value of $100, 45 percent had an implicit reservation price of $50 or less, 61 percent had a price of $100 or less, and 73 percent had a price of $200 or less.[9].

The cumulative frequency distributions indicate that the reservation prices elicited under the WTA questions are much higher than those estimated using the WTP questions. For example, of those Nevada respondents asked for their willingness to pay (using $2,000 as the initial value), 64 percent had a reservation price of less than $1,000 and 73 percent had a reservation price of less than $2,000. In contrast, only 28 percent of the respondents in the willingness-to-accept for $1,000 condition report a reservation price less than $1,000, and 38 percent report a reservation price less than $2,000. More generally, in both samples, all three of the WTP conditions generate lower estimates of reservation price than any of the WTA conditions. For example, the median reservation price is estimated to be less than $1,000 under each of the WTP conditions, while it is greater than $2,000 under each of the WTA conditions.

4.5. WTP–WTA Discrepancies

The finding that individuals assign higher personal costs to a repository under a willingness-to-accept paradigm than under a willingness-to-pay paradigm is consistent with many other studies on contingent valuation of risk. For example, Viscusi, Magat, and Huber (1987) found that while consumers of an insecticide were willing to pay only a relatively small premium to reduce their health risk by a given amount, they generally refused to buy a much cheaper product that imposed only a very slight increase in risk. These findings suggest a very high WTA-based estimate of reservation price. Similarly, a survey by Gerking, De Haan, and Schulze (1988) found that the amount of extra pay that workers demanded to shift to a job with increased risk was two and a half times greater than

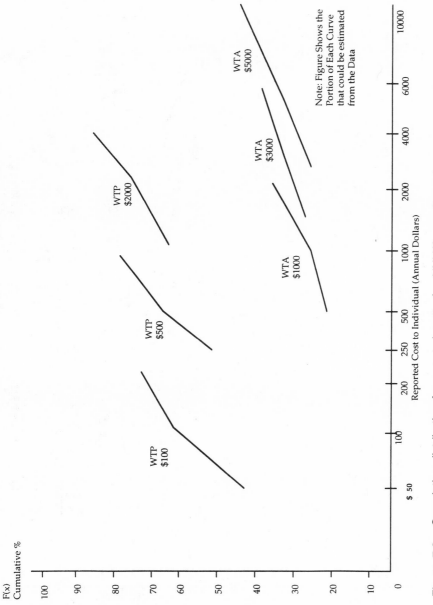

Figure 7.2. Cumulative distribution for reported cost of a HNLW repository at Yucca Mountain (Nevada sample).

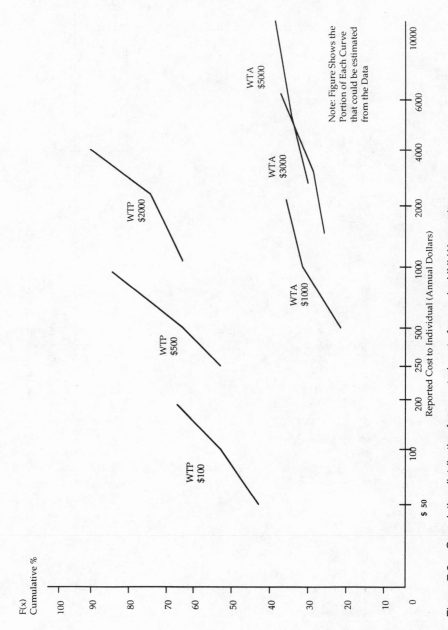

Figure 7.3.   Cumulative distribution for reported cost of a nearby HNLW repository (Nevada sample).

the amount they would be willing to give up to bring about an equivalent decrease in risk. This research documenting the discrepancy between WTP valuations and WTA valuations has a number of counterparts in domains other than risk — lottery tickets, common consumer goods such as pens, and societal goods such as forests (Thaler, 1980, 1985; Knetsch and Sinden, 1984; Cummings, Brookshire, and Schulze, 1986; Coursey, Hovis, and Schulze, 1987; Knetsch, Thaler and Kahneman, 1988; McClelland and Schulze, in press).

It is interesting to consider a number of possible sources of the discrepancy between the WTA-based assessments of repository cost and the WTP-based assessments. This helps us to draw some conclusion regarding the actual costs associated with living near a repository, and indicates the practical limitations of employing benefits packages such as rebates to elicit local acceptance. We explore the viability of five potential reasons in this section: 1) income effects, 2) loss aversion, 3) a general reluctance to pay for risk avoidance, 4) strategic behavior, and 5) objections to compensation.

Income effects.   From the standpoint of economic theory, the only reason one would expect to observe such a great discrepancy between WTP amounts and WTA amounts is an income effect. However, this explanation is refuted by the fact that income was not a significant predictor of either the WTP responses or the WTA responses. In a series of regression analyses that controlled for perceived risk, we found that poor respondents were just as likely to make payments and to reject rebates as were well-off respondents. This lack of a strong income effect strongly suggests that some other factor accounts for the large discrepancy between the results of the WTA and WTP conditions.

Loss aversion.   A second possible explanation for the WTA-WTP discrepancy concerns differences in the assumed *status quo* in the two questions. In the WTA question, the respondent begins in the situation where the repository has not yet been sited; he or she is asked what benefit is required to allow the repository to be built nearby. In this case, the respondent is asked to value a loss: how much compensation will offset the loss imposed by a repository? In contrast, the WTP question starts the respondent off in the situation where the repository is tentatively scheduled to be built nearby; he or she makes a payment to prevent the decision from being carried out. Here the commodity being valued, the removal of the repository, is a gain. This distinction between losses and gains has proved particularly useful in explaining behavior that appears anomalous, especially discrepancies between WTA and WTP (Kahneman and Tversky, 1979; Tversky and Kahneman, 1981; Thaler, 1985).

According to prospect theory advanced by Kahneman and Tversky's (1979), losses are move aversive than gains are pleasant. Such a theory helps explain the discrepancies observed in the current data. Those in the WTA condition are asked to forego a level of safety that they have taken for granted, whereas those in the WTP condition already operate under the assumption that they have lost this assurance.

Protest responses.　Another possible reason that WTP reservation prices are so much lower than the WTA values has to do with objections to the policy of paying an extra tax to avoid a risk. Some individuals who refused to pay $50 per year may regard the actual cost of the repository as greater than $50, but feel that there are strong technical reasons that the facility should not be built. In refusing to pay the prescribed amount, they are protesting the fact that they are forced into a position in which their willingness to pay dictates that the repository will be built somewhere else. The presence of these "protest responses" has been documented in other studies that have employed willingness-to-pay questions to assess the value assigned to risk reduction (Smith and Desvousges, 1987; Gerking, et al., 1988).

Strategic Behavior.　It is also possible that respondents may mold their responses in such a way as to extract better deals from the federal government. An individual who reports that he or she would be unwilling to accept $5,000 per year in return for voting in favor of a nearby repository may think that this response may elicit a more favorable offer from the government. In other words, there is a real incentive to respondents in the WTA condition to overreport their true reservation price.

The corresponding incentive to underreport in the WTP condition — to refuse to pay $X when one's reservation price is in fact greater than $X — is much less pronounced. In this condition, a false report fails to gain any strategic advantage. Refusing to accept an offer does not necessarily lead the federal government to offer a better deal, since the government has no real need to obtain these preemptive payments; if local residents refuse to make the payments, the default is that the repository is built at the proposed site.

Reluctance to Accept Payments.　Much of the discrepancy between WTA and WTP values appears to reflect a tendency for individuals to regard a rebate offer as a bride. In other words, respondents are unwilling to trade an increase in risk for an increase in dollars. This reluctance to make such a choice may run very deep in people. For instance, Calabresi and Bobbitt (1978) suggest that individuals may wish to preserve the belief that life is special. One way to address this concern for the increase in risk is to recast the benefit package in such a way that the benefits directly offset the aggregate health risks faced by local residents, rather than compensating for the excess risk with dollars. By channeling funds to local and state government for improved public services (e.g., better health care), residents of communities near the facility may attain higher levels of health *with* the facility than *without* it. Data from the repository surveys suggest that this form of benefit package is somewhat more acceptable to the public. Whereas rebates led the repository to be accepted by 29 percent of the Nevada sample, grants increased this rate to 33 percent. This difference is significant at $p < .05$, using a test of correlated proportions.

The reluctance to accept rebates in the present case is at odds with behavior commonly observed for other risks. In practice, individuals frequently engage in trade-offs between money and personal risk. For example, workers often voluntarily accept a premium on their wages in return for incurring an extra risk to their health — 'hazardous duty pay'. Indeed, economists evaluating the benefits of environmental and occupational regulation often rely on observed wage differentials to estimate the value that the public places on a (statistical) life.

A number of factors distinguish the occupational case from the siting case. First, there is a difference in the number of persons placed at risk by a decision to accept money. In the occupational case, the worker incurs a personal risk, whereas in the siting case the decision to accept a repository exposes a large number of individuals — most of whom are currently unborn, and thus unrepresented — to the risk. The opposition to rebates suggests that benefit packages must address the issue of intergenerational equity. One possibility is establishing a trust fund that ensures that benefits will be disbursed to all those who suffer from the repository.

Payments in return for a repository are also likely to provoke opposition from respondents who oppose the construction of a repository in general, quite aside from the fact that their personal impacts might be offset by the payments. To those who believe that a repository is somehow illegitimate because it poses unacceptable risks to future generations, accepting economic incentives condones an unethical policy choice. This consideration gives many respondents more than adequate cause to refuse rebate offers, regardless of their value. Evidence for such an effect comes from an experiment by McClelland and Schulze (in press), in which subjects whose actions dictated tree-cutting policy were more likely to refuse compensation offers that offset their own personal costs.[10]

4.6. Prospects for Benefits Packages

This section has highlighted a number of factors that call into question the viability of monetary payments to eliminate opposition to a noxious facility. First and foremost, for a benefit-sharing strategy to be successful, those who are directly affected by the facility must believe that the package makes them personally better off than under the *status quo*. Because of the public's reluctance to make trade-offs between risk and dollars, economic incentives are most likely to be successful in situations in which the risks are perceived to be very low. In France, for example, residents living near nuclear reactors were offered special reductions on their electricity rates as compensation for having the facility nearby. These offers generally were welcomed by communities selected to host reactors, but only because the French perceived nuclear power to be much less risky than did residents of other countries. In fact, the reduction was withdrawn by the French government several years ago because power obtained from nuclear reactors was considered to be as safe as electricity generated from other sources.

The requirement of *safety first* was also documented by Peelle and Ellis (1987) in their study of the Department of Energy's attempt to site a monitored retrievable storage (MRS) facility for high-level nuclear waste in Oak Ridge, Tennessee. A local task force was unwilling to talk about compensation until they received strong assurances that the facility would be safe. We find a similar situation in the case of a permanent geologic repository for nuclear waste. Former Nevada Governor Richard Bryan remarked on the inability of benefits packages to elicit public acceptance in the absence of safety assurances:

> [i]n order for any state to ever be able to accept a repository, a situation must be created whereby the leaders and citizens in that state are able to see and believe that the site selected was the product of an impeccable, scientifically objective screening process. No amount of compensation or federal "incentives" can ever substitute for safety and technical suitability in the site selection effort (Bryan, 1987, p. 33).

It should be noted that satisfying this prerequisite level of safety is particular difficult in the case of radioactive waste facilities. Radiation risks are unfamiliar and dreaded, and thus often defy "reduction" to safe levels. The task of siting these facilities is made more difficult by the fact that the fear commonly associated with radiation risks may generate stigmatization, which in turn may produce economic losses to tourism, agriculture, and business recruitment that can spread throughout an entire state. In such a case, the developer may face the burden of gaining support from stakeholders outside the local community — including state officials. The proposed MRS facility provides an interesting case in point. Although DOE was able to gain a modicum of support among residents of Oak Ridge, officials at the state level rejected the proposal after considering the potential impact to economic development efforts in the eastern part of the state (Sigmon, 1987).

In addition, it appears from our data on willingness to accept rebates that a benefits package will be accepted only if residents are first assured that the package is fair — that it distributes benefits to everyone who will suffer, and that the facility is legitimate — it is an appropriate technological solution to the problem at hand. Consequently, one should not expect benefit sharing *by itself* to elicit acceptance from the public. Other policy tools must be invoked prior to benefits packages to make the facility minimally acceptable. We consider two particular tools here: mitigation and recruitment of volunteer communities.

5. Risk Mitigation

5.1. Purpose

We argued in the previous section that benefits packages can be effective in enhancing local tolerance for a facility only if the risks are perceived to be acceptably small. Thus, an essential early step in the siting process is the mitigation of facility risks (Morell and Magorian, 1982; O'Hare, Bacow and Sanderson, 1983; Carnes et al., 1983; and Peelle, 1987). Mitigation measures are important not only as a means of reducing the facility's risks, but also to involve the public in a positive way in the facility's development.

One of the more promising mitigation measures is to form a committee of local residents that is granted special oversight powers, including the power to suspend operations at the facility if the operating standards are not adhered to. In a survey of Wisconsin residents, Carnes et al. (1983) found that opposition to a high-level nuclear waste repository decreased if the facility was subject to this sort of local control.

We also found evidence within the survey of Nevada residents that local control could enhance the acceptability of a repository. In this section of the survey, respondents indicated how important they thought various mitigation and compensation measures would be "in making a repository more acceptable to nearby residents." For each measure, table 7.4 reports the percentage of the Nevada sample who responded with the highest rating, "very important." Because of the importance of addressing the concerns of facility opponents, the percentages are computed separately among those respondents who voted *against* Yucca Mountain and those who voted in favor.

Not surprisingly, both groups overwhelmingly regard it to be very important to have strict safety standards in place and an inspector on site. That is, 89 percent of the opponents believed this, as did 93 percent of those in favor. The more interesting result is that opponents consider the committee with shut-down power to be nearly as important a measure (80 percent regard it to be very important), while those currently in favor see much less need for such a committee (41 percent consider it very important). The lack of control by the public of radiation and chemical risks is one of the key features that makes these risks appear to be so serious (Slovic, 1987).

Table 7.4. Perceived Importance of Mitigation and Compensation Measures in Making a Repository 'More Acceptable' to Nearby Residents

| Measure | Percentage Who Rate the Measure as Very Important in Gaining Support | |
	Among Those Who Voted AGAINST Yucca Mountain	Among Those Who Voted FOR Yucca Mountain
Strict safety standards set by federal government, plus an inspector on site	89%	93%
Local committee has power to shut down repository	80%	41%
Local committee gives safety advice to management	74%	62%
Property values are protected	61%	61%
Large grants for community facilities	48%	49%
Rebates to residents within 100 miles of repository	40%	26%
High-tech project with new jobs near repository	38%	54%

5.2. Trust

With respect to mitigation, the key objective is to gain the trust of the local residents. For the public to have confidence in the safety of the facility, the developer must have a reputation for assessing risk accurately, for constructing the facility according to a rigorous design, and for managing the facility competently. To the extent that the developer is not trusted to fulfill these responsibilities, the perceived level of risk will remain high.

Trust plays an especially important role in influencing perceived risk in the case of novel facilities such as radioactive waste repositories. Because these facilities have no history, it is difficult for the general public — and scientists — to estimate with confidence the likelihood of mishaps. With this level of ambiguity, the credibility of the facility developer will be an especially salient determinant of perceived risk.

The lack of trust is obvious in the case of the federal government's attempt to site a HLNW repository in Nevada. The Department of Energy has suffered through a litany of investigative reports documenting safety lapses at nuclear weapons facilities throughout the country (e.g., Schneider, 1988a; 1988b). In addition, a number of articles have reported that DOE has based its analyses of the repository on incomplete and ambiguous data, and in fact has suppressed data that call into question the suitability of the Yucca Mountain site (Wald, 1988; Wingard, 1988; Norris, 1988).

The mistrust has, not surprisingly, affected the public's perceptions of the safety of the repository (Kraft and Cleary, 1989). Table 7.5 shows the correlation between the various risk measures and an item that asked respondents to rate the degree to which they trust the federal government to make a repository as safe as possible. The correlations are all significantly positive, with the trust measure explaining between 5 percent and 10 percent of the variance in the various risk measures. This indicates that risk perceptions are indeed sensitive to the perceived competence of the developer. On the other hand, the fact that the correlations are much less than one indicates that respondents also view the repository risk as depending upon factors over which the government can exercise little control — the intrinsic limits of the technology and unforeseen geologic events.

6. Competitive Siting Processes

As long as the developer pursues the typical siting model of first identifying a favored site, and then involving the local public, the overriding perception

Table 7.5. Relation Between Trust in Federal Government and Various Indicators of Perceived Risk in Nevada

RISK INDICATOR	CORRELATION
Likelihood of Release:	
Accident at repository	−.311
Release during transport	−.297
Wastes leak into groundwater	−.373
Sabotage	−.236
Severity of Consequences:	
Certain death	−.241
Kill many people at once	−.218
Risk Appraisals:	
Seriousness of risk to self	−.274
Risk to future generations is serious	−.330
Benefits outweigh risks to nearby residents	.318

Note: All correlations significant at p < .01.

will be that the risks are involuntarily imposed on the host community. A more promising approach is for the developer to set up a siting process in which communities will have a positive incentive to serve as the host. Only those communities that voluntarily express an interest in being considered should be actively involved as partners in the operation of the facility. The emphasis on community control is maintained throughout the entire siting process; a community that initially expresses interest is free to withdraw at any point along the way.

For this siting strategy to succeed in identifying willing communities, the developer must recruit communities whose needs closely match the potential benefits that the particular facility package could provide. This approach has recently been advocated for siting a number of disposal facilities, including hazardous waste incinerators (McGlennon, 1983; Ruckelshaus, 1988), landfills, and low-level radioactive waste repositories.

6.1. Bidding Procedures

Siting procedures need to balance economic and political tensions by attempting to satisfy efficiency considerations while still being perceived as fair by the relevant parties. If only one community is being considered as a site, then its residents can demand a higher amount of compensation than they would actually require to accept the facility. Ideally, more than one community will be willing to entertain the prospect of hosting the facility. This would allow the developer to invoke some sort of bidding mechanism as part of the final selection procedure, thereby reducing the facility's costs while also reaching a more efficient solution.

It is likely that the community specifying the smallest benefit-sharing package will be relatively poor, since poorer communities normally require a smaller package to improve their welfare over the *status quo*. This may be perceived as unfair by some, even if it is viewed as eminently fair by the volunteering community.

Two key features of the voluntary procedure may mitigate this concern. Since communities maintain control at all points along the way, a community will only remain a candidate site if it bids an amount that makes it better off with the facility than without. The process must also contain an open fact-finding process so that all relevant information about the facility — especially the level of risk and the degree of uncertainty about the risk — is publicly aired. Only in this way can the siting strategy satisfy the requirement of informed consent that attaches to any legitimate definition of fairness.

A bidding mechanism may prove effective not only for cases where a firm or government needs to build a disposal facility, but also in cooperative ventures where communities collaborate to develop a central facility — say for recycling household refuse. Consider several (n) communities that each ship their waste to an expensive outside contractor, and thus could benefit from building their own recycling facility. Assume that each community is willing to serve as the host if the benefits are high enough. The low-bid auction proposed by Kunreuther et al. (1987) represents an efficient means of finding an acceptable site in this case. Under this auction, each community specifies a bid B_i that reflects the amount that it would require to host the facility. The community with the lowest bid, call it 1, wins the auction and thus becomes the host for the facility. This particular community also receives the specified benefits (B_1). The remaining $n - 1$ communities each pay a fraction of their bid, $B_i/(n - 1)$, to a regional authority. The "winner" receives the B_1 which by definition is less than $\sum_{i \neq 1} B_i/(n - 1)$. The excess amount can be used to provide other services to the region.

The auction has the feature that the more a community bids, the higher will be the amount it has to pay if it is not selected. This creates an incentive for communities to bid an amount B_i that is not much greater than the estimated cost involved in its actually hosting the facility.

An emerging set of cases suggests that this approach of combining competitive procedures with voluntary participation is a promising avenue for facility developers to pursue. In Alberta, extensive voluntary participation by community representatives in a siting evaluation program is credited with having three communities compete with each other to host a large waste-treatment facility (McGlennon, 1983).

Recently ECOS, a company based in the state of Washington, developed a procedure for finding a hazardous-waste handling facility for the state. After screening the state for acceptable sites, communities were publicly asked whether they were interested in being a candidate site. Although a number initially responded positively, several withdrew from the process. Residents in two communities, however, felt that the mitigation measures addressed their safety concerns and that the benefits package was sufficiently attractive. As a result, over 60 percent of the voters favored the proposal.

6.2. Consensus Siting Rules

It remains to be seen whether the voluntary approach will succeed in finding host communities willing to accept especially noxious facilities such as radioactive waste repositories. In the monitored retrievable storage (MRS) facility case, the benefits package was negotiated without the threat of reversion. That is, the federal government would *not* step in and build the facility without local consent. The city of Oak Ridge possessed extensive leverage in determining the mitigation and monetary measures that would accompany the repository (Sigmon, 1987). While community officials were willing to consider the prospect of hosting the MRS, local support was insufficient to reach an agreement (Peelle, 1987).[11]

At present, it seems wise to maintain a contingency plan for siting facilities regarded as especially noxious but nonetheless necessary from a societal standpoint. Such a default siting plan should take the form of a set of clear rules by which a location will be selected if *no* community volunteers. For this policy to constitute a viable default plan, all stakeholders must be convinced that the *status quo* is untenable as a potential solution. In addition, a sound and objective procedure should be employed to select a site. This procedure should balance equity and efficiency considerations, incorporating such factors as population density, geological suitability, and the level of waste generated.

The crafters of the original 1982 Nuclear Waste Policy Act recognized the difficulty of gaining voluntary support for a repository from any state, and thus developed a set of siting rules that could be defended as fair (Colglazier and Langum, 1988). One provision called for the construction of both an eastern and a western repository. An eastern site was deemed especially appropriate since the vast majority of high-level nuclear waste is generated by reactors in that region of the country.

Building multiple repositories also enhances equity relative to a single-site policy in that there is less variance between states in the level of risk that each incurs. See Keeney and Winkler (1985) and Keller and Sarin (1988) for suggestive analyses of this issue. A second fairness feature of NWPA was the implicit directive to select the site that is technically most suitable. Although fairness was built into the siting policy, these two provisions were revoked during the implementation of NWPA as discussed above.[12]

It is possible that even if no community initially volunteers for the facility, thus requiring the implementation of the contingent siting policy, a volunteer might eventually be found. In particular, once the contingent siting policy has been employed to designate a site and set the benefits level, the developer could re-open the siting process to see if any other community would like to place a lower bid. In this way, the facility could be located in an area that rendered *ex post* consent, portending a more favorable working relationship between the operator and the host community. No less important is the feature that the cost to the developer will decrease if a lower bid is submitted.

An especially interesting extension of this strategy is the case where the default siting rule is a lottery. Here, the "winning" community would negotiate what it considered to be a fair benefits package with the developer. However, at this point, all the communities in the lottery—including the "winner"—are given an opportunity to compete for the privilege of hosting the facility by bidding downward. The lowest bid gets the facility (Kunreuther and Portney, 1990). One might consider whether the use of a lottery in the case of the HLNW repository would have elicited a favorable response from any of the three candidate states.

7. Conclusion

In summarizing what we know about siting noxious facilities, it is crucial to emphasize the importance of communicating the implications of the status quo ante to the entire public. In other words, everyone needs to appreciate the consequences of not building the facility. For example, the status quo may impose higher levels of risk on all communities than would obtain with the facility. On the other hand, it may turn out that the developer is promoting a facility that fails to represent the best solution to the problem. In either case, detailing the consequences of the possible actions will produce a more informed discussion of what states of the world are feasible and desirable.

The Washington ECOS experience may serve as a prototype for market-based siting strategies that could be invoked by many other states and regions. By stressing safety first and benefits second, it may be possible to create a situation in which a community that failed to get chosen to host the facility actually felt it had lost out on something. In such cases we will have modified the common acronym NIMBY to the unheard of acronym YIMBY — Yes in My Backyard.

Notes

1. Nine percent of the sample responded "don't know" and were excluded from the following analysis.

2. A similar graph can be drawn to depict the effect of the third predictor, risk versus benefits to nearby residents.

3. Rosenman, Fort, and Budd (1988) present a related model for analyzing the costs associated with a radioactive waste repository.

4. The model can be expanded to allow for the more natural case of multiple risks, without changing the basic result. By considering only a single risk, the calculations are greatly simplified and the implications of the model are more transparent.

5. This was actually the first of a two-part question. If the person voted in favor of locating the repository with the rebate, the follow-up asked whether he or she would accept the repository for half the amount. If the person was opposed in the first question, the amount was doubled.

6. The 27% figure reported here differs from the 24% reported in the previous section because the current analysis is restricted to the sub-sample who answered the rebate question, whereas the 24% figure corresponds to the entire sample.

7. Respondents received either the rebate or the extra-tax question, not both.

8. If the respondent agreed to pay the surcharge, the amount was doubled and the question was repeated. Those unwilling to pay the initial amount were given a follow-up question in which the amount was cut in half.

9. At first glance, it might seem reasonable to assume that all reservation prices are greater than 0. This would imply $F(0) = 0$ and would allow us to begin the curves begin in the lower left hand corner of the quadrant. However, such an assumption would imply that everyone prefers to move the repository if it can be done at no cost, which is at odds with the referendum data reported earlier (some Nevada residents would rather have the repository at Yucca Mountain than at other sites, i.e., the facility has a positive net value to them).

10. While there is a moral imperative to avoid pay-off in return for explicitly consenting to a facility, there is much less of a duty to pay in order to prevent an illegitimate policy from being enacted. This could be construed as a omission-commission distinction, there being

less blame in the case of failing to act preventively than in acting positively (Spranca, M., Minsk, E., and Baron, J., 1991.

11. As noted, actions at the state level would have precluded any agreement reached between Oak Ridge and the federal government.

12. An analysis of the current data set in Easterling (in press) suggests that if the federal government had explicitly identified the safest site for a repository, opposition would have been reduced within the host state.

References

Bryan, R. H. 1987. "The Politics and Promises of Nuclear Waste Disposal: The View from Nevada," *Environment* 29(8), 14−17; 32−38.

Calabresi, G., and P. Bobbitt. 1978. *Tragic choices*. New York: Norton.

Carnes, S. A., E. D. Copenhaver, J. H. Sorensen, E. J. Soderstrom, J. H. Reed, D. J. Bjornstad, and E. Peelle. 1983. "Incentives and Nuclear Waste Siting: Prospects and Constraints," *Energy Systems and Policy* 7(4), 324−351.

Carter, L. J. 1987. "Siting the Nuclear Waste Repository: Last Stand at Yucca Mountain," *Environment* 29(8), 8−13; 26−31.

Colglazier, E. W., and R. B. Langum. 1988. "Policy Conflicts in the Process for Siting Nuclear Waste Repositories," *Annual Review of Energy* 11, 317−357.

Coursey, D. L., J. J. Hovis, and W. D. Schulze. 1987. "The Disparity Between Willingness to Accept and Willingness to Pay Measures of Value," *Quarterly Journal of Economics* 102, 679−690.

Cummings, R. G., D. S. Brookshire, and W. D. Schulze. 1986. *Valuing Environmental Goods: An Assessment of the Contingent Valuation Method*. Iotowa, NJ: Rowman & Allanheld.

Dunlap, Riley E., and Rodney K. Baxten. 1988. "Public Reaction to Siting a High-level Nuclear Waste Repository at Hanford: A Survey of Local Area Residents." Pullman, WA: Washington State University.

Easterling, D. V. 1990. "Fair Rules for Siting a High-level Nuclear Waste Repository." *Journal of Policy Analysis and Management* (in press).

Ewing, T. F. 1990. "Guarantees near a landfill," *New York Times*, July 8.

Fischhoff, B., P. Slovic, S. Lichtenstein, S. Read, and B. Combs. 1978. How Safe Is Safe Enough? A Pscyhometric Study of Attitudes Toward Technological Risks and Benefits," *Policy Sciences* 8, 127−152.

Gerking, S., M. de Haan, and W. Schulze. 1988. "The Marginal Value of Job Safety: A Contingent Valuation Study," *Journal of Risk and Uncertainty* 1, 185−199.

Kahneman, D., and A. Tversky. 1979. "Prospect Theory: An Analysis of Decision Under Risk," *Econometrica* 47, 263−291.

Kasperson, R. E., and B. L. Rubin. 1983. "Siting a Radioactive Waste Repository: What Role for Equity?" In R. E. Kasperson, (ed.), *Equity Issues in Radioactive Waste Management*. Cambridge, MA: Oegleschlager, Gunn, and Hain.

Keeney, R. L., and R. L. Winkler. 1985. "Evaluating Decision Strategies for Equity of Public Risks," *Operations Research* 33, 955−970.

Keller, L. R., and R. K. Sarin. 1988. "Equity in Social Risk: Some Empirical Observations," *Risk Analysis* 8, 135–146.

Kneese, A., S. Bend David, D. Brookshire, W. Schulze, and D. Bold. 1983. "Economic Issues in the Legacy Problem," In R. E. Kasperson, (ed.), *Equity Issues in Radioactive Waste Management*. Cambridge, MA: Oegleschlager, Gunn, and Flain.

Knetsch, J. L., and J. A. Sinden. 1984. "Willingness to Pay and Compensation Demanded: Experimental Evidence of an Unexpected Disparity in Measures of Value." *Quarterly Journal of Economics* 102, 507–521.

Knetsch, J. L., R. Thaler, and D. Kahneman. 1988. "Experimental Tests of the Coase Theorem and the Endowment Effect," unpublished manuscript.

Kraft, M. E., and B. B. Clary. 1989. "Public Testimony in Nuclear Waste Repository Bearings: A Content Analysis." Paper presented at the Annual Meeting of the American Association for the Advancement of Science, San Francisco, CA, January 14–19, 1989.

Kunreuther, H., and D. Easterling. 1990. "Are Risk-Benefit Tradeoffs Possible in Siting Hazardous Facilities?" *American Economic Review: Papers and Proceedings* 80, 252–257.

Kunreuther, H., D. Easterling, and P. Kleindorfer. 1988. "The Convention Planning Process: Potential Impact of a Repository in Nevada." Working Paper, Wharton Risk and Decision Processes Center, published by Nevada Nuclear Waste Project Office.

Kunreuther, H., P. Kleindorfer, P. J. Knez, and R. Yaksick. 1987. "A Compensation Mechanism for Siting Noxious Facilities: Theory and Experimental Design," *Journal of Environmental Economics and Management* 14, 371–383.

Kunreuther, H., and P. Portney. 1991. "Wheel of Fortune: A Lottery Auction Mechanism for the Siting of Noxious Facilities." *Journal of Energy Engineering* 3: 125–32 (December).

Lindell, M. K., and T. C. Earle. 1983. "How Close Is Close Enough: Public Perceptions of the Risk of Industrial Facilities," *Risk Analysis* 3, 245–253.

MacLean, D. 1983. "Radioactive Wastes: A Problem of Morality Between Generations." In R. Kasperson, *Equity Issues in Radioactive Waste Management*. Cambridge, MA: Oegleschlager, Gunn, and Hain, pp. 175–188.

McClelland, G. H. and W. D. Schulze. (in press). "The Disparity between Willingness-to-Pay and Willingness-to-Accept as a Framing Effect." In D. R. Brown and J. E. K. Smith, (eds.), *Frontiers in Mathematical Psychology*. New York: Springer-Verlag.

McClelland, G. H., W. D. Schulze, and B. Hurd. (1990). "The Effect of Risk Beliefs on Property Values: A Case Study of a Hazardous Waste Site. *Risk Analysis* 10, 485–497.

McGlennon, J. 1983. "The Alberta Experience ... Hazardous Wastes? Maybe in My Backyard," *The Environmental Forum* 2, 23–25.

Merkhofer, M. W., and R. L. Keeney. 1987. "A Multiattribute Utility Analysis of Alternative Sites for the Disposal of Nuclear Waste." *Risk Analysis* 7, 173–194.

Metz, W. C., M. Morey, and J. Lowry. 1990. "Hedonic Price Theory: Concept and Applications." Paper presented at First Annual International High-Level Radioactive Waste Management Conference, Las Vegas, April 8–12.

Morell, D., and C. Magorian. 1982. *Siting Hazardous Waste Facilities: Local Opposition and the Myth of Preemption.* Cambridge, MA: Ballinger.

Mufson, M. 1982. "Three Mile Island: Psychological Effects of a Nuclear Accident and Mass Media Coverage." In *Psychosocial Aspects of Nuclear Developments.* Washington, D.C.: American Psychiatric Association.

Norris, M. 1988. "Agency Blasts DOE on Yucca: NRC: Waste Site Data Are Flawed, Procedures Weak," *Reno Gazette Journal,* March 24, pp. 1C, 2C.

O'Hare, M., L. Bacow, and D. Sanderson. 1983. *Facility Siting and Public Opposition.* New York: Van Nostrand Reinhold.

Peelle, E. 1987. "The MRS Task Force: Economic and Noneconomic Incentives for Local Public Acceptance of a Proposed Nuclear Waste Packaging and Storage Facility." In R. C. Post, (ed.), *Waste Management 87.* Tucson, AZ: University of Arizona.

Peelle, E., and R. Ellis. 1987. "Hazardous Waste Management Outlook: Are There Ways Out of the 'Not-in-My-Backyard' Impasse?" *Forum for Applied Research and Public Policy* 2(Fall), 68–88.

Popper, F. 1983. "LP/HC and LULU's: The Political Uses of Risk Analysis in Land Planning," *Risk Analysis* 3, 255–263.

Rennick, P. H., and R. L. Greyell. 1990. "Opting for Cooperation: A Voluntary Approach to Siting a Low-level Radioactive Waste Facility." Working Paper, Siting Task Force on Low-Level Radioactive Waste Management. Ottawa, Ontario, Canada: Energy, Mines and Resources Canada.

Rosenman, R. R., Fort, and W. Budd 1988. "Perceptions, Fear, and Economic Loss: An Application of Prospect Theory to Environmental Decision Making." *Policy Sciences* 21, 327–350.

Ruckelshaus, W. D. 1989. "The Politics of Waste Disposal," *Wall Street Journal.* September 5.

Schneider, K. 1988a. "Operators Got Millions in Bonuses Despite Hazards at Atom Plants," *New York Times,* October 26, pp. A1, B9.

Schneider, K. 1988b. "Defects in Nuclear Arms Industry Minimized in Early Reagan Years: Safety Overhaul Follows Course Rejected in '81," *New York Times,* November 6, pp. A1, B12.

Shapiro, F. C. 1988. "A Reporter at Large: Yucca Mountain," *New Yorker,* May 23, pp. 61–67.

Sigmon, E. B. 1987. "Achieving a Negotiated Compensation Agreement in Siting: The MRS case," *Journal of Policy Analysis and Management* 6, 170–179.

Slovic, P. 1987. "Perception of Risk," *Science* 236, 280–285.

Slovic, P., M. Layman, N. N. Kraus, J. Chalmers, G. Gesell, and J. Flynn. 1989. "Perceived Risk, Stigma, and Potential Economic Impacts of a High-level Repository in Nevada." Carson City, Nevada: Decision Research for Nevada Nuclear Waste Project Office.

Smith, V. K., and W. H. Desvousges. 1987. "An Empirical Analysis of the

Economic Value of Risk Changes," *Journal of Political Economy* 95, 89–114.

Spranca, M., E. Minsk, and J. Baron. 1991. "Omission and Commission in Judgement and Choice," *Journal of Experimental Social Psychology* 27, 76–105.

Svenson, O., and G. Karlsson. 1989. "Decision-making, Time Horizons, and Risk in the Very Long-term Perspective," *Risk Analysis* 9, 385–400.

Sweet, W. E., R. D. Ross, and G. V. Velde. 1985. "Hazardous Waste Incineration: A Progress Report," *Journal of Air Pollution Control Association* 35(2), 138–143.

Thaler, R. 1980. "Toward a Positive Theory of Consumer Choice," *Journal of Economic Behavior and Organization* 1, 39–60.

Thaler, R. 1985. "Mental Accounting and Consumer Choice," *Marketing Science* 4, 199–214.

Tversky, A, and D. Kahneman. 1981. "The Framing of Decisions and the Psychology of Choice," *Science* 211, 453–458.

Viscusi, W. K., W. A. Magat, and J. Huber. 1987. "An Investigation of the Rationality of Consumer Valuations of Multiple Health Risks," *RAND Journal of Economics* 18, 465–479.

Wald, M. L. 1988. "Work Is Faltering on U.S. Repository for Nuclear Waste," *New York Times*, January 17, pp. A1, B10.

Weidenbaum, M. 1989. "Protecting the Environment," *Society* 27: 49–56.

Weinstein, N. D., P. M. Sandman, and M. L. Klotz. 1987. *Public Response to the Risk from Radon, 1986*. Final report to the Division of Environmental Quality, New Jersey Department of Environmental Protection.

Willig, R. D. 1976. "Consumers' Surplus Without Apology," *American Economic Review* 66, 589–597.

Wingard, L. 1988. "Scientist Says DOE Should Dump Site," *Las Vegas Review-Journal* January 22, p. 1A.

8 OCCUPATIONAL SAFETY AND HEALTH IN THE 1990S

W. Kip Viscusi*

The Occupational Safety and Health Administration (OSHA) continues to be justifiably maligned as one of the least effective federal regulatory agencies. Congress initiated this agency with the Occupational Safety and Health Act of 1970. The impetus for the establishment of this new branch of the U.S. Department of Labor was based in part on a misleading rise in some measures of industry risk levels. In spite of these ominous trends, most measures of risks to occupational safety and health continued to display a downward trend. Specifically, the *total* injury frequency rate for manufacturing rose 2.4 percent annually from 1958 to 1970, but several measures of disabling injuries and death rates were either constant or exhibited a steady decline (Viscusi, 1983). This pattern is consistent with a possible reporting bias due to the problem of defining what constitutes a job-related injury. The advocates of the establishment of OSHA did not assess the mixed statistical signals, but focused on the one rising injury trend as an indication of an alarming escalation in workplace risks.

* George G. Allen Professor of Economics and Director of the Program on Risk Analysis and Civil Liability, Duke University.

Congress saw the establishment of OSHA as a mechanism for reversing what was in fact an illusory upsurge in injuries. In addition, Congress envisioned that OSHA would have sweeping effects on the control of risks in the workplace.

The high expectations accompanying the establishment of OSHA were similar to those for other efforts launched at the time. Seat-belt regulations instituted by the U.S. Department of Transportation are another prominent example. In each case, there was a widely held belief that the technological solution to our safety problems would yield dramatic gains. This usually meant, it seems, the expectation that it would be possible to reduce risks by at least half from their existing levels.

The reality has been quite different. OSHA began its operations in response to the structure established by its enabling legislation. The agency, predictably enough, adopted as its regulatory strategy an approach of setting regulatory standards that would be treated as mandatory guidelines to be enforced by inspectors with the authority to assess penalties on non-complying firms. The original safety standards consisted of the adoption of thousands of previously voluntary industry standards. These industry standards had been developed as discretionary guidelines — as conventions or norms — with little apparent thought to the idea that they might become mandatory throughout industry. OSHA's only modification to these standards was largely editorial — it replaced the discretionary *should* to a more mandatory *shall*. With these minor editing changes in place, OSHA was in business — armed with thousands of regulations — on a broad front of safety issues.

Not surprisingly, the agency became the object of widespread ridicule. Many of the standards were not well conceived and were most inappropriate as mandatory guidelines. Bridge workers were required to wear orange life vests regardless of whether the riverbeds over which they worked were dry. Detailed specification standards for ladders, handrails, and machine guards dictated specific workplace design without regard for alternatives that might have provided greater safety. Across a wide range of technological choices, OSHA assumed the role of a technology-forcing agency.

The enormity of the regulatory task, coupled with the infeasibility of promulgating uniform design standards that would be cost−effective in all contexts, led to a predictable backlash by the firms that had to pay the price for this regulation. Since stringent and sweeping regulations were coupled with weak and inconsistent enforcement, OSHA came to epitomize bureaucratic incompetence rather than a positive force for safety.

The second era of OSHA operations is marked by the advent of the

Carter administration. First, the Department of Labor undertook a number of substantial revisions in the OSHA standards. This effort resulted in the elimination of many petty regulations that had been the most dramatic examples of regulatory excess. The second theme was a shift in the agency's focus from safety issues to health issues. This seemed justified in view of the relatively greater likelihood of poorly understood health hazards as opposed to more readily monitorable safety risks. This shift in emphasis was coupled with an overambitious commitment to the stringency of such regulations. As a result many of the proposed OSHA standards were involved in battles within the Carter administration or in the courts.

With the coming of the Reagan administration in 1981 the emphasis throughout the federal government shifted to deregulation. Unfortunately, this new emphasis did not involve a restructuring of OSHA's regulatory approach but rather a retrenchment across a broad spectrum of regulatory activity. OSHA did not try to do different things, or the same things better. Rather, the mandate was to do less of what it had already been doing—and not very well at that.

One exception to this pattern was in the area of hazard communication standards. This innovation, proposed at the end of the Carter administration, was finalized during the Reagan administration. This new information standard greatly expanded the domain of OSHA regulations to include the provision of risk information. The intent was to foster involvement of worker actions to promote and encourage greater workplace safety. Overall, however, the Reagan administration's plan for OSHA involved little more than a scaling back of the agency's efforts. This retrenchment led to a new wave of criticism of OSHA. Having done little to improve safety and health conditions in the workplace, the agency was now seen as abandoning even its minimalist role. Although such criticism had long been prominent in the economics literature, the strong proponents of job-safety regulations became quite vigorous in their attacks. These attacks might be understood if we consider, in greater detail, the regulatory standards used by OSHA.

1. The Structure of OSHA Standards

It is commonplace for legislation to mandate rather broad performance goals, and to direct the relevant governmental agency to develop explicit rules and requirements whereby—it is hoped—those goals might be achieved. This was certainly the case with occupational safety and health legislation. OSHA's enabling legislation required that it issue standards, yet the nature of the standards was not specified by Congress. Indeed, there were few legislative constraints other than a general exhortation to promote worker health and safety. OSHA was given the mandate "to assure as far as possible every working man and woman in the nation safe and healthful working conditions"[1] and "to set mandatory occupational health and safety standards."[2] Several key dimensions are involved in the choice of the regulatory strategy within these broad limits. The first pertains to the focus of the standards, while the second concerns the character of particular regulations.

1.1. The Focus of Standards

The first concern is whether or not there should be any differential emphasis on particular types of hazards in the workplace. Recall that the economics literature draws a sharp distinction between health hazards and safety hazards. From an economic standpoint, the greatest gains are to be reaped by intervening in the situations in whcih the market failure is the most substantial. The general consensus in the literature is that such failures are likely to be greater for health risks than they are for safety risks. That is, in the case of safety hazards, workers have a variety of sources of information to assess their exposure to risk. Included here would be the injury record of the firm in particular industries, as well as monitorable aspects of specific jobs.

On the other hand, health hazards tend to be less visible. Moreover, because of the long time lags involved—and problems of multiple causality—health hazards tend to both poorly documented and little understood. As a general rule, therefore, the rationale for public policy involvement in the area of health hazards should be more compelling than for safety hazards.

In spite of this a priori logic, the focus of the agency's regulatory efforts has been quite the opposite. As noted above, the original OSHA standards focused almost exclusively on safety hazards. Moreover, even though there was a shift in emphasis toward health hazards during the Carter administration, these newer regulations were issued at an exceedingly slow pace. The delays in adoption, to a large extent arising from their stringency, arose because of court challenges and internal OSHA battles. The cotton dust standard, for example, was originally opposed by the economists in the Carter White House. Additionally, the textile industry pursued litigation all the way to the U.S. Supreme Court. As a result, OSHA has remained largely a safety-oriented agency.

1.2. The Character of Standards

The second issue in designing performance standards pertains to the precise character of the particular regulations to be put in place. The choice is between 1) a performance standard whereby the industry is required to meet a certain standard of safety or 2) a design standard that mandates specific technological aspects of workplace design. Design standards have the advantage in that they can be more readily enforced. However, their disadvantage is that design standards may impose inefficiencies since the required design may not be the most cost-effective mechanism for promoting safety in specific instances. It is not uncommon to find design standards that mandate that handrails must be $30-34''$ high, at least $2''$ thick for hardwood and $1\frac{1}{2}''$ thick for metal, spaced no more than 8 feet apart, and have at least $3''$ of clearance from a wall.

While some specifications are innocuous, others may be either ineffective or woefully incomplete. A principal disadvantage of narrow specifications is that they may not be broadly applicable mechanisms for promoting safety. For example, President Ford's task force on OSHA concluded that the machine-guard standards were so narrowly defined that they pertained to only 15 percent of all machines (MacAvoy, 1977).

In addition to the usual distinction between performance and design standards, standards can vary in the degree to which they call for protective equipment and other mechanisms that are alternatives to changes in the technology of the workplace. For instance, it will often be more cost-effective to have workers use protective equipment to reduce the risk of hearing loss than it will be to require a reduction in the overall noise level of the workplace. We observe this strategy among baggage handlers at airport gates. Similarly, individual respirators will often reduce worker exposure to hazardous substances at far less cost than will large-scale engineering controls. Finally, providing workers with information on risks and associated precautions allows individuals to take cost-effective safety precautions that do not require expensive alterations in the technology of the workplace.

Although performance-oriented alternatives are frequently attractive, their obvious drawback is that they rely on changes in worker behavior. There is no assurance that workers will wear the protective equipment or will take the suggested safety precautions. If such equipment is onerous or uncomfortable to wear or if it interferes with job operations, there will be a tendency for individuals to ignore the guidelines, thus undermining the desired effect. This tendency is compounded when workers are reimbursed on an output-based system. The reduction in productivity forces workers to face a difficult incentive problem—exhortations to be safe versus the financial inducement to boost output.

Even without monetary conflicts, problems with precautionary behavior may arise. The experience with automobile seat belt regulations is a telling illustration of failure to undertake apparently desirable safety precautions. Despite the substantial safety gains from seat belt use, a majority of motorists forego the use of seat belts and thereby make individual decisions that appear to be less than fully rational.

The second disadvantage of performance-oriented regulations arises in those instances in which risk perceptions are inadequate. Here, workers will not properly value the safety benefits from precautions and hence some mandatory rules may be needed to induce the ideal safety behavior. When such perceptions are not fully shared, safety measures will have a tendency to be opposed by unions. In a competitive market, wages will adjust in the long run to reflect the increased burdens imposed by such jobs. In unionized markets, with wages already somewhat above their competitive level, there is no assurance that there will be such an adjustment. A feasible solution in such settings may be increased negotiation between unions and firms over safety policies that are combined with contractual commitments to compensation. The issue here is added discomfort to workers versus centralized changes in technology and processes.

One final contentious aspect of design standards has been their stringency. One instructive measure of the cost-effectiveness of regulations is given by the cost per life saved. Table 8.1 provides a summary of the cost per life saved for a variety of OSHA regulations. At the low end of the scale we find highly efficient regulations that save lives very cheaply. One such example is the service standard for oil and gas wells with a cost per life saved of $100,000. At the high end is a proposed OSHA formaldehyde standard with a cost per life saved of $72 billion. As table 8.1 suggests, there is a wide range in the cost effectiveness of alternative government regulations, and the task for the regulatory agencies is to strike an appropriate balance between the costs and benefits of these standards.

To date, OSHA has made little attempt to make such distinctions in spite of well-established mechanisms for doing so. A substantial literature on labor market valuations of life and limb indicates the value that workers themselves place on small risks of death, and these numbers can serve as a general benchmark for establishing the benefit values for averting such risks. If one uses as the reference point a value of life figure in the range of $3 million to $5 million (Moore and Viscusi, 1990), then the judgment as to which standards are desirable and which are not becomes apparent. Using these value-of-life figures, all OSHA standards

Table 8.1.   Cost Per Life Saved for OSHA Regulation*

Regulation	Year	Status	Annual Lives Saved	Cost Per Life Saved (Thousands of 1984 $)
Oil & Gas Well Service	1983	Proposed	50.000	$100
Underground Construction	1983	Proposed	8.100	300
Servicing Wheel Rims	1984	Final	2.300	500
Crane Suspended Personnel Platform	1984	Proposed	5.000	900
Concrete & Masonry Construction	1985	Proposed	6.500	1,400
Hazard Communication	1983	Final	200.000	1,800
Grain Dust	1984	Proposed	4.000	2,800
Asbestos	1972	Final	396.000	7,400
Benzene	1985	Proposed	3.800	17,100
Ethylene Oxide	1984	Final	2.800	25,600
Acrylonitrile	1978	Final	6.900	37,600
Coke Ovens	1976	Final	31.000	61,800
Asbestos	1986	Final	74.700	89,300
Arsenic	1978	Final	11.700	92,500
Acrylonitrile	1978	Rejected	0.600	308,000
EDB	1983	Proposed	0.002	15,600,000
Formaldehyde	1985	Proposed	0.010	72,000,000

* *Source*: John F. Morrall III, "A Review of the Record," *Regulation*, Vol 10 (1986), p. 30.

in the top part of table 8.1 — including the grain dust regulation — are economically defensible. On this metric, notice that those standards with a cost per life saved at the level of the asbestos standard or greater would not pass a benefit-cost test.

The wide dispersion in the estimated cost per life saved in table 8.1 suggests the gross nature of the policy decisions that must be made. Notice, however, that it is not necessary to ascertain whether the appropriate value of life is $3 million, $5 million, or $7 million. It is often sufficient to know that the value of life is in excess of $1 million, yet falls considerably below a number such as $20 million. The ultimate objective is to select those policies that promote risk reduction and yet achieve that objective at the least cost. Focusing regulatory efforts in this manner will further this objective.

Since the figures in table 8.1 pertain to average costs per life saved, additional refinements may be possible. Ideally, one should equate the marginal benefits of a regulation with its marginal costs. Doing so may affect the optimal degree of stringency of many of the regulations listed. Indeed, it may be the case that regulations that are attractive on benefit-cost grounds could be improved, while some regulations with exorbitant costs per life saved could be made more acceptable by altering their stringency.

2. Efforts at Reforming OSHA Standards

Although recent years have brought increased emphasis on regulating health hazards, and OSHA has made an effort to eliminate the more onerous regulations, the original emphasis of OSHA regulations has remained largely intact. Workplace standards remain directed largely toward safety-related problems. There have, however, been a number of changes in the character of OSHA regulations which provide important lessons with respect to the kinds of regulations that might be beneficial in the future.

The preponderance of OSHA's regulations continue to consist of the 4,000 general industry standards initially adopted by the agency. As noted earlier, the basis for these standards was the set of national consensus standards developed as voluntary guidelines by the American National Standards Institute, the National Fire Protection Association, and Federal Maritime safety standards. Under the Carter administration approximately one-fourth of these were eliminated or modified with the effect of muting the harshest criticisms that had been levied against OSHA.

As mentioned previously, the most innovative regulation in the history of OSHA, proposed at the end of the Carter administration but later to become the most costly social regulation promulgated by the Reagan administration, was the OSHA hazard communication standard. The focus of the standard was not on technological aspects of workplace design. Rather, OSHA began to realize that the number of potentially hazardous substances in the workplace was too great to address with substance-by-substance regulations. As a result, a broader approach was needed to control the risks. In overdue recognition of the role of worker actions, OSHA sought to involve worker behavior in the enhancement of safety through a hazard communication program that would alert workers to the risks and the associated precautions pertaining to chemicals in the workplace.

This regulation had several components. First, it required the labeling of hazardous chemicals used in manufacturing industries. Second, it required that workers be given safety training in the handling of such chemicals and the procedures to be followed in different warnings contexts. Third, chemical producers had to distribute material safety data sheets, and user firms had to maintain these sheets so that the ingredients to which workers were being exposed would be known. This information is most consequential in cases requiring medical treatment. Overall, the hazard communication effort represented a comprehensive and highly innovative program to make better use of precautionary behavior to enhance safety.

The potential role of worker actions in promoting safety is enormous. Although division of responsibility between workers and workplace technologies is somewhat arbitrary, all major studies of the contributors to workplace safety indicate that worker actions are important. Studies have indicated that workplace accidents account for 45 percent of all the workers' compensation cases in the state of Wisconsin, 84.3 percent of the job accidents in England, the majority of deaths of deep sea divers in the North Sea, almost two-thirds of all the accidents in the workplace that are monitored by the National Safety Council, and 95 percent of all workers' compensation cases in the state of Pennsylvania (Viscusi, 1983).

The most recent detailed study of the causation of workplace accidents is the Bureau of Labor Statistics investigation of almost 600 injuries arising in longshoring operations. Table 8.2 summarizes the different assignments of causation. Seventy-one percent of all workers cited some aspect of the worksite conditions that contributed to the accident, but some of these conditions, such as poor weather, are difficult or impossible to control. Nevertheless, many of the leading contributors to accidents, such as slippery and uneven work surfaces, are among the main targets of OSHA regulations. It is of particular interest to note that 68 percent of all workers cited factors other than worksite conditions as contributing to the accident. The speed of workplace operations, the lack of information about hazards, and co-worker actions were the main other factors contributing to the accident.

The information in table 8.2 suggests that job accidents are the result of a complex interaction of the technology of the workplace, the nature of job operations, and the safety precautions undertaken by workers. A successful safety policy must address all facets of this accident-generating process, not just one. During its initial years of operation, OSHA focused only on one of these contributing classes of factors—those pertaining to technological design. The hazard communication standard represents an

Table 8.2. Conditions or factors contributing to the accident: Injuries involving longshore operations, selected reporting periods, 1985–86

Conditions or factors workers felt contributed to accident	Percent[1]
Worksite conditions	
Total, 582 injured workers	100
Too noisy	2
Poor weather conditions	6
Cluttered work area	8
Slippery work surface	17
Uneven work surface	19
Equipment broke or didn't work properly	16
Working in too small or tight an area	13
Hard to see or bad lighting	9
Work area not properly safeguarded	5
Other worksite condition	8
None	29
Other contributing factors	
Total, 582 injured workers	100
Co-worker's actions	14
Hurrying or being rushed	22
Being tired	2
Material too heavy or bulky	11
Carelessness on part of injured worker	10
Not aware of danger	20
Tool(s) in bad shape or not right for job	6
Not wearing right safety gear	2
Other factor	4
None	32

[1] Because more than one response is possible, the sum of the percentages exceeds 100. Percentages are based on the total number of persons who answered the question.

NOTE: The reporting period is October 1985 for New York: April 1986 for all other ports. See appendix A for the scope of the survey. Due to rounding, percentages may not add to total.

Source: U.S. Department of Labor, Bureau of Labor Statistics, "Injuries Involving Longshore Operations," Bulletin 2326 (1989), p. 10.

important effort to expand the range of considerations to include the nature of job operations and the precautionary actions taken by workers.

Interestingly enough, OSHA had little basis for assessing the likely impact of the hazard communication standard before it was undertaken.

Subsequent analyses suggest that the behavioral response may be substantial. The potential effect of labels is illustrated by the data in table 8.3. In this case, workers at four different chemical plants were shown chemical labels for chemicals that they were told would replace the chemicals with which they now worked. The sample of workers at each plant was divided into four different groups and, on a random basis, workers in each of these groups were shown a particular hazard-warning label. One of the chemical hazards was intended to be safe — sodium bicarbonate (household baking soda). The three remaining chemicals posed various kinds of risks. Chloroacetophenone is an irritant that causes tearing, TNT is a well-known explosive, and asbestos is perhaps the best-known carcinogen. Asbestos is responsible for the majority of all product liability litigation currently in the federal courts.

What would be the effect of this new information on risk perceptions? As expected, exposure to sodium bicarbonate reduced the fraction of workers who considered their jobs to be above average in riskiness. Equally likely, exposure to the three other chemicals increased the fraction of workers who considered their jobs to be more risky than average. While none of the workers in the sodium bicarbonate labeling group required a wage increase to work with this substance, many of the workers in the other three chemical groups did require a wage premium. Moreover, in these latter groups, some workers refused to work with the chemicals at any price.

If workers were not paid extra to compensate for the added risk, there would be an effect on their likelihood of quitting. That is, exposure to the three relatively risky chemicals in the absence of a compensating wage differential would increase workers' propensity to quit from 13 percent in the case of chloroacetophenone to as much as 63 percent in the case of asbestos. Working with sodium bicarbonate instead of the current chemicals to which workers were exposed would reduce their quit rates by 23 percent. The market response to chemical labels engendered by the shift in risk perceptions is manifested in wage-risk trade offs and an impact on quit rates that follow economic predictions. In addition, for the analogous consumer risk communication case, these efforts have the expected impact on precautionary behavior as well (Viscusi and Magat, 1987).

Another innovative regulation of a performance-oriented character, but not specifically related to precautionary behavior, is the 1984 revision of OSHA's dust standard for grain elevators.[3] The objective of this standard is to reduce the level of grain dust in grain elevators so as to lower the probability of explosions. Under OSHA's traditional regulatory approach the solution would be simple: OSHA would mandate a uniform

Table 8.3. Worker Responses to Hazard Warnings

	Sodium Bicarbonate (n = 31)	Chloroacetophenone (n = 106)	Asbestos (n = 102)	TNT (n = 96)
Initial risk	.12	.10	.09	.10
Risk after receiving warning	.06	.18	.26	.31
Annual risk premium required ($1982)[a]	0.0	1,919.01	2,995.59	5,158.31
Would not stay on job at any wage	.00	.02	.11	.17
Intend to quit if no wage increase	.00	.23	.65	.73
Would take the job again if no wage increase	.90	.58	.11	.07

Source: W. Kip Viscusi and Wesley Magat, *Learning About Risk: Consumer and Worker Responses to Hazard Information* (Cambridge: Harvard University Press, 1987), p. 113.

[a] The risk premium figures are conditional upon facing an increased risk and being willing to accept a finite risk premium.

requirement to be met nationwide. Instead, OSHA offered a technological solution — pneumatic dust control equipment — but it also offered alternative approaches that firms could adopt. In particular, a firm could choose to clean up the dust whenever it reached a 'specified action level' of one-eighth of an inch, or it could choose to clean up the dust on a time-based schedule of one cleanup per shift. Thus, OSHA gave the industry three different options to meet a desired safety objective thereby allowing firms to choose the option that would promote safety at the least cost.

While allowing firms to select the most cost-effective option certainly represents a remarkable shift in OSHA policy, we should note in passing that this particular regulation was not necessarily ideal. Specifically, OSHA mandated that these standards be met throughout the industry, including those grain elevators with low throughput ratios, so that all opportunities for promoting more cost-effective policies were not exploited. The same regulations applied regardless of whether or not grain dust posed an explosion hazard. That is, those elevator facilities used primarily for grain storage were liable to the same standards as elevators engaged in grain handling; the risks of explosion are much higher in the latter facilities. Cost-effectiveness requires that the compliance options should have been varied to reflect the differing severity and nature of risks depending on the dominant function of the facility.

The final example of beneficial revisions in regulatory structure pertains to the updating of regulations. Because the standards are technology based, they must be continually revised and modified to reflect the state-of-the-art technologies actually used in various industrial sectors. Hence, inefficiencies arise for firms that must make capital-investment decisions on a basis that may not coincide with the cycle of OSHA regulations. The general approach has been to base compliance on the previously existing regulatory standards through grandfather clauses. In this way, capital investments made before the new regulations are in effect can be exempt. Notice that an increased reliance on performance-oriented regulations would make the updating of firms' efforts to enhance safety more of a continual process than one that responds to the highly infrequent cycle of OSHA standards updates.

One controversial standard promulgated during the Carter administration concerned cotton dust. Perhaps this controversy encouraged the Reagan administration to undertake a reassessment of the performance and the merits of the regulation.[4] A retrospective assessment of the actual benefits and costs of the standard indicated that some loosening of the standard appeared to be desirable. The difficulty arose because noncomplying firms were found to have had very high costs of compliance as compared with the firms that readily complied. In addition, changes in workplace operation — and worker rotation — were found to accomplish the same level of health benefits as investing in new capital equipment under the existing OSHA standard.

Despite the strong economic case for variation or relaxation of the standard, OSHA chose not to relax the standard. This inaction may seem difficult to reconcile with other Reagan administration actions intended to scale back regulatory initiatives. However, a main reason for maintaining the existing standard is that the major firms in the industry, which had originally lobbied against the standard and had taken their appeals to the U.S. Supreme Court, had by that time made the investments necessary for compliance. Having undertaken expensive investments to comply with the standards, these firms now opposed any effort to relax the standard. Of particular concern was the prospect for introducing greater use of protective equipment or worker rotation that would enable other firms to avoid the safety-oriented capital investments they had already been incurred by part of the industry. Of such logic are arguments of fairness constructed.

The lesson in the cotton dust case is clear. However ill-conceived industry officials claimed the OSHA standards to be, once those standards are in place it is unlikely that there will be a constituency for reverting to the preregulation world of the 1960s. Instead, reform efforts should focus on how the current approach can be modified, recognizing that the same firms that once vigorously opposed OSHA now have a substantial stake in OSHA's past policy actions.

3. The Need for Effective Enforcement

The primary lesson of regulation is that promulgating regulations does not ensure compliance. If owners and managers of firms are rational, as most economists assume, they will base their compliance decisions on whether the expected benefits of compliance exceed the expected costs of non-compliance. In particular, firms will comply with an OSHA regulation if

$$\begin{matrix} \text{Expect Costs of} \\ \text{Compliance} \end{matrix} < \begin{matrix} \text{Probability of} \\ \text{Inspection} \end{matrix} \times \begin{matrix} \text{Expected No.} \\ \text{of Violations} \\ \text{per inspection} \end{matrix} \times \begin{matrix} \text{Average Penalty} \\ \text{per Violation.} \end{matrix}$$

The gains from complying with OSHA regulations depend on the sanctions that will be avoided, while the costs of complying with OSHA regulations will often include substantial investments as reflected in the cost per life saved statistics presented in table 8.1. Unfortunately, OSHA has coupled fairly stringent regulations with lax enforcement. The enforcement effort consists of two components. The first component is that of the probability of an inspection and discovery of a violation. It follows that without an inspection, OSHA will not become aware of a workplace violation. Yet the probability of seeing an OSHA inspector has been likened by one author to the chance of spotting Halley's comet (Smith, 1976). More recently OSHA is said to have a probability of inspecting any given firm of 1/100 per year (Viscusi, 1983). Although OSHA inspections rose from 28,900 in 1972 to 90,300 by 1976, during the latter half of the 1970s the level of inspections declined to an average of about 60,000 per year.

Given a low probability of inspection and discovery, the sanctions for a violation must be substantial to induce firms to make a major investment in safety. These incentives have, for the most part, been minuscule. OSHA penalties reached a peak of $25.5 million in 1980, but have generally been much less, with amounts such as $6.4 million in 1983 or $8.2 million in 1975. Although fines in the millions may appear to be substantial, they provide little financial incentive when compared with the other mechanisms now in place. For instance, the marketplace provides for $70 billion in compensating differentials for job risks, which in turn generates powerful incentives for safety (Viscusi, 1983). In addition, the workers' compensation system imposes premiums in excess of $20 billion which also provide for safety incentives.

As a consequence, the net impact of OSHA regulations and penalties on safety has been rather minimal. Many studies of the effect of OSHA regulations indicate that there has been no statistically significant effect on safety. Indeed, recent estimates of the effect of OSHA—which are among the highest in the literature—indicate that on a percentage basis the effect of OSHA on the injury rate is at most 2.6 percent. OSHA's effect on the total rate of lost workdays, which captures more severe injuries, is at most 6 percent (Viscusi, 1986). In contrast, a recent study of the safety incentives generated by workers' compensation indicates a much more dramatic effect on worker death risks from the workers' compensation program (Moore and Viscusi, 1990). That study indicated that in the absence of workers' compensation, fatality rates in the U.S. workforce would increase by 20 percent. Contrasted with the consensus estimate of no significant effect of OSHA on safety—indeed, even given the most favorable estimates of the safety effect of OSHA—one finds that there is much less impact of OSHA's efforts than the billions of dollars of safety incentives created through the merit rating structure of workers' compensation. It is also noteworthy that the safety effects of workers' compensation are particularly great in the case of large firms. This finding further bolsters the case for incentive effects since large firms are more likely to be strongly merit-rated with premiums tied very closely to their injury experience.

Although OSHA's inspection strategy has undergone some refinement, it has generally remained unchanged. An OSHA inspection has always remained a rare event, and there is no indication that it will change. This need not be the case, and it generally is not in other Federal agency contexts. For example, the EPA water pollution program has a similar kind of regulatory approach, relying on discharge permits rather than on regulatory standards. In the case of EPA effluent standards, the agency not only requires that firms submit monthly reports of pollution discharges to the agency, but it also inspects all major pollutors an average of once per year. Not surprisingly, the compliance rates are much higher, and the effect of inspections is much greater, in water pollution cases (Magat and Viscusi, 1990).

It is also noteworthy that EPA gathers water pollution information on a regular basis while OSHA receives injury-rate information for each firm as part of the data surveys of the Bureau of Labor Statistics (BLS). During the Reagan administration, OSHA officials would visit firms in an effort to obtain data that the Bureau of Labor Statistics would not share with the agency. It seems obvious that much could be gained in targeting inspections if Congress would give OSHA the authority to require the reporting of injury rate data directly to OSHA rather than to the BLS. Although some biases in reporting may result, the gains in worker safety would probably offset such biases. Indeed, current data series may already be biased by the effect of records check inspections (Ruser and Smith, 1989).

Although the Reagan administration's drastic reductions in the penalty structure have been reversed by the Bush administration, agency officials have never expressed any sense of the importance of increasing the level of financial incentives. In the absence of such changes, the financial incentives for safety will continue to be low. That means that OSHA will remain a minor player in the drive for greater safety in the workplace.

4. Where Now for OSHA Policy?

Research indicates that the impact of OSHA regulations has consistently been very modest, with many studies indicating no significant effect on worker safety. This finding is not altogether surprising in view of the modest financial incentives generated by OSHA enforcement efforts. In addition, the considerable financial incentives generated by market forces, and by workers' compensation, create powerful incentives for increased worker safety. Hence, OSHA regulations are operating in an environment that is not far removed from substantial levels of safety. If the risk reduction incentives of the status quo, and of workers' compensation premiums, were not in effect, then the scope for OSHA to influence worker safety would be much greater. The unrealistically high expectations for OSHA can be traced, at least in part, to legislators' failure to appreciate the importance of the other safety incentives already in place.

The substantial effect on fatality rates of workers' compensation premiums highlights the potential role that can be played by an injury tax. Economists have long advocated a pollution tax in environmental policy and there have also been advocates of the imposition of an injury tax for workplace injuries. The basic idea is that such a tax would create financial incentives for safety that would be directly linked to workplace injuries. These incentives for safety are no less influential in promoting workers' well-being than would be the penalties levied by OSHA through its current inspection process. In addition, because these penalties could be levied on a decentralized basis, it would be possible to increase considerably the scale of the financial incentives generated from the meager incentives that now result from OSHA enforcement efforts.

Thus, any discussion of improving the OSHA approach to worker safety must start with the concept of an injury tax. While annual collections from this tax could run in the billions of dollars, it would be much larger if the other dimensions of worker safety did not exist. The advantage of an injury tax extends beyond the ability to impose financial incentives on hazardous firms without incurring the cost of a large cadre of inspectors. The additional benefit is that injury taxes are performance-related rather than based on design standards. Firms can choose how they will reduce workplace injuries using alternative techologies, provision of safety training, or changes in workplace operations. Thus, the injury tax is the ultimate performance-oriented policy in contrast to the rigid specification standards administered by OSHA. Moreover, in a world in which the technological options are changing, the injury tax always gives the appropriate incentives for introducing new technologies, whereas revisions of OSHA standards often occur with a substantial lag.

The introduction of an injury tax does not eliminate the need for OSHA standards, but it does greatly reduce the relative responsibility that must be borne by those standards in terms of promoting safety. Unfortunately, long-term health hazards that result in illnesses are not

readily amenable to the injury tax approach since these cannot be monitored. The main difficulty is that most job-related illnesses can also be
caused by other influences as well. Moreover, in situations in which there
are long time lags before the illness becomes apparent, it is generally not
feasible to distinguish which illnesses are due to the job and which are
due to other causes.

Shifting much of the responsibility for safety to an injury tax would
enable inspectors to focus more on health hazards than they have previously. Throughout OSHA's history fewer than one-fifth of all inspections
have been devoted to health risks with the bulk of all inspections focused
on safety-related concerns (Viscusi, 1986b). The current emphasis on
safety stems, in part, from the fact that safety conditions are more readily
monitorable than health risks. Safety violations can be more easily ascer-
tained by OSHA inspectors who, not unexpectedly, focus their efforts on
these more obvious hazards.

With the introduction of an injury tax, OSHA inspectors could focus
almost exclusively on health risks. To the extent that safety risks are of
continuing concern, inspections could focus on the extreme safety violations
as well as providing consultative services to advise firms on promising
alternative mechanisms for promoting safety.

A second component of any reform effort is to establish a more
consistent balance in OSHA regulations. As the figures in table 8.1
indicated, OSHA regulations are wildly inconsistent in terms of their
degree of stringency. A greater number of lives could be saved at less cost
by establishing a more uniform marginal cost per life saved. Although
OSHA is explicitly prohibited from basing its regulations on a formal
benefit-cost test, it is not prohibited from ensuring that the cost-effectiveness of alternative policies is equalized in a more sensible manner than
under the present regulatory regime. Some balancing that falls short of a
benefit-cost test is clearly needed so that society will benefit as much as
possible from the regulations OSHA promulgates and enforces.

The third needed reform is an increased reliance on performance-
oriented regulations to the extent that they can be specified in a manner
that will be enforceable. By shifting more of the burden to an injury tax,
the scope of safety regulations will be reduced since the financial incentives
of the tax will bear the primary burden for establishing safety incentives.
There also will be a stronger performance orientation in the health
standards that will continue to be enforced in their present manner.
Typical OSHA standards delineate permissible exposure limits, which by
their very nature tend to be more performance-oriented than safety risks
that specify particular kinds of machine guarding and other technological

devices in the workplace. The performance orientation could be increased further through the use of protective equipment when such choices represent a feasible compliance option. Greater attention to the potential role of safety training and hazard information of various kinds also would be a promising addition to OSHA's strategy.

Finally, by putting OSHA's regulation on a sounder footing, one would then be able to enforce the regulations that OSHA does administer more stringently. Token fines and infrequent inspections will do little to enhance safety. If OSHA has a broad injury tax to capture minor infractions—and if it focuses its inspectors' efforts on truly serious violations for which it will levy substantial penalties—then the overall impact of OSHA regulation will be enhanced.

Overall, it is clear that there is a legitimate role for OSHA to play in the economy. Worker safety and health information is not perfect, and there are a variety of gaps in market operation. Unfortunately, OSHA has not fulfilled its potential because it has focused primarily on safety risks that tend to be handled relatively well by the market, and it has coupled its focus with a weak enforcement effort. As OSHA enters its third decade, the time has come for a serious reexamination of the fundamental objectives of the agency and a reorientation of its regulatory strategy.

Notes

1. Section 26 of the Occupational Safety and Health Act of 1970, USC § 651 (1976).
2. *Ibid*, Section 26, part 3.
3. Office of Management and Budget, OSHA's Proposed Standards for Grain Handling Facilities (1984), unpublished memorandum, and 49 Federal Register 996 (1984).
4. For a description of this study prepared for OSHA see the article by the two principal authors of the report prepared for OSHA, Kolp and Viscusi (1986).

References

Bacos, W. Lawrence. 1980. *Bargaining for Job Safety and Health*. Cambridge: MIT Press.
Kolp, Paul, and W. Kip Viscusi. 1986. "Uncertainty in Risk Analysis: A Retrospective Assessment of the OSHA Cotton Dust Standard." In V. Kerry Smith, (ed.), *Advances in Applied Microeconomics*, Vol. 4. Greenwich: JAI Press, pp. 105–130.
MacAvoy, Paul. 1977. *OSHA Safety Regulation: Report of the Presidential Task*

Force. Washington, D.C.: American Enterprise Institute.

Magat, Wesley A., and W. Kip Viscusi. 1990. "Effectiveness of EPA's Regulatory Enforcement: The Case of Industrial Effluent Standards," *Journal of Law and Economics* 33(2): 331–60.

Mendeloff, John. 1979. *Regulating Safety: An Economic and Political Analysis of Occupational Safety and Health Policy*. Cambridge: MIT Press.

Moore, Michael J., and W. Kip Viscusi. 1990. *Compensation Mechanisms for Job Risks: Wages, Workers' Compensation and Product Liability*. Princeton: Princeton University Press.

Morrall, John F. 1986. "A Review of the Record," *Regulation*, Nov/Dec 25–34.

Nichols, Albert, and Richard Zeckhauser. 1981. "OSHA After a Decade: A Time for Reason," In Leonard Weiss and Michael Klass, (eds.), *Case Studies in Regulation: Revolution and Reform*. Boston: Little, Brown & Company, 202–234.

Ruser, John W., and Robert S. Smith. 1989. "The Effect of OSHA Records-Check Inspections on Reported Occupational Injuries in Manufacturing Establishments," *Journal of Risk and Uncertainty* 1(4), 415–435.

Smith, Robert S. 1979. "The Impact of OSHA Inspections on Manufacturing Injury Rates," *Journal of Human Resources* 14, 145–170.

Smith, Robert S. 1976. *The Occupational Safety and Health Act: Its Goals and Achievements*. Washington, D.C.: American Enterprise Institute.

Viscusi, W. Kip. 1983. *Risk by Choice: Regulating Health and Safety in the Workplace*. Cambridge: Harvard University Press.

Viscusi, W. Kip. 1986a. "Reforming OSHA Regulation of Workplace Risks." In L. Weiss and M. Klass, *Regulatory Reform: What Actually Happened*. Boston: Little, Brown & Company, 234–268.

Viscusi, W. Kip. 1986b. "The Impact of Occupational Safety and Health Regulation, 1973–1983," *Rand Journal of Economics* 17(4), 567–580.

Viscusi, W. Kip, and Wesley Magat. 1973. *Learning About Risk: Consumer and Worker Responses to Hazard Information*. Cambridge: Harvard University Press.

Index